中国在行动

CHINA IN ACTION

全球视野下的中国低碳绿色发展新征程

GLOBAL PERSPECTIVES ON CHINA'S NEW JOURNEY
TO LOW CARBON
AND GREEN DEVELOPMENT

中国日报社中国观察智库　主编
China Daily China Watch Institute Ed.

SPM
南方传媒

广东人民出版社
· 广州 ·

图书在版编目（CIP）数据

中国在行动：全球视野下的中国低碳绿色发展新征程：中英双语版 / 中国日报社中国观察智库主编. —广州：广东人民出版社，2024.1

ISBN 978-7-218-17082-4

Ⅰ.①中… Ⅱ.①中… Ⅲ.低碳经济—绿色经济—经济发展—概况—中国—汉、英 Ⅳ.①F124.5

中国国家版本馆CIP数据核字（2023）第204397号

ZHONGGUO ZAI XINGDONG：QUANQIU SHIYE XIA DE ZHONGGUO DITAN LüSE FAZHAN
XINZHENGCHENG（ZHONG-YING SHUANGYUBAN）

中国在行动：全球视野下的中国低碳绿色发展新征程（中英双语版）

中国日报社中国观察智库　主编

出 版 人：肖风华

策划编辑：张　芳
责任编辑：黄洁华
装帧设计：友间文化
责任技编：吴彦斌

出版发行：广东人民出版社
地　　址：广州市越秀区大沙头四马路10号（邮政编码：510199）
电　　话：（020）85716809（总编室）
传　　真：（020）83289585
网　　址：http://www.gdpph.com
印　　刷：珠海市豪迈实业有限公司
开　　本：787mm×1 092mm　1/16
印　　张：19.75　插页：6　字　数：280千
版　　次：2024年1月第1版
印　　次：2024年1月第1次印刷
定　　价：88.00元

如发现印装质量问题，影响阅读，请与出版社（020-85716849）联系调换。
售书热线：（020）87716172

编写说明 ❀

2020年9月22日，习近平主席在第75届联合国大会上宣布，中国将力争在2030年前二氧化碳排放达到峰值，努力争取在2060年前实现碳中和目标。2021年全国两会，碳达峰和碳中和被首次写入政府工作报告。2022年政府工作报告中，更是明确指示出台碳达峰行动方案，启动全国碳排放权交易市场，为实现碳中和路径明确了发展方向。"言必信，行必果。"中国以实际行动肩负起大国担当，积极探索发展与减排两不误的可持续发展模式，推动多领域的绿色多边合作，为推动构建人类命运共同体作出重要贡献。

新冠肺炎疫情和气候环境变化都是全人类共同面对的巨大危机。在疫情后的经济复苏方面，中国有望成为绿色复苏的领跑者，例如，在城市空气污染防治、西北地区沙漠绿化、人口密集地区土地保护等方面，中国已经取得了巨大进步，积累了丰富经验，总结制定出了许多行之有效的科学方法和制度安排。

本书邀请全球气候治理、碳排放和绿色发展等领域的中外专家学者撰文，从国际视野审视中国在"双碳"承诺背后的务实行动和巨大成效，结合统计数据和典型案例，多角度讨论中国如何以行之有效的政策、标准和具体行动为全球碳排放和气候治理体系带来新风，阐述了中国"双碳"目标对世界可持续发展发挥的积极影响和引导作用，尤其是对发展中国家加速绿色低碳能源和技术应用的重大意义，充分体现了中国"双碳"实践为推动全球环境治理、构建人类命运共同体作出的巨大贡献。本书精准把握习近平生态文明思想的深刻内涵，蕴含了中国对人类文明形态的前瞻性思考，向世界分享中国经验、中国智慧、中国方案，具有重要的现实意义和参考价值。

本书分为四大部分，第一篇"势在必行：'双碳'目标的世界意义与挑战"的主旨是把中国的"双碳"目标置于世界可持续发展的大潮流中，宏观地探讨中国实现低碳绿色发展的世界意义与面临的挑战，指出多边合作是共同应对全球环境风险的前提。第二篇"中国行动：'言必信，行必果'"围绕中国积极参与全球气候治理，在保护生物多样性、节能和减排、绿色技术应用方面制定国内外政策和方针，以实际行动带动带动全球绿色转型。第三篇"绿色探索：多领域齐头并进改革创新"汇集了中外专家就中国如何取得可持续发展和经济发展平衡、各产业减排转型的探索，以及在绿色创新技术的国际合作等多个关键议题展开多角度的讨论，从真实案例和数据入手，为推动全球疫情后绿色复苏和激励各国共同加快绿色转型提供了丰富的思考和客观理性的分析。第四篇"多边合作：探索低碳绿色发展无国界"是对人类发展的绿色未来的路径和国际间合作的展望，分析中国"双碳"目标实现过程中可能遇到的困难与挑战，国际社会对中国减排和绿色转型影响的看法和具有前瞻性的建议。

Introduction

On September 22, 2020, President Xi Jinping announced at the 75th United Nations General Assembly that China would strive to peak its carbon dioxide emissions by 2030 and to achieve carbon neutrality by 2060. In the 2021 Annual Assemblies of the National People's Congress and the Chinese People's Political Consultative Conference, carbon peaking and carbon neutrality were written into the government work report for the first time. The government work report of 2022 even explicitly indicated that it is to issue a carbon peaking action plan, to launch a national carbon emission right exchange, clearly specifying a path to realization of carbon neutrality. "Deeds, but not words." China shoulders the responsibility of a major country with practical actions, proactively explores for a sustainable development model balancing development and emission reduction, promotes multilateral cooperation in various fields of green development, and makes important contributions to the building of a community with a shared future for mankind.

The COVID-19 pandemic and climate change are both huge crises facing the whole of mankind. In terms of economic recovery after the pandemic, China is expected to become a forerunner in green recovery. For example, China has made great progress and accumulated rich experience in urban air pollution control, desert greening in its Northwest region, and land protection in densely populated areas. It has also formulated and validated scientific methods and institutional arrangements in such endeavor.

In this book we invited experts and scholars from home and abroad in the fields of global climate governance, carbon emissions and green development to contribute articles, revealing the practical actions and significant achievements of China's commitment of dual carbon goal from a global perspective. With specific statistics and cases, this book discusses the new and effective measures of global carbon emission and climate governance brought from China's exploration on policies, specifications and actions. It also explicates the positive and leading influence of China's dual carbon goal to the world's sustainable development, especially in accelerating application of green technologies and low-carbon energies for developing countries, which shows the significant contribution of China's exploration on dual carbon goal to the global environment governance and the building of a community with a shared future for mankind. This book accurately grasps the profound connotation of Xi Jinping's thoughts on ecological civilization, contains China's forward-looking thinking on the form of human civilization, and shares China's experience, China's wisdom and China's solutions with the world, which has important practical significance and reference value.

This book is composed of four parts. Part One "The Imperative Act: the Importance of Dual Carbon Goal to the World and the Challenge" places China's dual carbon goal in the general trend of world sustainable development, macroscopically discusses the world significance and challenges of China's realization of low-carbon and green development, and points out that multilateral cooperation is the premise of jointly dealing with global environmental risks. Part Two "China's Action: 'Deeds, not words'" elaborates China's active participation in global climate governance, how China formulated domestic guidelines and foreign policies for biodiversity protection, energy conservation, emission reduction, and green technologies application, and how it takes practical actions to drive the global green transformation. In Part Three "Green Exploration: Reform and Innovation in Various Fields", experts from home and abroad discuss multiscopically on how China can achieve a balance between sustainability and economic development, and explore ways for emission reduction transformation in various industries and international cooperation in green innovation technology. The discussions featuring real cases and data provide profound thinking and objective analysis on how to promote post pandemic green recovery and provide inspiration on how countries can jointly accelerate green transformation as well.

Part Four "Multilateral Cooperation: Exploring Low-Carbon Green Development Without Borders" is a vision for the green future of human development and the prospect of international cooperation. It analyzes the difficulties and challenges that China might encounter in the strive to realize the dual carbon goal and describes international society's views on the impact of China's emission reduction and their forward-looking recommendations on China's green transformation.

中国观察智库

  中国日报社中国观察智库，是中国日报依托遍布全球的高端资源和传播渠道，倾力打造的传播型智库。该智库汇聚全球中国问题研究的意见领袖、政治人物和商界精英，集纳海内外"最强大脑"的权威观点，建设中国研究的全球"朋友圈"，促进交流互鉴，提升研究水平，推动形成新理论、创造新智慧，影响并引领全球中国问题研究方向。致力于成为内容具有聚合性、权威性和工具性，传播效果具有穿透性的高端智库平台，并使其成为全球中国议题最权威的平台和风向标，服务于传播中国、影响世界、促进沟通和理解、推动建设人类命运共同体的使命。

  《中国日报》是国家英文日报，创刊于改革开放之初。经过40年的发展，已经建成覆盖全球的集平面媒体、网站、移动新媒体、社交媒体、电邮简报以及系列品牌产品的全媒体传播网络，有效进入海外主流社会，形成传播优势，并积累了丰富的专业人才、分发渠道、运营经验和人脉资源优势，旗下的《中国观察报》与20余个国家的30余家权威媒体开展深度合作，期均发行500万份。《中国日报》是国内外高端人士首选的中国英文媒体，是讲述中国故事、传播中国理念、塑造中国改革开放形象的重要媒体平台。

China Watch Institute

China Watch Institute is a communication channel facilitating research and analysis for China-focused institutions and thinkers around the world.

Powered by China Daily's core strength as a national flagship of international communication, China Watch Institute is a top-notch conduit for timely, detailed and thought-provoking research on China-related issues. It's in the best position to leverage its vast experience in communicating the China story to the world, especially to political influencers, opinion makers and business leaders by utilizing our incomparable network of China watchers and thinkers across the globe.

China Watch's global presence across a broad spectrum of media partners in more than 20 countries publishing in seven languages -- such as The Washington Post, The Wall Street Journal, The Daily Telegraph, Le Figaro, Süddeutsche Zeitung, El Pais, Rossiyskaya Gazeta and The Mainichi Shimbun – which gives it unrivalled reach around the world to increase cross-cultural communication.

The institute is committed to establishing itself as a high-end think tank platform which is inclusive, authoritative and a benchmark for global China issues.

China Daily, established in 1981 as the national English-language newspaper, has developed into a multi-media information platform combining newspapers, websites and apps with a strong presence on Facebook, Twitter, Sina Weibo and WeChat. It serves more than 200 million readers all over the world and is a default choice for people who read about China in English. The group plays an important role as a channel for information exchanges between China and the rest of the world.

策划编辑团队
Editorial and Production Team

撰稿人

庄巨忠　Zhuang Juzhong

国际金融论坛学术委员，亚洲开发银行前副首席经济学家

Academic Committee Member of the International Finance Forum and Former Deputy Chief Economist of Asian Development Bank

张建宇　Zhang Jianyu

"一带一路"绿色发展国际研究院执行院长

Executive President of the Belt and Road Initiative Green Development Institute

仇保兴　Qiu Baoxing

国务院参事、中国城市科学研究会理事长

Advisor of the Chinese State Council and the President of the Chinese Society for Urban Studies

安德烈·库尔曼　Andreas Kuhlmann

德国能源署署长

Chief Executive of the Deutsche Energie-Agentur (the German Energy Agency)

白雅婷　Beate Trankmann

联合国开发计划署驻华代表

Resident Representative of the United Nations Development Programme in China

格热戈日·科沃德科　Grzegorz W. Kolodko

波兰前副总理兼财政部长、波兰华沙科兹敏斯基大学教授、北京师范大学"一带一路"学院特聘教授

Poland's Former Deputy Prime Minister and Minister of Finance, Professor at Kozminski University in Warsaw, and Distinguished Professor of the Belt and Road School at Beijing Normal University

谢屹　Xie Yi

北京林业大学经济管理学院教授

Professor at the School of Economics and Management at Beijing Forestry University

杰瑞米·里夫金　Jeremy Rifkin

欧盟委员会顾问、《零碳社会》作者

Advisor to the European Commission, the author of *The Zero Carbon Society*

弗拉基米尔·诺罗夫　Vladimir Norov

上海合作组织前秘书长

Former Secretary-General of the Shanghai Cooperation Organization

袁家海　Yuan Jiahai

华北电力大学经济与管理学院教授、新能源电力与低碳发展研究北京市重点实验室副主任

Professor at the School of Economics and Management at North China Electric Power University and Deputy Director of the Beijing Key Laboratory of New Energy and Low-carbon Development

石建斌　Shi Jianbin

保尔森基金会顾问、北京师范大学环境学院副教授

Advisor to the Paulson Institute and Associate Professor of the School of Environment at Beijing Normal University

王文卿　Wang Wenqing

厦门大学环境与生态学院副院长、教授

Professor and Associate Dean of the College of Environment and Ecology at Xiamen University

丽贝卡·卡特　Rebecca Carter

世界资源研究所气候适应性发展实践项目气候适应负责人

Acting Director of the World Resources Institute's Climate Resilience Practice

余甜　Yu Tian

世界资源研究所原初级经济分析师

Former Junior Economics Analyst at the World Resources Institute

张达　Zhang Da

清华大学能源环境经济研究所副教授

Associate Professor of the Institute of Energy, Environment, and Economy at Tsinghua University

黄俊灵　Huang Junling

中国长江三峡集团国际清洁能源研究室负责人

Director of the International Clean Energy Research Office at the China Three Gorges Corporation

牛志明　Niu Zhiming

亚洲开发银行驻中国代表处高级项目官员

Senior Project Officer at the Asian Development Bank's Resident Mission in China

杜晖贤　Frederick C. Dubee

罗马俱乐部成员、中国生物多样性保护与绿色发展基金会国际工作顾问

Member of the Club of Rome and International Affairs Expert Adviser to the China Biodiversity Conservation and Green Development Foundation

朱力　Zhu Li

保尔森基金会生态保护项目主任

Director of the conservation program at the Paulson Institute

牛红卫　Niu Hongwei

保尔森基金会生态保护项目总监

Chief Conservation Officer at the Paulson Institute

唐瑞　Terry Townshend

保尔森基金会顾问

Adviser to the Paulson Institute

艾瑞碧　Rebecca Ivey

世界经济论坛原大中华区首席代表（2021—2022）

Chief Representative Officer at the China Office of the World
Economic Forum Beijing（2021-2022）

俞子荣　Yu Zirong

商务部国际贸易经济合作研究院副院长

Vice-President of the Chinese Academy of International
Trade and Economic Cooperation under the Ministry of
Commerce

阎甜　Yan Tian

永续全球环境研究所海外投资、贸易与环境项目官员

Program Officer in the Overseas Investment, Trade and the
Environment program at the Global Environmental Institute

龙冬荃　Long Dongquan

永续全球环境研究所对外联络项目官员

Communications Officer at the Global Environmental
Institute

石教群　Shi Jiaoqun

联合国粮农组织亚太区域办公室特别顾问（南南及三方合作）

Special Advisor at the Food and Agriculture Organization Regional Office for Asia and the Pacific

龙迪　Dimitri de Boer

克莱恩斯（ClientEarth）欧洲环保协会亚洲区主任、中国环境与发展国际合作委员会特邀顾问

Regional Director for Asia at environmental law organization ClientEarth and Special Advisor of China Council for International Cooperation on Environment and Development

王珂礼　Christoph Nedopil Wang

复旦大学泛海国际金融学院经济学副教授、绿色金融与发展中心主任

Associate Professor and Director of the Green Finance & Development Center at Fanhai International School of Finance at Fudan University

林伯强　Lin Boqiang

厦门大学中国能源政策研究院院长

Dean of China Institute for Energy Policy Studies at Xiamen University

王元丰　Wang Yuanfeng

中国发展战略学研究会副理事长、中国城市科学研究会可持续土木工程专业委员会理事长、北京交通大学教授

Vice-Chairman of Chinese Association of Development Strategy Studies and Chairman of Sustainable Civil Engineering Committee of the Chinese Society for Urban Studies, Professor at Beijing Jiaotong University

谢茜　Xie Xi

世界经济论坛北京代表处"海洋行动之友"项目负责人

Project Lead of Friends of Ocean Action of China at the World Economic Forum's Beijing Representative Office

陈冀俍　Chen Jiliang

创绿研究院高级研究员

Senior Researcher of the Greenovation Hub

马骏　Ma Jun

中国金融学会绿色金融专业委员会主任、北京绿色金融与可持续发展研究院院长、二十国集团可持续金融工作组共同主席

Chairman of the Green Finance Committee of China Society for Finance and Banking, President of the Institute of Finance and Sustainability, Co-Chair of the G20 Sustainable Finance Working Group

周勤　Zhou Qin

落基山研究所中国高级研究员

Senior Fellow at the Rocky Mountain Institute China

刘雨菁　Liu Yujing

落基山研究所中国部门总监

Manager at the Rocky Mountain Institute China

尼古拉斯·斯特恩　Nicholas Stern

伦敦政经学院政治经济学帕特尔（IG Patel）讲席教授、格兰瑟姆气候变化和环境研究所主席

I.G. Patel Professor of Economics and Government and Chair of the Grantham Research Institute on Climate Change and the Environment at the London School of Economics and Political Science

邹骥　Zou Ji

能源基金会首席执行官兼中国区总裁

Chief Executive and President of the Energy Foundation China

唐纳德·拉莫塔　Donald Ramotar

圭亚那前总统、人民进步党前总书记

Former President of the Cooperative Republic of Guyana and Former General Secretary of the People's Progressive Party

埃里克·索尔海姆　Erik Solheim

"一带一路"绿色发展国际研究院联合主席、联合国环境署前执行主任

President of the Belt and Road Initiative Green Development Institute and Former Executive Director of the United Nations Environment Programme

齐晔　Qi Ye

香港科技大学（广州）碳中和与气候变化学域署理主任、清华大学公共管理学院教授

Acting Head of Carbon Neutrality and Climate Change Thrust, Hong Kong University of Science and Technology (Guangzhou) and Professor of environmental policy at Tsinghua University

黄杰夫　Jeff Huang

AEX控股公司创始合伙人、芝加哥气候交易所前副总裁

CEO of AEX Holdings Ltd (HK) and former VP for Asia of the Chicago Climate Exchange

戴青丽　Deborah Lehr

保尔森基金会副主席兼总裁

Vice-Chairman and Executive Director of the Paulson Institute

杰弗里·萨克斯　Jeffrey Sachs

美国哥伦比亚大学可持续发展中心主任、经济学教授

Economics Professor and Director of the Center for Sustainable Development at Columbia University

芮悟峰　Wolfgang Röhr

德国驻上海前总领事、同济大学德国研究中心特聘研究员

Former member of the German Foreign Service, Researcher at the German Studies Center at Tongji University.

费翰思　Hans　Friederich

国际竹藤（INBAR）前总干事

Former Director-General of the International Bamboo and Rattan Organization

杨力超　Yang　Lichao

北京师范大学社会学院副教授

Associate Professor at the School of Sociology at Beijing Normal University

罗伯特·沃克　Robert　Walker

北京师范大学社会学院教授、牛津大学格林坦普尔顿学院名誉研究员

Professor at the School of Sociology at Beijing Normal University and Emeritus Fellow of Green Templeton College at Oxford University

目 录
Contents

第二篇 **中国行动**

Chapter II **"言必信，行必果"**

China Steps Up
Deeds, Not Words

第三篇 绿色探索
Chapter III
多领域齐头并进改革创新

Green Exploration
Reform and Innovation Trials in Various Fields

第四篇　多边合作
Chapter IV　探索低碳绿色发展无国界

Multilateral Cooperation
No Border for the Exploration of Low Carbon and Green Development

前　言

曲莹璞

中国日报社社长兼总编辑

　　近年来，全球低碳绿色转型发展遭遇严峻挑战。新冠疫情持续反复，俄乌冲突威胁能源和粮食安全，世界经济衰退风险加大，应对气候变化举措乏力。联合国秘书长古特雷斯在《联合国气候变化框架公约》第二十七次缔约方大会（COP27）上表示，地球正在迅速接近临界点。"我们正踩着油门，一路驶向气候灾难。"

　　尽管处于气候政策"开倒车"、减排力度不足的国际环境中，中国仍坚定不移地选择生态优先的高质量发展道路，主动承担推动绿色低碳转型的大国担当。

　　2022年10月16日，举世瞩目的中国共产党第二十次全国代表大会在北京开幕。习近平总书记在大会报告中指出："大自然是人类赖以生存发展的基本条件。尊重自然、顺应自然、保护自然，是全面建设社会主义现代化国家的内在要求。必须牢固树立和践行绿水青山就是金山银山的理念,站在人与自然和谐共生的高度谋划发展。"这为中国走生态优先的高质量发展道路,实现人与自然和谐共生的现代化建设提供了方向指引和根本遵循。

1972年,联合国人类环境会议召开,这是首届以环境为主要议题的世界会议,也开启了中国参与和融入世界环境保护合作的篇章。自那时以来,中国一直都是全球气候环境治理的积极参与者和贡献者。作为全球最早签署和批准《联合国气候变化框架公约》《生物多样性公约》的缔约方之一,中国积极开展气候变化、生物多样性、野生动植物、荒漠化防治等领域的国际合作。如今,中国已经站在全球气候环境治理舞台的中央,成为世界绿色转型发展的引领者。联合国环境规划署前执行主任埃里克·索尔海姆赞扬中国这一角色的转变:"在城市空气污染防治、西北地区沙漠绿化、人口密集地区土地保护等方面,中国已经取得了巨大进步,积累了丰富经验,总结制定出许多行之有效的科学方法和制度安排。中国已经是全球绿色环保领域的领导者。"

在此背景下,中国日报社旗下中国观察智库和广东人民出版社合作出版了这本有关中国绿色发展实践及其世界性意义的评论集——《中国在行动:全球视野下的中国低碳绿色发展新征程》,圭亚那前总统唐纳德·拉莫塔,波兰前副总理兼财政部长格热戈日·科沃德科,美国哥伦比亚大学可持续发展中心主任杰弗里·萨克斯,伦敦政治经济学院格兰瑟姆气候变化和环境研究所所长尼古拉斯·斯特恩,国务院参事、中国城市科学研究会理事长仇保兴,中国金融学会绿色金融专业委员会主任马骏等国际知名人士应邀撰文。他们或依据学术研究,或结合亲身经历,详细介绍了中国绿色转型的经验,生动描绘了中国引领国际合作的成果,并肯定了中国践行可持续发展承诺的责任与担当。

时任世界经济论坛大中华区首席代表艾瑞碧写道："过去十年里，任何一个呼吸过北京空气的人都可以证明，通往蓝天的道路从来不是笔直平坦的，瞩目的成就背后是中国的坚持和投入。空气污染治理的成功预示着中国有能力应对气候变化，也让世界各国相信，一个更加包容、有韧性并且可持续的未来并非遥不可及。"

美国知名经济学家杰弗里·萨克斯认为：中国处于向零排放模式快速转型的有利位置，因为它在一系列重要领域拥有强大的技术水平和制造能力，如光伏、风电、水电、远距离高压输电网、5G、人工智能、电动汽车、电池等。在"十四五"期间，中国还将加大关键技术领域的资源投入，这将使其能够以更低成本、更快实现低碳转型。

"气候经济学之父"尼古拉斯·斯特恩、能源基金会首席执行官兼中国区总裁邹骥在联合撰文中称："中国已经在气候变化问题上展现出全球领导力。中国还可以向其他国家展示，一个庞大的经济体如何摆脱化石燃料，实现能源转型。"

数十位作者从不同角度对中国绿色低碳发展进行了剖析，话题囊括应对气候变化、生物多样性保护、美丽中国建设、山水林田湖草沙共治、产业结构调整升级、污染治理、能源转型、绿色"一带一路"、绿色金融等，力图真实、立体、全面地呈现当代中国绿色转型的细节和全貌。

环境气候关系人类未来的命运福祉。各个国家都在寻求适应各自政治社会环境的可持续发展解决方案。世界迈向"碳中和"离不开中国智慧。"人与自然和谐共生"是习近平总书记提出的"全球发展倡议"核心原则之一。秉持这一理念，中国积极应对环境污染、气候变化、生物多样性丧失三重全球性危机，贡献中国方案、中国智慧、中国力量。

中国式现代化是人与自然和谐共生的现代化，促进人与自然和谐共生是中国式现代化的本质要求。区别于西方发达国家"先污染后治理"的老路，中国选择了一条生态优先、绿色发展之路。同时，中国还向世界分享绿色技术和绿色发展经验，与美国、欧洲、上海合作组织成员国、东南亚国家联盟成员国、非洲联盟成员国等开放合作，携手"一带一路"沿线国家改变经济增长方式，推动实现疫后绿色复苏。

绿色实力正在转化为绿色国际影响力。这十年，中国可再生能源发电装机容量突破10亿千瓦，水电、风电、太阳能发电、生物质发电装机量均居世界第一，清洁能源消费占比从14.5%提升到25.5%；这十年，中国还有效地保护了国内90%的陆地生态系统类型和74%的国家重点保护野生动植物种群，成为全球"增绿"的主力军。《生物多样性公约》第十五次缔约方大会（COP15）是联合国首次以生态文明为主题的全球性会议，中国作为主席国，推动"昆明—蒙特利尔全球生物多样性框架"达成，为全球生物多样性治理擘画了新蓝图。去年11月，《湿地公约》第十四届缔约方大会（COP14）在武汉举办，向全世界展现中国的湿地保护成就。

习近平总书记在第75届联合国大会上指出："中国将提高国家自主贡献力度，采取更加有力的政策和措施，二氧化碳排放力争于2030年前达到峰值，努力争取2060年前实现碳中和。"在宣布"双碳"目标后，中国的绿色转型进展更被世界所瞩目，提升国际话语权面临着千载难逢的时代机遇。

气候和环境问题已经超越科学本身，成为国际社会博弈角力的主战场之一。因此，生态文明、绿色发展理念的国际传播，不仅是讲好中国绿色故事、传播好中国声音、彰显中国自信的现实需要，也是中国引领并创建一种基于更加和平、公正、合理的国际秩序的地球生命共同体的必然选择。

习近平生态文明思想和中国探索低碳转型的实践成果，丰富了全球环境治理体系，是我们讲好中国故事、传播好中国声音，展现可信、可爱、可敬的中国形象的基础。在气候变化背景下，做好中国低碳转型、绿色发展的国际传播工作，全面阐述中国的生态观、发展观，彰显负责任的大国形象，是包括中国日报在内的中国媒体、智库的重要使命和时代责任。

Foreword

The global green and low-carbon transition has faced severe challenges in recent years. The response to climate change has been lackluster amid the COVID-19 pandemic, the threat to energy and food security posed by the Russia-Ukraine conflict and heightened risks of a global economic recession. United Nations Secretary-General António Guterres said at the 27th Conference of the Parties to the UN Framework Convention on Climate Change, or COP27, that the planet is fast approaching a tipping point. "We are on a highway to climate hell with our foot still on the accelerator."

Despite the backpedaling on climate policies and lack of progress in cutting emissions, China remains unwavering in its path of high-quality development and has taken the initiative to shoulder its responsibility to advance a green and low-carbon transition.

At the 20th National Congress of the Communist Party of China that opened in Beijing on Oct 16, 2022. Xi Jinping, general secretary of the CPC Central Committee, pointed out in his report to the Congress: "Nature provides the basic conditions for human survival and development. Respecting, adapting to, and protecting nature is essential for building China into a modern socialist country in all respects. We must uphold and act on the principle that lucid waters and lush mountains are invaluable assets, and we must remember to maintain harmony between humanity and nature when planning our development." This charts the direction and provides the fundamental guidance for China to follow a path of high-quality development that gives priority to ecological protection and enable the harmonious co-existence between man and nature.

The 1972 UN Conference on the Human Environment in Stockholm was the first world conference to make the environment a major issue and was also a starting point for China to participate in global environmental cooperation. So far, China has been an active participant and contributor to global climate and environmental governance. As one of the first parties in the world to sign and ratify the UN Framework Convention on Climate Change and the Convention on Biological Diversity, China has collaborated internationally in the fields of climate change, biodiversity, wild animals and plants, and desertification prevention and control. China has taken center stage and is playing an active role in global governance against climate change, and is increasingly seen as a torchbearer in the global green transition and development. Erik Solheim, former executive director of the UN Environment Programme, praised China's role: "China can share its unique ideas and experience, such as the huge progress fighting against air pollution in cities, the desert greening endeavor in Northwestern China, the redlining system that offers a scientific approach to land conservation in densely populated regions. China can be a global green leader by showing the world that a green recovery from the pandemic is possible."

In this context, the China Watch Institute of China Daily and Guangdong People's Publishing House have jointly published *China in Action: China's New Journey on Low-Carbon Green Development from a Global Perspective*, a collection of commentaries on China's green development practices and its significance to the world. Among the distinguished contributors to this book are former Guyanese president Donald Ramotar, former Polish deputy prime minister and minister of finance Grzegorz Kolodko, Jeffrey Sachs, director of the Center for Sustainable Development at Columbia University, Nicholas Stern, chair of the Grantham Research Institute on Climate Change and the Environment at the London School of Economics and Political Science, Qiu Baoxing, a counselor of the State Council and president of the Chinese Society for Urban Studies, and Ma Jun, chairman of the Green Finance Committee of the China Society for Finance and Banking. Based on their academic research or personal experience, the authors share details of China's experience in the green transition, vividly describe the outcomes of China's leadership in international cooperation, and affirm China's responsibility and commitment to sustainable development.

Rebecca Ivey, who was then chief representative officer of the World Economic Forum's China Office, wrote: "As anyone who has breathed Beijing air for the past decade can attest, the path to blue skies has not been linear, but China's commitments highlight measurable progress. The fight against air pollution is an example that foreshadows China's ability to take action on climate change and redeem global trust for a more inclusive, resilient and sustainable future."

Jeffrey Sachs, the well-known US economist, wrote: "China is very well placed to make a rapid transformation to net zero, because it has strong technological and manufacturing capacities in all of the most vital areas: advanced photovoltaics, wind turbines, hydroelectric power, long-distance high-voltage transmission grids, 5G broadband, artificial intelligence systems, electric vehicles, advanced batteries, among other technologies. Moreover, under its 14th Five-Year Plan (2021-25), China has committed added resources to technological advances in key areas, which will enable it to excel in low-cost rapid decarbonization."

Nicholas Stern, former chief economist of the World Bank, and Zou Ji, chief executive and president of the Energy Foundation China, wrote in a joint article: "China is already showing global leadership on climate change. China can also show other countries how a large economy can be transformed by moving away from fossil fuels."

The authors have analyzed China's green and low-carbon development from different perspectives. Their topics include coping with climate change, biodiversity protection, building a Beautiful China, a holistic approach to conserving and improving mountain, water, forest, farmland, grassland and desert ecosystems, the restructuring and upgrading of industries, pollution control, energy transition and green Belt and Road, and green finance. They present the details and overall picture of contemporary China's green transformation from an honest, multidimensional and comprehensive perspective.

The environment and climate are related to the future and well-being of mankind. Every country is seeking solutions for sustainable development to apply to its own political and social environment. The world can't move toward carbon neutrality without Chinese wisdom. Harmony between man and nature is one of the core principles of the Global Development Initiative proposed by General Secretary Xi. Adhering to this concept, China is actively responding to the triple global crisis of environmental pollution, climate change and biodiversity loss, and contributes Chinese solutions, wisdom and strength.

The Chinese path to modernization is the modernization of harmony between humanity and nature. Instead of following the traditional path taken by the West to treat pollution only after damage has been done, China has given priority to ecological protection and promoted green development. At the same time, China is also sharing green technology and its green development experience with the rest of world, cooperating with the US, Europe, and members of the Shanghai Cooperation Organization, the Association of Southeast Asian Nations and the African Union. The nation has worked together with countries taking part in the Belt and Road Initiative in transforming the model of economic growth and attaining a green post-pandemic recovery.

China's capacity in green development is being transformed into greater international influence in the sector. Over the past decade, the installed capacity of renewable energy in China has exceeded 1 billion kilowatts, the installed capacity of hydropower, wind power, solar power and biomass power generation has each topped the world, and the proportion of clean energy in total energy consumption has increased from 14.5 percent to 25.5 percent. China has ensured the effective protection of 90 percent of domestic terrestrial ecosystem types and 74 percent of national key protected wildlife species. The nation has become a key pillar for global greening efforts. The 15th Conference of the Parties to the Convention on Biological Diversity, or COP15, is the first global meeting of the UN with the theme of ecological civilization. China, as the host of the event, pushed forward the adoption of the Kunming Montreal Global Biodiversity Framework, which charted a new blueprint for global governance on biodiversity. In November last year, the 14th Meeting of the Conference of the Contracting Parties to the Ramsar Convention on Wetlands, or COP14, was held in Wuhan, which showcased China's wetland conservation achievements to the world.

General Secretary Xi pointed out at the 75th session of the UN General Assembly: "China will scale up its Intended Nationally Determined Contributions by adopting more vigorous policies and measures. We aim to have CO2 emissions peak before 2030 and achieve carbon neutrality before 2060." China's green transition has attracted the attention of the world after the announcement of the climate goals. The nation now faces a golden opportunity to enhance its influence in international discourse.

Climate and environmental issues have long gone beyond science and become a main battlefield in international competition. Therefore, the international communication of ecological civilization and green development concepts will not only contribute to efforts to tell China's green stories well, make China's voice better heard, and demonstrate its self-confidence, but also represent an inevitable choice for China to lead the building of a more peaceful, just and reasonable international order that features a community with a shared future for life on earth.

Xi Jinping Thought on Ecological Civilization and the outcomes from China's exploration of low-carbon transition have enriched the global environmental governance system. It is the basis for us to tell Chinese stories well, make Chinese voices better heard, and present Chinese theories and facts that are credible and appealing. In the context of global climate change, it is an important mission and responsibility for Chinese media outlets and think tanks, including China Daily, to do well in telling the world about China's low-carbon transition and green development, comprehensively explain China's concepts on ecology and development, and showcase the image of a responsible major country.

Qu Yingpu,
Publisher and editor-in-chief of China Daily

序 言 ●

埃里克·索尔海姆

怎样让地球母亲恢复美丽面庞？
中国经验值得借鉴

新冠肺炎的全球大流行向我们表明，当我们人类不再破坏大自然时，大自然就会迅速恢复活力。人们在南非开普敦的大街上看到企鹅，在西班牙巴塞罗那遭遇"熊出没"，在日本的城市里和鹿亲密接触，在美国国家公园里，野生动物也经常举行"派对"。

如果我们要恢复全球的生态系统，还有很多工作要做。在这方面，中国可以贡献不少经验，因为现在，全球最佳实践大多产生于中国。

这里我举四个例子来说明中国在这方面的领导力，可以为其他国家带来启发。

第一，一切政策的核心在于人。

据报道，内蒙古草原的植被覆盖率现已提高到45%，为上世纪90年代以来的最高水平。无数人通过共同努力，把库布其沙漠从"死亡之海"变成一片绿洲，把塞罕坝地区从不毛之地变成"美丽高岭"。

世界其他地方也有类似的举措。2005年前后，乍得的扎库玛国家公园偷猎泛滥，数千头大象被武装偷猎者杀害，甚至有整个大象族群被"灭门"的惨剧。

后来，扎库玛国家公园启动了一项全面的反偷猎计划，从当地社区雇用了100多名巡查员，对他们进行了广泛的培训，在现代技术装备和战术的加持下，最终使偷猎大象的活动得到控制。

在卢旺达，当地人也站在了野生动物保护的第一线，为大猩猩种群数量增加做出了贡献。游客近距离参观大猩猩，同大猩猩相处一个小时，花费大约是人民币1万元。这个价钱不便宜，但为当地人创造了巨大的商机，从酒店员工，到出租车司机和导游，跟野生动物相关的旅游观光业带动了成千上万人就业。

我担任挪威国际发展部长和环境部长时，每当要筹建新的国家公园，我都会去跟生活在公园周边的人们聊聊。虽然要花费很多时间，但这时间花得值，因为从当地人提出的意见和建议上可以看出他们保护大自然的意愿。

第二，要用人们听得懂的话来阐述保护自然的道理。

语言的目的在于交流，这个道理谁都明白，但在很多情况下，我们的讲话和文件里面充满了专业名词术语，不是饱学之士还真看不懂。

促成巴黎协定达成的时任法国外长洛朗·法比尤斯曾经半开玩

笑地问我："'生物多样性'是个什么东西？是一种病吗？"他说到点子上了——公文语言是动员社会大众保护大自然的障碍。

为了打赢这场自然保卫战，我们需要通过唤起人们内心对大自然的热爱来动员群众。"美丽中国"这个口号简明扼要、感情充沛，是在这方面的一次有益尝试。美国总统拜登最近在讲话中提到了"美丽美国"，显然是效仿了这一提法。这表明，这个口号产生了强烈共鸣，我们正在朝着正确的方向迈进。

第三，国际合作至关重要。

如今我们的生态系统面临的诸多威胁是跨越国界的，中国致力于携手其他国家应对共同挑战，积极推动协调合作。

中国在塑造当今产业格局方面具有无可比拟的影响力，在提高人们的环保意识方面，它也可以发挥关键作用，确保木材、棕榈油、大豆、牛肉等的供应方不会危及土地、水和森林。

例如，象牙贸易在中国曾经是一项利润丰厚的买卖，然而自2018年开始，中国政府对象牙实施严格的禁售令，这对非洲的大象偷猎活动是个有力的间接打击。

第四，生态保护需要拓展到城市地区。

在城市和人口稠密地区，如长三角、珠三角等地，生态保护挑战巨大，但中国正在研究对策。生态保护红线政策就是在科学评价生态系统价值的基础上，针对全国范围制定的。这是一项全球最佳实践，它将指导中国城市化程度最高、人口最稠密的地区进行生态保护工作。今年将在昆明举办的联合国生物多样性大会，为世界了解这个概念，让其他国家从中受到启发提供了机会。

中国还有很多做法值得称道。在深圳，"绿色走廊"穿城而过，湿地保护成效明显，成为候鸟由南向北迁徙途中的"驿站"。

从2020年1月1日开始长达十年的长江"禁渔令"也是一个富有

远见的决定。虽然"禁渔令"给部分群众造成了暂时的困难，但从长远看，"禁渔令"有助于河流生态系统恢复，有利于鱼类大量回归。

2005年，时任浙江省委书记的习近平在浙江安吉县考察时首次提出"绿水青山就是金山银山"。目前，浙江97%以上的村庄已将被污染的水道改造成可作为饮用水水源的清洁河流，惠及3000万居民。2018年，浙江省"千村示范万村整治"工程荣获联合国"地球卫士奖"。

我们总是把地球比作"母亲"，但现在我们发现，"母亲"似乎并不欢迎我们。20世纪的发展模式是"先污染后治理"。我们为了经济发展牺牲了自然环境。现在是时候停止破坏我们共同的家园，恢复人与自然的和谐，共同打造"美丽世界"了。

Preface

Nature's healing

China offers some best practices that can help us make Mother Earth beautiful again

The COVID-19 pandemic has shown us that nature bounces back fast when we humans stop overwhelming it. Penguins have been observed in the streets of Cape Town, bears in Barcelona and deer in Japanese cities. Wildlife have been having parties in the United States' national parks.

But there is much to be done if we are to restore the world's ecosystems. China has a lot to offer in this regard as now, more often than not, global best practice originates in China.

Here are four ways in which China may offer inspiration and leadership.

First, policy should be people-centered. In China, reports say that Inner Mongolia has raised the vegetation coverage for its grasslands to 45 percent, the highest since the 1990s. That came from the hard and smart collective efforts made by numerous people. Among them were those who transformed the Kubuqi Desert from a "sea of death" to a dazzling oasis, and those who turned the Saihanba region in Hebei province from a barren land to a "beautiful highland".

There are initiatives from elsewhere that offer the same lesson. In the mid-2000s a wave of poaching hit Zakouma National Park in Chad. Thousands of elephants were killed by armed poachers that would fire indiscriminately into densely packed elephant herds, killing entire family units.

Zakouma employed over 100 rangers from local communities and gave them extensive training. A comprehensive anti-poaching program that put people at the center, equipped with modern-day technology and tactics, finally brought the elephant poaching under control.

Likewise, Rwanda has succeeded in increasing the number of gorillas by making local people the frontline of protection. A visit to see the gorillas costs nearly 10,000 yuan ($1,564) for one person to spend one hour with the apes. It's expensive, but it creates a huge incentive for the locals. Thousands of people are employed as hotel staff, taxi drivers and tourist guides.

When I worked as minister of environment and international development in Norway, I spent long hours negotiating new national parks with the people living around them. Every hour was well spent as changes proposed by local people, gave them the will to protect nature.

Second, a new people-friendly narrative is needed. It may seem a platitude to say that the purpose of human language is to communicate. But it is not uncommon to find our speeches and documents full of technical jargon only intelligible to an erudite few.

Laurent Fabius, the French foreign minister who fathered the Paris climate accord once jokingly asked me: "What is biodiversity? Is that a disease?" He had a point. Bureaucratese is the obstacle standing in the way of mobilizing good people to protect our incredible nature.

To win the battle to protect nature, we need to mobilize people through their love of nature. The slogan "Beautiful China" is a brilliant emotional attempt in this regard. US President Joe Biden recently copied it, speaking about a beautiful

America. That shows how much the idea resonates and that we are moving in the right direction.

Third, many of the threats that our ecosystems face today are transnational and cross-border, making international cooperation critical. China is committed to concerted efforts to address common challenges and promote collaborative efforts.

And since China has incomparable influence in shaping today's industries, it can play a key role in raising awareness of the need to make sure the supplies of timber, palm oil, soybean or beef come from responsible sources that do not put land, water and forests in jeopardy. Other countries will add their weight. Indonesia has been very successful recently in reducing deforestation through efforts from a visionary government and determined business.

Ivory used to be a lucrative business in China before the government imposed a stringent sales ban on it. China's efforts to enforce the ban on sales of ivory have made a huge difference to elephant poaching in Africa.

Fourth, conservation needs to be taken to urban areas.

It's a big challenge to protect nature inside cities or in heavily populated areas such as the lower Yangtze River Delta or Pearl River Delta. But China is developing the necessary tools. The Ecological Conservation Red Line policy has been formulated with the aim of protecting areas all over China based on a scientific assessment of ecosystem value. This is best international practice. It will guide conservation in the most urban and most populated parts of China. The Kunming conference presents an opportunity to familiarize the world with the concept and inspire others.

A lot is happening in China. The city planners of Shenzhen, a tech city in South China, have introduced green corridors through the city and protected a wetland inside the town. The wetland allows birds from the southern hemisphere to rest en-route to the Arctic.

The fishing ban in the Yangtze River is another visionary decision. It will be tough for many people in the short run, but it will ensure that the river's ecosystems are restored and that fish return in abundance.

During a visit to Anji county in Zhejiang province, President Xi Jinping, who was the Party chief of Zhejiang at that time, said: "We do not promote economic development at the expense of the environment. Clear waters and green mountains are as valuable as mountains of gold and silver."

Today, over 97 percent of villages in Zhejiang have transformed their polluted waterways into clean and drinkable rivers, benefiting 30 million residents. They were awarded the United Nation's Champion of the Earth prize in 2018.

It is a cliché to say that human livelihoods depend on Mother Earth, but not so when we find ourselves no longer welcome in her arms. The 20th century development model was first we pollute, and then we clean up. We sacrificed the natural world for economic development. Now it's time to stop the damage we are doing to our common home and restore the harmony between man and nature. Let's shape a beautiful world.

Erik Solheim

势在必行

"双碳"目标的世界意义与挑战

多边对话建互信，共同应对全球环境风险

"一带一路"：绿色复苏之路

庄巨忠

国际金融论坛学术委员，亚洲开发银行前副首席经济学家

推动绿色发展是"一带一路"沿线国家实现疫后复苏的长期发展需要。沿线国家在推动绿色发展方面已经取得了长足进步，包括提高能效、发展可再生能源、降低二氧化碳排放强度、控制污染、保护森林和生物多样性等，但未来还有很长的路要走。相关国家应加快经济增长方式转型，加强环保执法，利用市场机制减少碳排放，发展绿色投资、绿色金融，促进国际合作。

新冠肺炎疫情给"一带一路"沿线国家带来了巨大的经济和社会影响。根据国际货币基金组织预测，66个"一带一路"沿线国家2020年GDP将平均萎缩2.5%，但2021年将增长6.5%（其中中国增长8.2%），2022年增长5.5%（中国增长5.8%）。这些预测假设

2021年大多数国家继续保持社交距离，但随着疫苗接种面的扩大和治疗手段的改善，保持社交距离的力度逐步下降，到2022年底疫情在全球范围内得到全面控制。从目前情形看，这些假设是合理的，谨慎又不失乐观。要使经济增长实现"V字形"复苏，各国必须继续保持积极的财政和货币政策，支持企业恢复生产和创造就业，增加基础设施投资，并向低收入家庭提供必需的社会保障。同样重要的是，经济复苏计划必须考虑和满足长期可持续发展的需要，推动绿色转型。

66个"一带一路"沿线国家占全球人口的63%，按购买力平价计算的全球GDP的47%，全球二氧化碳年排放的55%，全球遭受PM2.5空气污染超过世界卫生组织标准的人口的68%。这些数字表明，"一带一路"沿线国家的绿色转型对自身和全球的可持续发展至关重要。可以这么说：没有沿线国家的绿色转型，就没有全球的可持续发展。

/ 成绩与挑战 /

近年来，"一带一路"沿线国家在推动绿色发展方面付出了很大努力，包括提高能效、发展可再生能源、降低二氧化碳排放强度、控制污染、保护森林和生物多样性等。比如，在过去15—20年间，沿线国家单位GDP能耗和单位GDP二氧化碳的排放平均累计减少了20%（中国减少了30%）。

越来越多的国家正在把绿色转型放在国家发展战略的重要地位。中国就是一个很好的例子。2000至2019年间，中国可再生能源发电占比从17%提高到了29%。中国政府已宣布二氧化碳排放力争于2030年前达到峰值，并努力争取在2060年前实现"碳中和"。其他设定了"碳中和"目标的沿线国家还有匈牙利（2050年）、斯洛伐克（2050年）和新加坡（21世纪下半叶）。

尽管取得了令人鼓舞的进步，但沿线国家的绿色转型发展仍然任重道远。沿线国家单位GDP能耗比经合组织国家仍然要高40%—50%，单位GDP二氧化碳排放比经合组织国家要高80%。据估计，2019年沿线国家一次能源消费中石化能源的占比为89%，石化能源发电占比为70%以上。而在国际能源署"可持续发展的情景"下，全球石化能源消费在一次能源消费的占比到2040年要下降至56%，石化能源发电占比要下降至24%。

2019年全球PM2.5空气污染最严重的60个国家中，将近一半是"一带一路"沿线国家。考虑到未来经济发展的趋势，如果不改变增长模式，沿线国家二氧化碳和其他污染的排放还将快速上升。

/ 出路何在 /

为了进一步推进绿色转型和发展，"一带一路"沿线国家必须加强以下几个方面的政策措施：

第一是要改变经济增长方式，提高增长的质量。最重要的是要使增长方式实现由资源驱动向创新驱动的转变。同时要积极倡导循环经济，提高资源的利用效率。根据政府间气候变化专门委员会第五次评估报告，为了达到《巴黎协定》设定的在本世纪内将全球平均气温相对于工业化前水平增幅保持在2摄氏度以下的目标，到2050年，全球二氧化碳排放要比2010年减少40%—70%，本世纪末前所有国家必须实现"碳中和"。世界的可持续发展需要越来越多的"一带一路"沿线国家设定合适的"碳中和"目标。

第二是要加强环保立法，控制污染物排放，不走"先污染，后治理"的老路。大多数沿线国家都有环保立法，关键是要确保立法的严格执行。

第三是要利用市场机制，不但能减少碳排放，还能降低减排成本。一个途径是取消石化能源价格补贴。根据国际能源机构（IEA）的数据，2019年在全球石化能源补贴额最高的25个国家中，"一带一路"沿线国家占18个。减少石化能源补贴省下的财政资源可以用来补贴可再生能源。尽管近十年来可再生能源的成本大幅下降（如太阳能光伏发电的长期单位成本下降了80%，风电下降了30%—40%），这些新能源需要很高的初始投资，因而需要政府支持。另一个途径是征收碳税，实行排放总量管制和排放权交易。越来越多的国家正在发展碳交易市场，包括中国、印度、泰国和哈萨克斯坦等部分"一带一路"沿线国家。部分东南亚国家也在计划发展或正在发展碳交易市场。但是在大多数沿线国家中，碳交易市场尚处于初创阶段。

第四是要加强绿色投资。根据亚洲发展银行研究的推算，66个"一带一路"沿线国家在今后十年中，每年的基础设施投资需求约为2.3万亿美元。如何保证这些投资能促进绿色转型至关重要，这就需要加强对可再生能源、绿色交通、绿色农业，以及绿色科技的投资。

第五是要发展绿色金融。在大多数沿线国家中，公共投资远远不能满足绿色发展的投资需要。发展绿色金融是吸引私营部门对绿色发展投资的重要途径。中国近年来绿色金融发展迅速，2018年和2019年连续两年成为全球最大的绿色债券发行国。但在许多沿线国家中，绿色金融尚处于起步阶段。

第六是要加强国际和地区合作。大多数"一带一路"沿线国家是发展中国家，在全球累计碳排放中占比不太高，但受气候变化的影响却很大。发达国家有义务对它们的绿色转型和发展提供援助。

《巴黎协定》的预期是到2020年，发达国家每年提供1000亿美元资金援助，帮助发展中国家减缓和适应气候变化；到2025年，这一金额应达到一个更高的水平。尽管受到疫情的影响，发达国家仍应努力实现这一目标。

"一带一路"沿线国家之间相互合作推动绿色发展的潜力巨大。中国作为"一带一路"倡议的发起国和全球第二大经济体，通过政策对话、知识共享、基础设施互联互通、资金流通、贸易发展和科技合作，对推动"一带一路"沿线国家的绿色转型和发展可以起非常大的作用。

（此文首发于2020年12月15日中国日报中国观察智库）

2035"美丽中国"，不光是中国自己的事

张建宇

"一带一路"绿色发展国际研究院执行院长

　　十九大提出了2035年"美丽中国"建设目标，要实现这一目标，中国不仅要考虑自身的生态环境保护进程，还需要更多考虑国际形势与全球环境治理大局。当前许多国家和地区提出了低碳减排发展目标，中国的生态文明建设离不开世界，应从全球共建生态文明的高度来谋划，统筹解决国内与国际环境问题。

　　把生态环境保护纳入全面建成小康社会目标体系，是十八大以来中国生态文明建设的重要推动力。习近平总书记曾提出，"小康全面不全面，生态环境质量是关键"。为此，中国打响了三年污染防治攻坚战，并实现了生态环境质量的总体改善。在2020年全面建成小康社会的目标达成后，实现十九大提出的2035年"美丽中国"目标将成为下一个重要任务。

　　和以全面建成小康社会为驱动的生态环境治理不同，2035年"美丽中国"目标的制定需要更多地考虑国际形势与趋势，从全球生态文明建设的高度来谋划。

　　从全球生态环境治理进程来看，2035年是检验《巴黎协定》

2030年目标能否与2050年全球长期低排放发展目标有效衔接的关键时间点。为应对气候变化，2035年世界需要一个强有力的国际环境治理体系，以确保人类社会的可持续发展。

当前《巴黎协定》的签署国还在为2030年自主贡献目标而努力，但在2035年这个关键时间节点上，世界一些主要国家和地区已经开始推出自己的行动目标。虽然时任美国总统特朗普宣布退出《巴黎协定》，但美国众议院议长南希·佩洛西却提出要在"2050碳中和"目标下，到2035年实现新销售乘用车100%零排放；2020年当时的民主党总统候选人拜登则提出，到2035年使美国电力系统实现零排放、建筑部门碳足迹减半。

气候行动更为积极的欧盟则计划在"欧洲绿色新政"框架下，提出更具雄心的2035年气候目标。欧洲一些国家也提出了各自2035年行动目标。比如，德国将逐步淘汰煤炭的时间由2038年调整到了2035年；英国计划在2035年前禁止销售新生产的汽油和柴油车；芬兰计划于2035年达到碳中和，并随后实现温室气体负排放。

2035年将是实现世界可持续发展目标的一个重要时间节点，而共建全球生态文明是中国生态文明建设的重要组成部分，因此"美丽中国"目标应是一个开放的目标。中国不仅要考虑自身的生态环境保护进程，还要融入到国际环境治理进程中，统筹国内国外两个大局，在此基础上制定和实现"美丽中国"目标。

/ 中国与世界紧密相连 /

2035年中国经济总量将有望成为世界第一，国家的经济实力进一步增强。因此，中国在国际环境治理方面的责任也将更大。中国的生态文明建设不仅是要实现国内"美丽"，也影响着世界的可持续发展进程。更为重要的是，作为人类命运共同体的成员，中国的生态文明建设离不开世界，中国要深化和维护本国的生态文明成果，就必须与世界更加紧密地合作，一起解决全球面临的环境与气候挑战。

因此，制定一个什么样的2035年目标，以及选择一个什么样的实现路径，是中国需要考虑的一个问题，也是全球瞩目的大事件。

一方面，2035年"美丽中国"目标决定着中国2030年国际承诺能否兑现。2030年，中国要面对两个重要的国际承诺目标，即《巴黎协定》承诺的达峰目标和联合国可持续发展目标。2035年"美丽中国"目标对全球可持续发展目标和气候目标的实现路径、时间和实现程度将产生重大影响。

另一方面，2035年"美丽中国"目标决定着达峰后中国的气候行动走向。在温室气体排放达峰之后，中国如何定位自己在国际气候治理体系中的角色，以及能否与国际社会共同努力实现《巴黎协定》2摄氏度甚至1.5摄氏度的温控目标，2035年目标的确立将会为这些问题提供答案。

/ 共建全球生态文明 /

在习近平生态文明思想的指引下，中国的生态环境保护工作取得了全球瞩目的成就。从"绿水青山就是金山银山"的发展观到"山水林田湖草"的整体生态观，习近平生态文明思想正在中国逐渐从理论转化为实践。中国的2023年生态文明建设需要从全球共建生态文明的角度谋划，以统筹解决国内与全球环境问题为目标，不断拓展习近平生态文明思想的实践范畴和内容。

从全球生态文明建设的视角谋划"美丽中国"目标，需要协调多时空维度与多目标任务。在国内，需统筹经济、环境与社会发展多个发展目标，建立与中国经济、社会发展相适应的环境目标，从保护健康的角度，提高环境质量标准，推动实现生态环境质量的根本改善。在国际上，要对标与中国发展水平相匹配的可持续发展目标和温室气体控制目标，搭建起国际2030年与2050年气候与可持续发展目标之间的桥梁，成为国际气候治理的真正引领者。在制定和研究"美丽中国2035"的过程中，应坚持开放和包容的原则，博采国内外不同利益相关方的观点。

制定"美丽中国"目标的关键是坚信和坚持绿色发展理念。面对复杂的国际政治局势，要坚持绿色发展的战略定力，用"绿水青山就是金山银山"的理念指导气候变化行动，将国际温室气体减排负担转变为提升自身绿色发展竞争力的契机，把气候变化行动从成本分担驱动转化为利益分享驱动，从而确保中国制定一个具有雄心的2035"美丽中国"目标。

新冠肺炎疫情和逆全球化为生态文明建设带来了很大的不确定性。但也孕育着巨大的机遇。疫情之下，5G通信技术加速布局，数字技术快速发展和应用，加速了中国经济的数字化进程，为实现能源、制造业的绿色低碳转型带来了新动能。

在全球化的新趋势下，自五月份以来，中国确定以国内大循环为主体国内外市场互相促进的"双循环"发展格局，将有利于进一步加速国内高质量发展进程。利用抗击疫情、恢复经济的机遇，加快绿色基础设施投资，调整全球产业链，推动国内绿色消费，可以为中国制定和实现更高的"美丽中国"目标奠定坚实的基础。

（此文首发于2020年10月28日中国日报中国观察智库）

中德合作为"后疫情"时期经济
绿色转型注入动力

仇保兴

国务院参事、中国城市科学研究会理事长

安德烈·库尔曼（Andreas Kuhlmann）

德国能源署署长

疫情之后的经济复苏必须秉持绿色发展的理念，积极推动能源转型，为可持续经济复苏提供强劲的动力。中德两国在能源合作领域有着良好的传统和丰硕的成果，这场疫情危机也是双方日后加强合作的新契机，以实现经济的可持续转型，共同推进根本性创新和现代化进程，克服经济衰退，缓解环境和气候问题。

在经历了新冠肺炎疫情导致的经济下行之后，我们需要一个"绿色"的新开端：能源转型发展策略和相关行动方案，可以为双边和多边合作框架内的可持续经济复苏计划提供强劲动力。

/ 共同危机 /

突如其来的新冠肺炎疫情改变了世界，所有国家都在寻找应对这一重大危机的最佳方案。可以说，这些各种各样的挑战也激发了各类应对策略。然而一个关键的事实是在一个像今天这样的网络化世界，一场全球化的危机势必需要一个全球化的答案。

这次危机史无前例，但好在我们并非从"零"开始，国际合作早已有行之有效的形式。例如，中国和德国在能源转型和防止气候变化领域都取得了不小的成绩，并且开展了多年富有成效的合作。两国可以在此基础上再接再厉。

新冠危机和气候危机异中有同——它们不会按个体区别影响，而是真正的全球性挑战。奉行孤立主义、各行其是无法解决这两个危机，只有团结合作才能使我们获得强大力量，更快地走出现在的经济危机。由于疫情期间全球范围内的封控措施，我们正面临着历史性的全球经济衰退。我们必须迅速而又不失审慎地为这个特殊情况找到解决方法。

/ 找准目标 /

要想走出危机，首先要选对方向。

已经有很多人在大声疾呼，要求世界各国政府在新冠危机过后，以可持续的发展目标来复苏经济。2015年联合国通过的"可持续发展目标"为此提供了一个很好的指导方针。

现在需要因势利导，以投资未来的可持续发展为导向制定经济复苏计划。有了"绿色复苏"的良好定位，就能进一步推动一体化综合能源转型意义上的跨产业转型并扩大其影响。必须要加大力度推动能源转型，这对旨在气候保护的"零碳经济"可做出至关重要的贡献，也能创造就业机会，提振经济前景。相比之下，在已经过时的化石能源领域继续投资将无法达到这些目标。

因此，我们应在此时此刻设定明确的可持续发展目标，以国际化的视野和更高的标准，运用经济激励手段，为美好生活创造条件。

/ 成绩颇丰 /

德国能源署已经与来自中国的合作伙伴开展了十余年的合作，项目涵盖节能建筑、城市可持续发展、工业能效、可再生能源、智能能源系统和大气污染治理等。与中国城市科学研究会、中国住建部科技与产业化发展中心等合作伙伴的长期、务实、互信和成功的合作，印证了中德两国推动绿色转型进程的共同努力。这些合作以可持续发展为特点，着眼于全球气候保护，伴随着社会的发展而与时俱进。

随着时间的推移，早期的节能建筑领域合作催生了"中德生态城市"、能源一体化园区等令人振奋的项目。特别是2008年开始的超低能耗"被动房"建筑项目，取得了巨大的成果，如今在中国已经得到了广泛的推广应用。上述这些在合作中取得的成绩和相互之间建立的信任，正是中德两国在气候领域进一步加强合作的坚实基础。

被动房（passive house）：指通过自然采光、太阳能辐射等被动式节能措施，与建筑外围结构保温隔热节能技术相结合，不使用主动的采暖和空调系统就可维持舒适的室内热环境的建筑。

中德两国都不乏巧思佳策，目前双方合作正围绕着"正能房"、旧区改造以及城市未来等专题展开。诸如住宅区"集成式节能改造"等创新方法也可以在两国得到发展和推广。

正能房（plus-energy house）：指采用可再生能源（如太

阳能、生物质能等），除满足自身所需能源之外，还可以向外输出能源的建筑。

/ 投资未来 /

能源转型和气候保护在可持续经济的意义上为未来的合作提供了多种多样的模式。数字化和新的应用型技术的研究（例如氢能的研究）等课题正变得越来越重要。中德两国在这些领域都很活跃，并且可以相互支持。

在国际上，绿色金融作为气候保护的杠杆正发挥着越来越大的作用——中国和欧盟作为这一领域的先行者，应在创建分类方案等具体领域保持密切的沟通和交流。

需要特别指出的是，在气候保护领域的投入，不仅是对未来的投资，也是解决当前很多紧迫问题的有力措施。譬如，对大量的既有建筑进行节能改造，就可以立即创造成千上万的就业岗位，并且或多或少解决使用化石能源采暖造成的大气污染问题。

我们应把这场危机作为加强合作的契机，实现经济的可持续转型，共同推进根本性创新和现代化进程，以克服正在发生的经济衰退，同时缓解环境和气候问题。我们已经通过国际协定确定了这些目标，我们手中已掌握着很好的解决方案，我们还可以创造更多的可能性。我们可以通过更加密切的合作取得丰硕成果。

（此文首发于2020年7月20日中国日报中国观察智库）

〔第二章〕
绿色发展顺应世界发展潮流

全球气候行动"不差钱"，
关键是要用对地方

白雅婷（Beate Trankmann）

联合国开发计划署驻华代表

2021年11月13日，第26届联合国气候变化大会延期一天落幕。可持续发展的道路是我们唯一的生存之路，世界各国急需朝着低碳绿色经济转型。这需要巨大的投资，然而问题的关键并不在于资金短缺，而在于资金流向是否合理。各国应通过终止化石燃料补贴、征收碳税、调整能源价格等手段，将公共开支引向保护气候和自然，并撬动更多私营资本加入能源转型工作。

在第26届联合国气候变化大会（COP26）结束之际，气候危机使人类正站在命运的十字路口，面临着生死攸关的抉择。我们不能再继续走原来的老路了，因为这样下去会导致数百万物种灭绝，而最终灭绝的恐怕会是人类自己。但是，我们如果抓住机遇，选择另外一条可持续的道路，仍可为人类和地球创造一个共享的美好未来。

中国国家主席习近平曾说："气候变化是大自然对人类敲响的警钟。"对亚洲来说尤其如此，因为全球受气候变化影响最大的人口，80%都在亚洲。仅2021年一年，中国河南省发生巨大暴雨灾害，印尼南加里曼丹省也同样遭遇几十年来最严重的洪水，还有欧洲及美国发生的严重干旱和灾难性森林大火等。这几起事件仅是2021年全球频发的极端天气灾害中的一小部分。

可持续发展是唯一的生存之道，需要我们为之付出前所未有的努力。为避免气候灾难，《巴黎协定》制定了将全球变暖限制在1.5摄氏度的理想目标，这意味着世界应在未来八年内将温室气体的年排放量减半。然而，即便COP26已经召开，全球依然没有为实现该目标步入正轨。如果全球不继续加大减排力度，到21世纪末人类可能面临全球气温上升2.7摄氏度的灾难性后果。在过去的一周里，各国陆续做出承诺，我们的目标正接近2摄氏度，但我们完全可以更具雄心。如果我们不努力将全球变暖限制在1.5摄氏度以内，后果仍将十分严重。

化石燃料（主要是煤、石油和天然气）是全球变暖的罪魁祸首，全球四分之三的温室气体排放量都来自于此。但世界各国每年却要花费4230亿美元的巨款用于化石燃料补贴——这些钱本可以让世界上每个人都接种上新冠疫苗，也是消除全球极端贫困每年所需资金的三倍。当务之急是把这些资金转用于增进人类和地球福祉，而不是为其带来危害。用联合国开发计划署署长施泰纳的话说："如果我们不能使全球经济增长与污染排放脱钩，人类的后果将不堪设想。"

中国已做好准备进行能源改革。在太阳能、风能等可再生能源技术和绿色金融方面，中国已处于世界领先水平。在2020年和2021年的联合国大会上，中国先后宣布了两项重要决议，即"在2030年实现碳达峰、2060年实现碳中和"，以及"停止在海外新建燃煤电厂"，这进一步增强了应对气候变化的承诺。鉴于中国目前是世界上最大的二氧化碳排放国，这些举措将为世界带来重要的改变。不过，一切都必须以具体的行动计划为支撑。

中国政府最近发布了两份重要文件——《中共中央国务院关于完整准确全面贯彻新发展理念做好碳达峰碳中和工作的意见》和《2030年前碳达峰行动方案》。这就是对其承诺的重要支持，也为中国实现净零排放提供了更清晰的路线。尤其是，文件提出了钢铁、能源和运输等关键行业的具体排放目标，这对实现净零排放至关重要。

为了使得全球变暖限制在1.5摄氏度的目标不再遥不可及，我们应该抓住机遇，加速气候行动。这要求最好能在2030年之前尽早实现碳达峰，并减少化石燃料（尤其是煤炭）的消费。同时应该引导投资从脱碳难度较高的重工业领域转移到绿色科技的研发，因为科技的变革有可能成为解决气候变化问题的关键。这些领域的开销不应被视为额外的成本，而是我们对未来的投资——因为对人类以及地球的福祉而言，不采取行动的代价将高得多。

向绿色、低碳经济转型固然重要，但更重要的是应该保证转型期间的公正，因为转型期间有可能会对能源安全和人们的生计产生一定影响。但转型也带来了很好的契机，能够创造更好的工作岗位，开拓新发展领域，进一步减少不平等现象。在中国，绿色产业发展迅速，新能源产业创造的工作岗位已经超过了化石能源产业。据预估，到2030年，各领域公正、绿色的转型可在全球范围内创造

3.95亿个就业机会，每年产生的经济价值可达10万亿美元。

诚然，无论是在中国还是其他任何一个国家，要实现向低碳直至净零排放的公正转型，所需的投资都会是巨大的。若要在2050年前实现全球净零排放，每年在清洁能源和能源效率上的投资需求高达4.4万亿美元。然而，问题并不在于资金短缺，而在于资金流向是否合理。根据美国智库大西洋理事会的数据，在过去的18个月里，为缓解疫情对经济产生的不利影响，世界各国仅在量化宽松政策方面就花费了9万亿美元。所以，我们并非没有能力负担拯救地球所需要的资金，解决问题的关键是要让公共部门、私营企业和金融市场在资金使用上能够考虑对自然的影响。

以下有五项具体的行动能为之助力：

一是必须调整可再生能源和化石能源的相对价格，如逐步取消化石燃料补贴、开征碳排放税等。这将创造必要的财政空间来降低低碳转型对人们（尤其是弱势群体）的生计有可能造成的影响。

二是公共支出必须用于保护气候和自然，而不是破坏它们。政府资金的参与能够降低私营经济参与的风险与成本，更好地撬动私营资本参与必要的转型工作。

三是各国应强制披露气候相关信息，将气候变化纳入所有金融决策的考量范畴。中国最大的两家银行——中国工商银行和中国银行，已经加入了气候相关财务信息披露工作组（TCFD），我们希望未来有更多的企业和机构能够效仿。

四是必须为高排放企业和投资者设置"气候行动KPI"，为净零排放指明方向。

五是未来的政策应该为每个人创造机会，包括对转型过程中生计受到影响的工人提供再就业培训。这些措施所需要的资金，可以由重新调整的"自然向好"型公共预算和实行新的碳定价政策筹集的资金来提供。

联合国开发计划署（UNDP）支持包括中国在内的世界各国采取转换化石燃料的阶段性措施，实现公正平等的能源转型。我们已准备好在这一关键领域与各国深化合作。

人类走向共同未来的路只有一条，那就是可持续发展道路。这是一条艰辛的"上坡路"，世界各国都责无旁贷。我们相信，中国具备采取即刻行动的规模、资源和机遇，也能够帮助其他国家一起做出正确的选择。这可能是人类为自己及地球上的生生万物做出努力的最后一次机会了，为了我们共享的美好未来，我们必须抓住这个机会。

（此文首发于2021年11月15日中国日报中国观察智库）

发达国家的气候环境"历史欠账"还清了吗？

格热戈日·科沃德科（Grzegorz W. Kolodko）

波兰前副总理兼财政部部长（1994—1997，2002—2003），华沙科兹敏斯基大学教授，北京师范大学"一带一路"学院特聘教授

气候环境问题是2021年G20峰会最重要的议题。应对气候变化，不仅需要科学研究、制订方案，更需要切实采取行动。美国等一些西方发达国家逃避减排责任，企图混淆视听，转移矛盾，限制中国等后发国家的发展。要在气候问题上做到公平公正，就应首先敦促发达国家承担更大责任，还清"历史欠账"。

2021年10月底在罗马举行的2021年G20峰会向世界传达了这样一个信息：当今时代，世界各国需要密切合作，通过确立和实施共享、协调、公平的反应机制来共同应对挑战。而这需要远见、对话和互信，以及一份深刻的全球共同责任感。我们需要展望新冠肺炎疫情危机后的未来，向着实现经济复苏、解决人民需求的目标前进。这意味着我们需要减少社会不平等，关注女性赋权和年轻一代的成长，以及保护最弱势群体。这还意味着我们需要创造更多就业岗位，提升社会保障，促进粮食安全。

由7个发达国家所组成的七国集团（G7）仅仅关注发达国家自身利益，而金砖国家（BRICS）之间则缺少共同点。相比之下，G20机制无疑更能反映出当下全人类的总体利益和世界经济的变化趋势。

其实"G20"这个叫法不太准确，或许更应该叫做"G43"，因为该机制由19个国家和欧盟组成，而欧盟包含27个国家，除了本身已经是G20成员的法、德、意三国之外还有24个国家。如今，G20已经成为了一个独立于国际组织之外的全球政策协调机制，而这种政策协调正是当下这个不稳定的世界所急需的。一直以来，人们对G20峰会总是寄予厚望，但是它的成果却总是不尽如人意。不过，纵使是有限的成果也同样重要。

2021年由意大利主办的G20峰会聚焦的议题可概括为"3P"，即People（人民）、Planet（地球）、Prosperity（繁荣）。峰会决定对企业设立15%的最低税率，这一决定看似微不足道，实际上影响很大，因为它旨在遏制有损于发展的税收逐底竞争。不过，本届峰会更重要的一项决定是为欠发达国家和极端贫困国家免费提供疫苗。其实早在其他G20成员就此达成一致之前，中国就已经在这样做了，而且比其他国家做得都要好。我们不妨回想一下，2020年以前，当疫苗还没有正式问世的时候，中国国家主席习近平便率先向世界呼吁：新冠疫苗必须成为公共产品。但可惜的是，由于缺乏良好的全球性协调机制，提供疫苗的援助行动开展得太晚，并且进展缓慢。

步入21世纪的第三个十年，由人类经济活动所导致的气候变化，依然是全人类所面临的最大生存威胁。气候变化是本次G20峰会最重要的议题，意大利总理德拉吉以务实的态度领导了关于该议题的讨论。2021年的G20峰会和联合国气候变化大会（COP26）

刚好是前后脚举行，一些国家领导人刚出G20会场，就直接飞赴英国格拉斯哥，参加气候变化大会。这样看来，气候议题的重要性更加凸显。

为了制定正确的行动目标以应对当前灾难性的气候变化形势，人们不但需要了解科技在加快可持续能源转型上能做什么，还需要强有力的政治承诺来保障行动落实，以及明确谁应该为当前的气候形势负责、负多大责任。各国和各国家集团在今后几年内的行动成本分摊，必须以这一正确评估为基础。那么谁应该在遏制全球变暖的行动中承担最大责任？应该是历史排放量最大的国家，而不是当前最大的排放国。

有人经常把这个问题高度政治化，拿带有欺骗性的答案来混淆视听。他们的逻辑是这样的：排放温室气体——尤其是排放二氧化碳最多的国家是造成气候危机的罪魁祸首，而众所周知，中国是当前排放二氧化碳最多的国家，因此理应将矛头对准中国。就这样，他们试图掀起新一轮世界反华舆论。这种做法不利于全球化的包容性发展，反而加剧了某些国家的恐华情绪。中国的二氧化碳排放量约占全球总量的28%，大约是美国（15%）的两倍。但从人均排放量上来看，中国每年人均二氧化碳排放量约为8.1吨，只相当于美国（15.5吨）的一半左右，这个指标更能说明问题。

从1750年开始算起，中国的二氧化碳累计排放量只占全球的13.7%，而美国几乎是中国的两倍，达25.5%。欧盟加英国占22.7%，印度占3.2%，非洲占2.9%，南美占2.6%。太平洋小岛国遭受气候变化影响最为严重，甚至面临沉没风险，但它们的历史累计排放量仅占全球的1.2%。

从这个角度来看，穷国要求富国在气候问题上做出更大贡献是合情合理的，我们必须公平地支付历史账单。因此，在本届联合国气候变化大会（COP26）上，印度总理莫迪宣布把印度实现"净零排放"的时间表定在2070年也就不足为奇了。

习近平主席曾表示，中国将努力争取在2060年之前实现碳中和，而发达国家的目标一般是2050年——当然，他们可能会争取更早实现这一目标。我们不应对所有国家施加同等压力，迫使他们缩短实现"净零排放"的时间，而主要应敦促发达国家加快脚步。毕竟，我们之所以今天走到了灾难的边缘，他们的责任最大。

（此文首发于2021年11月10日中国日报中国观察智库）

生物多样性竟成"诅咒"，
环保与发展如何平衡？

谢屹

北京林业大学经济管理学院教授

生态环境保护与地方经济发展的矛盾，是全球生物多样性保护领域普遍面临的挑战。生物多样性丰富地区大多发展基础薄弱，发展动能不足。中国努力建设人与自然和谐共生的现代化，通过精准扶贫，寻找地区经济发展新动能，解决制约自然保护与社区发展协同共进的资源与环境约束问题，实现了生物多样性和地区经济的平衡发展。

自然保护与社区发展的冲突，是全球生物多样性保护领域普遍面临的挑战，影响到联合国2030年可持续发展目标的实现。位于生物多样性丰富地区的社区，大多发展基础薄弱，发展模式单一，发展动能不足，加之保护生物多样性形成的资源与环境约束，它们往往处于经济发展水平相对落后与生物多样性丰富的怪圈中，形成难以摆脱的"生物多样性诅咒"。

2021年10月在昆明召开的联合国生物多样性大会第15次会议上通过了《昆明宣言》，"共建地球生命共同体、迈向生态文明"已经成为全球共识。

中国努力建设人与自然和谐共生的现代化，自然保护与社区发展协同共进水平及能力不断提升，野生动植物及生态系统多样性丰度持续增长，当地经济社会得到快速发展，正在步入生产发展、生活富裕、生态良好的文明发展道路。

中国实行最为严格的自然保护制度，建立以国家公园为主体的自然保护地体系，织密自然保护网络体系。迄今，中国已建立超过1万处自然保护地，面积约占中国陆地国土面积的18%；涵盖了90.5%的陆地生态系统类型、85%的野生动植物种类和65%的高等植物群类，以及300多种重点保护的野生动物和130多种重点保护的野生植物主要栖息地。

为在生物多样性保护和当地社区发展之间寻求平衡，中国付出的努力主要有以下方面。

第一，为生物多样性丰富地区的经济社会发展寻找新动能，构建自然保护与社区发展的利益公平格局，使社区人口共同分享自然保护与经济社会发展的收益。通过坚持创新发展理念，引入新技术、新工艺和新生产组织形式，支持当地社区创新自然资源利用类型、方式和模式，改变了传统的自然资源无序、过度和低效利用对自然保护的威胁，形成基于自然资源高效综合利用的绿色经济业态，践行了绿色发展理念。

例如，贵州省龙里县是典型的喀斯特地貌地区，生态系统独特，生物多样性丰富，也曾是国家贫困县。该县通过发展刺梨产业，打造由种植、加工、生态旅游组成的全产业链，带动全县7100名贫困人口脱贫，改变了原本"靠山吃山，靠水吃水"的对自然保护不利局面，实现了全民共享发展和城乡协调发展。

第二，实行政府主导下的自然保护与经济发展政策联动，解决制约自然保护与社区发展协同共进的资源与环境约束问题。通过精准扶贫产业政策，改善基础设施，提升当地人口劳动技能，发展观光和体验农业、林下种植、林下养殖和森林景观利用等新型生产活动，推动产品深加工和提高附加值，支持当地人口提高经营性收入。通过精准扶贫政策与当地生态系统保护的有机结合，为贫困人口提供生态工程建设和管护就业机会，参与森林抚育、天然林管护和野生动植物保护巡护，实现工资性收入。通过加大政策支持力度，提高生态公益林补偿和退耕还林还草还湿补助标准，提高当地人口的政策性收入。此外，通过实施财政转移支付兜底，将缺乏劳动力的当地人口纳入社会保障体系。

第三，发挥市场在提升资源配置效率中的主体作用，使得生物多样性丰富地区的自然资源利用活动得以提质增效，社区人口实现增收致富，并形成社区发展反哺自然保护的有利格局。

陕西省洋县是中国国家重点生态功能县，被誉为"世界天然物种基因库"，也一度是国家贫困县。1981年，洋县发现了一窝7只朱鹮，这是在日本等国宣告该物种"灭绝"后全球仅有的一个种群。作为与人类高度伴生的物种，朱鹮以当地人口的冬水稻田作为栖息地和觅食场所。为避免水稻种植使用的农药化肥影响朱鹮繁殖与种群恢复，当地联合大米加工和销售企业、种植农户和自然保护机构，共同发展没有化学肥料和杀虫剂的有机大米产品，采用生物技术防治病虫害和提高土壤肥力，弥补了产量下降导致的收入下降，并围绕观鸟开展农家乐和民宿游，使得当地农户收入快速增长，朱鹮种群数量得以持续扩大，从7只增加到5000多只，摆脱了灭绝危险，成为全球保护濒危物种并维持当地经济发展的最为成功的案例之一。

第四，提升全体公众的生态文明素养和自然保护参与意愿，拓展公众参与渠道、方式和形式，集合全社会力量，为生物多样性丰富地区的自然保护与社区发展协同共进注入新动能，解决由于当地经济社会发展水平相对较低导致的财政投入不足等问题。

无论是地处中国东北的东北虎豹国家公园、西北的三江源国家公园，还是东南的武夷山国家公园，都有一批社会公众作为志愿者，参与到国家公园的科普宣传、巡护监测，以及支持社区发展等工作中来，成为专业人才队伍的有力补充。云南省是全球生物多样性最为丰富的地区之一，也是亚洲象在中国的唯一分布地区。为支持亚洲象栖息地质量提升，当地保护组织通过网络平台发起了面向公众的资金募集专项计划，实际募集资金远超预期，发挥了公众在自然保护中的积极作用。

通过以上努力，中国生物多样性的丰富程度和地方经济实现了同步、稳步增长。

（此文首发于2022年1月12日中国日报中国观察智库）

〔第三章〕

共同构建公平合理、合作共赢的 全球气候治理体系

加快开启"生态文明"之路， 别让"恐龙灭绝"历史重演

杰瑞米·里夫金（Jeremy Rifkin）

欧盟委员会顾问，著有《零碳社会：生态文明的崛起和全球绿色新政》

当前人类正处于新一轮工业革命的前沿，但同时由于多年来持续的环境恶化和气候变化，"第六次全球生物大灭绝"的可能性正在上升。为避免这一危险变为现实，人们必须以"生态文明"和"绿色新政"的理念为指引，利用这次工业革命之机，完成从化石能源时代到"零碳社会"的跨越。这不仅有利于自然环境的恢复，也将产生巨大的经济效益。

科学家警告我们，人类长期大量使用化石燃料所导致的气候变

化已经引发了第六次全球生物大灭绝。全球警报已经拉响。

哈佛大学著名生物学家爱德华·威尔逊说："人类活动正造成物种加速灭绝，到本世纪末——也就是当今天蹒跚学步的娃娃变成耄耋老人的时候，地球上的物种数量将减少一半。上一次如此大规模的物种消失，还要追溯到6500万年前的恐龙灭绝事件。"

/ 警钟文明交替的当口 /

全球气候危机不仅已成为重要的政治话题，在商业界也产生了巨大影响，将在未来几年动摇全球经济的基础。许多关键经济部门已经开始与化石燃料脱钩，转而青睐更廉价的太阳能和风能，以及相关的清洁能源技术和绿色商业实践，注重能源的可循环性和韧性——这些都是生态文明的核心特征。

随着应用规模的扩大，太阳能和风能的平均装机成本大幅下降，现在已经低于核能、石油、煤炭和天然气成本，把传统能源和相关技术甩在了后面。最新研究发现，价值数万亿美元的化石能源资产已经"搁浅"，可能会产生一个"碳泡沫"，这个泡沫预计将在2028年左右破裂，导致"化石能源文明"的崩溃，这给我们敲响了警钟。迄今为止，超过11万亿美元的化石燃料行业投资已经或正在进行剥离。"受困资产"不仅包括仍深埋地下的煤、石油等化石能源本身，还包括油气管道、海上钻井平台、存储设施、炼油厂、发电厂、石油化工加工设备、加油站，以及众多同"化石能源文明"紧密相关的行业。

主要产油国将遭受双重打击：一方面是太阳能和风能价格大幅下降，另一方面是石油需求达峰和石油行业资产积压。包括中国在内的其他严重依赖化石能源的国家也将面临类似的经济和社会危机。各国要想求生存、求繁荣，政府就必须迅速适应市场变化——毕竟市场说了算。

显然，中国和世界需要一个新的经济愿景，并部署相应的计划，以便在不到一代人的时间内迅速实现"零碳社会"。人类正站在新旧时期交替的当口：身后是延续了200年的化石能源文明，面前是可再生能源的新时代。为了更好地理解这一历史性的时刻，我们需要回顾历史，看看过去那些伟大的经济转型是如何发生的。只有了解了它们如何发生，我们才能为当今的世界各国制定一张通往未来的路线图——这张路线图在西方叫做"绿色新政"，在中国则叫做"生态文明"。

/ 变局工业革命的前沿 /

纵观世界历史，每一次重大的经济基础设施革命都离不开三个要素：一种新的通信媒介来"沟通"社会、一种新的能源来"驱动"社会和一种新的交通运输体系来"联结"社会。这三个要素相互作用，才能使社会系统作为一个整体运行。基础设施的变革也改变了人类的生存环境，催生了新的经济体系和新的治理模式。

19世纪，蒸汽印刷和电报机"沟通"了社会，丰富的煤炭"驱动"了社会，火车和国家铁路系统"联结"了社会。第一次工业革命就是在这三者的共同作用下轰轰烈烈地开始了。于是更多的人进入城市生活，资本主义经济蓬勃发展，国家市场和民族国家治理模式开始出现。

到了20世纪，集中供电网络、电话、广播电视、廉价的石油和全国公路系统上的内燃机，为第二次工业革命提供了基础。而伴随着第二次工业革命，郊区得到了更大的发展，全球化和全球治理体系兴起。

当前我们正处于新一轮工业革命的风口浪尖。未来数字化的宽带通信互联网将与电力网、物流网紧密融合。其中，太阳能和风能将为电网提供电能，驱动无人驾驶电动汽车，而电动汽车将是数字化物流网的重要组成部分。

我们人类社会活动所产生的所有数据信息，都将被各种各样的传感器实时记录下来，从生态系统、农田、仓库、道路、工厂生产线、商店，特别是从住宅、商业楼宇和公共设施上，不间断地上传到这三张"网"上，让人们可以随时随地、更加高效地"沟通""驱动"和"联结"社会经济生活的方方面面。

——这，就是"物联网"。

在即将到来的新时代，建筑物需要进行改造，以节约能源，适应气候变化。它们还将被嵌入物联网设备，配备边缘数据中心，使公众能够在通信管理、能源生产、物流运输等方面更快捷地共享数据。这些智能建筑还将作为微型绿色发电厂、能源存储站，以及电动汽车交通枢纽，成为未来更加分散化的"零碳社会"的一部分。

在这场新的工业革命中，建筑将不再是封闭的私人空间，而可能成为一个个能源节点，按照建筑物拥有者和使用者的意愿，更加积极地参与能源的生产、存储和分配，以及其他更广泛的经济社会活动。

/ 转机零碳社会的大门 /

通过生态文明基础设施将所有的人和物联结起来，将带来巨大的经济效益。随着数字经济的规模不断扩大，不论个人还是企业，不论在家中还是在工作单位，都将能够与物联网相连接，自由访问网上流动的海量数据，这些数据将影响到他们的供应链、生产和服务，以及社会生活的各个方面。他们可以对这些大数据进行深度挖掘与自主分析，利用不同的算法开发出各种应用程序，以此提高总体效率，减少碳足迹，降低生产、分配、消费和回收废物过程中的边际成本，使他们的工作和生活方式更环保，更具韧性，更符合"零碳社会"的要求。

"数字化3.0"基础设施的大规模部署将涉及中国几乎所有产业部门，并将创造数百万个新就业机会。2020—2040年的未来20年内，在这类基础设施上每投资一美元，预计将产生3.3美元的GDP回报。同时，在改善公共卫生水平和缓解气候变化对经济的影响方面，中国还将节省数万亿美元。

气候变化给了我们一个重要教训，那就是我们所做的每一件事，其影响可能超越自己所在的社区、地域和国家，直至影响到地球上的每一个人，以及其他物种，乃至维持所有生命的整个生态系统。眼下真正的问题是：全人类是否能及时团结起来，阻止这一轮全球物种大灭绝？这是一个新的现实，将为中国的"生态文明"愿景和欧盟的"绿色新政"提供动力。

（此文首发于2020年7月27日中国日报中国观察智库）

应对气候变化，将带来实实在在的效益

弗拉基米尔·诺罗夫（Vladimir Norov）

上海合作组织前秘书长

气候环境问题及其引发的一系列社会经济问题，对上合组织国家影响巨大。当前各成员国都在努力减少碳排放，实现碳中和，进而保障粮食安全，预防自然灾害，加强能源自主，促进民生福祉。中国现已成为全球创新中心和最大的脱碳技术供应国，低碳转型将给中国带来切实的经济效益。

由气候变化所引发的问题日益严重，这已成为整个国际社会关注的焦点。要减少碳排放，实现碳中和目标，必须采用更先进的技术。

专家们一致认为，温室效应是由人类活动，即燃烧石油、天然气和煤炭等化石燃料造成的，这似乎导致了全球平均气温不可阻挡地上升，给人类带来许多负面后果，特别是生态状况恶化，加速了生物多样性的丧失，以及许多人畜共患疾病的出现。

据世界卫生组织统计，每年有20亿人患上传染病，其中1400万人死亡。联合国也表示，近几十年来，由于气候变化，世界范围内的沙漠化速度在加快。目前，沙漠化已导致全球20多亿公顷肥沃土地退化，这个数字还在以每年1200万公顷的速度增加。

荒漠化和土地退化、水资源短缺和粮食安全等问题影响着整个上海合作组织地区，尤其是中亚地区，也就是该组织的核心区域。这一地区的社会经济稳定对上合组织所有成员国至关重要。

说到这里，不得不提一下曾经的世界第四大湖——位于哈萨克斯坦和乌兹别克斯坦之间的咸海。自20世纪下半叶以来，咸海逐渐干涸，这场环境灾难不仅具有地区影响，而且具有全球影响。

2019年上合组织比什凯克峰会通过的《上海合作组织成员国元首理事会比什凯克宣言》强调，气候变化、饮用水短缺等安全挑战和威胁日益加剧并跨越国界，要求国际社会高度重视，并开展紧密协调和建设性协作。

鉴于维护上合组织区域生态平衡、恢复生物多样性、保障人民福祉和可持续发展的重要性，为了践行上合组织成员因在环保领域的合作理念，实行2020年上合组织莫斯科峰会上的行动计划，乌兹别克斯坦总统米尔济约耶夫提出了《上合组织绿色之带纲要》。该纲要旨在促进温室气体低排放技术在多个经济领域的应用和实施，增加可再生和低排放能源的占比，以便降低温室气体排放。2021年9月16日至17日在杜尚别举行的上海合作组织成立20周年纪念峰会上通过了这一纲要。

如今，上合组织所有成员国都在努力大幅减少碳排放，实现碳中和，这将对保障粮食安全、预防自然灾害、加强能源自主、促进人民福祉产生一系列重大而深远的积极影响。

2020年9月，习近平主席在联合国大会上做出承诺，努力争取在2060年前实现碳中和，这对中国和上合组织其他成员国以及全球应对气候变化都是个好消息。对世界而言，中国做出这一承诺，意味着国际社会离实现《巴黎协定》将全球升温幅度控制在2摄氏度以内的目标更近了一步。

实施积极应对气候变化的行动，将给中国带来实实在在的经济效益。

根据现有计算，实现升温幅度控制在1.5摄氏度以内的目标，到2050年将拉动中国GDP增长2％至3％，减少化石燃料需求80％左右，降低排放75％至85％。中国的脱碳计划为加速技术创新和现代化生产创造了巨大的机遇，这将进一步增强中国的经济实力。同时我们还要看到，中国是全球制造业和创新中心，通过为自己设定减排目标，正在成为世界上最大的脱碳技术供应国，帮助其他国家实现温室气体"净零排放"。

（此文首发于2021年9月16日中国日报中国观察智库）

中国可再生能源发展那么快，
为什么国际上还是"看不见"？

袁家海

华北电力大学经济与管理学院教授，新能源电力与低碳发展研究北京市重点实验室副主任

> 中国可再生能源总装机已突破10亿千瓦大关，水、风、光、生物质发电规模均位居全球第一。但从一次能源消费结构来看，可再生能源占比仍然很低。未来中国可再生能源的部署将呈加速态势，在成为全球可再生能源制造、创新和产业服务中心的同时，也将为全球能源转型做出巨大贡献。

官方数据显示，截至2021年10月底，中国可再生能源发电累计装机容量已达10.02亿千瓦，首次突破10亿千瓦大关，在2015年底基础上实现翻番，占全国发电总装机容量的比重达到43.5%，比2015年底提高10.2个百分点。其中，水电、风电、太阳能发电和生物质发电装机分别达到3.85亿千瓦、2.99亿千瓦、2.82亿千瓦和3534万千瓦，均持续保持世界第一。

这是中国能源转型进程中重要的里程碑，也是全球能源转型的大事件。

/ 飞速成长 /

事实上，中国自2004年起就在水电开发领域领跑全球，自2012年起就在风电和太阳能发电领域占据世界领先地位。

而目光回到2005年，中国刚通过可再生能源法时，风电光伏装机只有106万千瓦。在此后短短15年的时间里，中国的风电光伏装机总规模增长到了5.9亿千瓦。

得益于可再生能源法、极具雄心的可再生能源中长期发展规划和有力的上网电价政策，中国的可再生能源装机规模呈直线式增长。

在保障电量需求上，"十一五""十二五""十三五"期间，风电光伏在新增电量中的占比稳步提升，分别为2.7%、11.7%和27%。中国坚定推进能源转型、积极应对气候变化的决心和力度可见一斑。

在此过程中，可再生能源产业在中国也经历了从无到有、从弱到强，逐步发展壮大的过程。中国的可再生能源产业实现了从"跟跑"到"并跑"再到"领跑"的超越。自2017年起，中国已成为全球可再生能源装备制造大国，形成了全球最完备的可再生能源产业体系，并随着自主技术创新而逐步发展为可再生能源技术创新的第一方阵。

在全球前10的风电制造商中，中国占据7席；全球前10的光伏制造商中，中国占据6席；在动力电池领域，中国占据了全球前10中的7席。

/ 转型"悖论" /

然而，尽管进步巨大，可再生能源在中国一次能源供应中的占比仍然很低。2020年，中国的非化石能源占一次能源消费的占比仅为15.9%，除核电以外，水、风、光、生物质等可再生能源的发电总量的占比仅为13.7%。

这或许可以回答为什么中国能源转型取得巨大成就，但国际社会却看不到的悖论。

让我们还是用数据来回答这一悖论。2020年中国风电、光伏装机年净增加1.19亿千瓦，对应年满发电量1900亿千瓦时。同年中国一次能源消费总量49.8亿吨标准煤，新增风光装机产生的发电量对应的一次能源仅占比为1.1%。而截至2020年底，作为全球能源转型的模范生，德国的可再生装机总规模不超过1.3亿千瓦，英国的可再生能源装机不超过4800万千瓦。

作为全球人口最多的发展中国家和当之无愧的世界制造中心，工业化和快速城镇化对能源产生了巨大的需求。这意味着可再生能源在一次能源消费中占比的提高，以及最终完成对化石能源消费的替代，必然是一个漫长的过程。而中国政府做出的2030年前实现碳达峰、2060年前实现碳中和的承诺，已为这一过程划定了明确的终点。

/ 未来发展 /

中国"双碳"政策的落地，为可再生能源的未来发展打开了无限的想象空间。根据2021年10月底中国政府发布的"双碳"目标顶层设计政策文件，2060年非化石能源在能源消费中的占比要达到80%以上。除了一小部分来自于核电以外，主力都将来自于可再生能源。

这意味着未来中国可再生能源的部署将呈逐步加速的态势。我们预测，"十四五"时期，仅风电光伏年均容量的增加会达到1.2亿千瓦，"十五五"时期会达到1.4亿千瓦，而"十六五"时期会达到1.6亿千瓦。这意味着，再过7年，即到2028年时，中国将出现下一个10亿千瓦的新增可再生装机。

中国在成为全球可再生能源制造、创新和产业服务中心的同时，也在为全球能源转型做出巨大贡献。

一是中国强大的制造能力对全球可再生能源成本的快速下降做出了巨大贡献，未来中国的可再生能源产业创新能力将进一步为全球可再生能源经济性的改善提供强大助力。二是中国的太阳能和风电装备出口份额全球最大，分别占全球出口总量的28%和13%，直接推动了全球可再生能源技术的快速部署。三是水电、风电和光伏项目一直是中国海外电力项目"篮子"中的重要力量。据波士顿大学全球发展政策中心的数据，2000—2021年间中国海外电力投资的36.6%是水电、风电、光伏等可再生项目。

近年来，中国制定了更加严格的对外投资绿色工作指引和"一带一路"绿色项目发展指南，在9月份联合国大会上习近平主席宣布，中国将停止海外燃煤发电厂的建设。中国参与的海外电力规划项目重心已转向可再生能源，在2020年，水、风、光等项目容量占比超过50%。我们完全有理由相信，中国在可再生能源装备制造、技术创新、市场部署和系统整合方面的鲜活经验与成果，都是广大"一带一路"发展中国家在构建电力基础设施，保障可负担的现代能源服务方面中值得学习、借鉴的"最佳实践"。

（此文首发于2021年12月14日中国日报中国观察智库）

中国

"言必信，行必果"

行动

〔第一章〕
为全球气候治理贡献中国智慧

救救"海岸卫士"！

石建斌

保尔森基金会顾问，北京师范大学环境学院副教授

王文卿

厦门大学环境与生态学院副院长、教授

被誉为"海岸卫士"的红树林正在全球范围内呈现退化趋势。近20年来，中国在红树林保护和恢复方面取得了实质性的成就，相关研究也处于世界领先水平，但仍面临多重挑战。红树林保护和恢复应从红树林湿地生态系统整体着眼，建立健全相关技术标准、评估体系和规章制度，鼓励社区参与。红树林保护和研究可成为中国发展对外合作的新平台。

被誉为"海岸卫士"和"海上森林"的红树林是地球上最高产的生态系统之一，提供了许多重要的生态服务功能，包括防止海岸

侵蚀、抵御风暴潮和海平面上升的危害、净化水质、固碳、为众多生物提供栖息地和为人类提供重要的生计来源等。

据测算，每公顷红树林每年产生的生态功能价值约为3.3万至5.7万美元。

尽管红树林具有惊人的价值，但由于人类活动干扰，全球范围内的红树林遭受了严重破坏，呈现退化的趋势，而气候变化更加剧了这一趋势。过去的半个世纪里，全球红树林总面积减少了约一半。按照这种速度，如果我们不立即采取行动以扭转这种趋势的话，全球红树林将在本世纪内消失殆尽。

/ 成就 /

最近一项由保尔森基金会、老牛基金会与深圳红树林保护基金会发布的联合研究表明，尽管全球红树林面积仍在快速下降，但中国近20年来在红树林保护和恢复上却取得了积极成就。中国制定了《森林法》《海洋环境保护法》《湿地保护修复制度方案》等一系列政策法规，从制度上对红树林进行保护。

与此同时，中国加大了红树林恢复力度，实施了一系列举措，如2001年启动的"全国红树林保护工程"、2017年发布实施的《全国沿海防护林体系建设工程规划（2016-2025年）》等。这些举措使得中国的红树林面积从2000年的2.2万公顷增加到2019年的近2.9万公顷，成为世界上少数几个红树林面积净增长的国家之一。中国大陆目前建有38个以红树林为主要保护对象的保护地，50%以上的红树林已被纳入自然保护地范围，远远超过全世界25%的平均水平。

/ 挑战 /

然而，该联合研究也同时表明，中国的红树林保护、恢复和管理仍面临着许多挑战和难题。

首先，由于水产养殖业造成的污染、外来物种的入侵，以及人工海堤阻断红树林与堤内生态系统的联系，使得一些地方的红树林出现了严重的退化现象。

第二，过去20年里，中国主要通过在滩涂上人工造林的方式，使得红树林面积大大增加，但人工造林也存在着一些问题。例如，由于造林选址不当、环境不适宜和缺乏适当的后期维护等原因，人工种植的红树林成活率不高，但造林成本却很高。人工造林还有可能因为仅选择有限的红树树种，甚至外来红树树种，而带来一定的生态风险。此外，在潮间带滩涂上种植红树林可能会破坏或占据其他野生动植物（如迁徙水鸟和底栖动物）的重要栖息地。因此，需加大力度鼓励自然修复和整个红树林湿地生态系统修复。

恢复红树林生态系统功能的一种更为有效的方法是退塘还林。中国沿海地区存在大量的鱼塘，对其中适合恢复红树林的鱼塘进行改造，可以为恢复红树林提供空间。然而，补偿鱼塘经营者所需的巨额资金，以及当前退塘还林技术标准和操作指南的缺失，都妨碍了这种方法的推广。

/ 方案 /

红树林仅占中国森林总面积的很小一部分，却得到了中国领导人的高度重视。2017年4月19日，习近平主席到广西壮族自治区北海市金海湾红树林生态保护区考察时强调，一定要尊重科学、落实责任，把红树林保护好。2020年6月8日"世界海洋日"的活动主题在中国被定为"保护红树林，保护海洋生态"，旨在推动全社会提高对红树林重要生态价值的认识。中国正在形成一种有利于红树林保护和恢复的社会氛围。

2019年，自然资源部、国家林业和草原局联合组织开展了红树林资源现状和适宜恢复地的调查；正在组织编制全国红树林保护修复专项行动计划，将实施红树林生态修复。

2020年6月，中国发布了《全国重要生态系统保护和修复重大工程总体规划（2021–2035年）》，目标之一是通过实施包括红树林等典型海洋生态系统的保护修复在内的一系列重大工程，使海洋生态恶化的状况得到全面扭转，全国自然海岸线保有率不低于35％。

/ 倡议 /

鉴于此，我们相信中国将迎来红树林保护和恢复的"黄金机遇期"。根据上述联合研究的建议，为维持红树林生态系统的健康稳定，以下措施和行动应得到重视并及时落实：

第一，转变理念，将红树林作为一个完整的自然湿地生态系统进行保护和恢复，包括恢复鸟类、底栖生物和鱼类等其他野生动植物的栖息地，而不仅仅是一片树林。恢复工作应着眼于整个红树林湿地生态系统及其功能的恢复和提升。

第二，修改和完善以自然恢复为主、人工恢复为辅的红树林恢复标准和评估体系，在恢复红树林的同时采取措施提高林区周边居民的收入。

第三，对潮间带滩涂进行科学评估，只有通过评估、适于红树林造林的地区才可进行滩涂造林；禁止在海草床、重要鸟类栖息地实施滩涂造林。

第四，制定退塘还林技术标准和操作指南，进一步推进退塘还林。

第五，建立基于社区的红树林保护和生态恢复模式和机制，鼓励当地社区积极参与红树林生态系统的保护及恢复，并从中获益。

在红树林的保护和恢复过程中，中国应吸取其他国家的经验和教训。同时，鉴于中国的红树林研究在世界处于领先地位，相关知识和成功案例研究的对外分享也很重要。红树林的保护和恢复，有望成为中国与其他国家，特别是"一带一路"沿线有红树林分布的国家之间合作的新领域。

（此文首发于2020年7月7日中国日报中国观察智库）

应对气候变化，农业需要一场革命而不是微调

丽贝卡·卡特（Rebecca Carter）

世界资源研究所气候适应性发展实践项目气候适应负责人

余甜

世界资源研究所原初级经济分析师

气候变化已经对世界各地的粮食系统造成了破坏，严重影响着农民生计。在一些重点地区，农业生产体系需要进行变革性转变，以适应气候变化，保障粮食安全。关键手段包括：转移生产加工特定作物和牲畜的地理位置，使农业生产与生态系统和资源的变化形势相协调，以及大规模采用新方法、新技术。

气候变化已经对世界各地的粮食系统造成了破坏，导致全球饥饿加剧，许多农牧渔民的生计因此受到威胁。根据联合国粮农组织的报告，目前全球有6.9亿人处于饥饿状态，比2014年增加了6000万，而气候变化就是原因之一。气候变化还可能将另外1亿人口拉到贫困线以下，其中农民、牧民和其他农村人口占很大比例。

中国农业也受到气候变化的严重影响，其中受干旱影响最大，洪水和冰雹灾害次之。未来气候变化引起的气温和降水模式的改变

将继续直接或间接地造成作物减产。预计到2030年，季节性干旱将使中国三大主粮（水稻、小麦和玉米）减产8%。可以肯定的是，当前的农业模式将无法适应未来全球变暖的环境，特别是在沿海、干旱和半干旱地区，以及高度依赖冰川和积雪融水的农业地区。在这些地方，仅靠渐进式的适应是不够的，若不对农业系统进行根本性的改造，它可能将无法存续。

世界资源研究所近期发布报告《面临风险的粮食系统：长期粮食安全的变革性适应》，强调了农业变革性适应的必要性，并阐述了实现这一目标所需的措施。

何为"变革性适应"？政府间气候变化专门委员会对它的定义是：将重点放在更宏大、更深刻的系统性改变，而不是在维持现有系统的基础上进行渐进性微调，如引进更多的抗旱作物品种或使用更有效的灌溉手段。农业的变革性适应旨在改变农业系统的基本属性，以应对当前或预期的气候变化及其影响，其规模和目标往往大于渐进性活动。我们研究发现，实现农业变革性适应的关键手段主要有三种。

一是改变生产、加工和销售特定作物和牲畜的地理位置。例如，哥斯达黎加一些咖啡种植户正转而种植柑橘类水果，因为这些地区正变得过于温暖，不适合生产咖啡。在埃塞俄比亚，随着气温上升，小麦和画眉草等主要作物的种植正转移到海拔更高、温度更低的地区，而原来的土地上则开始大面积种植玉米。

二是使农业生产与不断变化的生态系统、可用的水和耕地资源相协调。例如，中国有40万公顷的盐碱地被用于种植海水稻，这是一种利用杂交育种和其他技术开发出来的耐盐碱水稻，可以在滩涂或其他高盐地区生长。与常规水稻相比，海水稻根系较深，植株较高，抗倒伏能力强，不易被上升的海水完全淹没，即使被淹没，海水退潮后仍能生长良好。因此，在气候变化导致海平面上升的地区，海水稻是一个不错的选择。2019年6月，中国和阿联酋专家实验发现，种植在迪拜沙漠中的海水稻产量达到每公顷9435公斤。中国专家指出，这个产量达到了沙漠盐碱地上水稻种植的国际先进水平。

三是大规模应用新方法和新技术，从而在特定地区实质性地改变农产品的类型以及现有农产品的生产和加工方式。例如，在印度部分地区，菜农已经开始使用低成本的塑料大棚来保护他们的农产品免受更极端的天气影响。他们发现，利用大棚可以种植更多种类的蔬菜，还能节约日益稀缺的水资源。

在农业变革性适应方面，中国已经有了成功范例，但随着气候变化影响加剧，中国需要做更多的工作，为进行系统性的变革做好准备。在上述例子中，较富裕的农户可能更容易获得信贷、相关信息和土地等关键资源，进而能够做出上述转变；而较贫困的农户将需要更多的支持，以确保他们不会掉队。例如，需要更多的投资，教授当地农民如何种植他们以前没种过的作物，饲养他们以前没饲养过的牲畜；还需要更多的财政资源和政策支持，以鼓励较贫穷的农民和社区做出这些变革性的变化，特别是确保那些最易受气候变化影响的群体，包括小农户、妇女和儿童，能够做出这些改变。

那么谁能推动这些行动，使粮食系统发生变革呢？

对大多数农民和社区来说，独立实施变革性适应虽说并非完全不可能，但难度很大。改变现有生产体系的基本要素以及市场和制度安排需要时间，而如果没有集中的行动，对粮食系统的转变往往需要更长时间才能实现。因此，支持和扩大粮食系统的变革性适应，需要决策者、资金提供者和研究机构共同采取行动，他们需要协同努力，加强粮食安全，把损失降到最低，并减少流离失所和发生冲突的风险。

采取变革性适应措施，可以让那些最易受气候变化影响的群体获得更充足的时间和空间，行使更大的决策权，自主选择最适合自身的解决方案——这一点可能是最重要的。制定规划要趁早，这样才有意义，不能等极端气候事件已经令现有系统不堪重负之后才去补救。对于易受影响的社区，还应该告诉他们哪些适应方法对他们更管用，从哪里能够获得长期、稳定的资金，以帮助他们自主制定解决方案。

今年，联合国秘书长古特雷斯将召开粮食系统峰会，这是在2030年前实现可持续发展目标的十年行动的一部分，旨在呼吁全世界共同努力，改变世界对粮食生产、消费和思考的方式。我们需要采取更加大胆的行动，在所有的17项可持续发展目标上取得进展，每项目标在某种程度上都依赖于更健康、更可持续和更公平的粮食系统，而变革性适应正是一项强有力的解决方案。

（此文首发于2021年7月26日中国日报中国观察智库）

〔第二章〕

绿色低碳发展新政策新举措

国有企业助力中国碳市场稳步发展

张达

清华大学能源环境经济研究所副教授

黄俊灵

中国长江三峡集团国际清洁能源研究室负责人

2021年7月正式启动的全国碳排放市场，是中国实现其气候目标的重要一步。中国碳交易系统基于中国国情，从最初只覆盖火电部门，循序渐进地扩展到其他排放密集型行业。国有企业，特别是国有电力企业，碳排放标准更严，长期投资规划和技术研发能力更强，在促进中国碳排放交易系统发展、推动长期绿色转型方面可以发挥中坚作用。

作为目前全球碳排放量最大的经济体，中国于2021年7月16日正式启动了全国碳排放权交易市场。这标志着向习近平主席2020

年9月提出的"二氧化碳排放力争于2030年前达到峰值，努力争取2060年前实现碳中和"的承诺迈出了重要一步。

碳市场允许纳入企业开展碳配额交易，从而激励企业以最低的成本实现碳减排。在碳市场中，面临更高减排成本的企业可以向有配额盈余的企业购买碳配额，也可以从与碳市场连接的抵消市场中购买自愿减排量抵扣配额。碳市场的设立将鼓励减排成本较低的企业减少排放、产生配额盈余出售，从而获得收益。因此，碳市场有望帮助高排放行业进行生产技术升级换代，提高非化石能源消费比重，并加强低碳技术的研发能力。同时，抵消市场则可通过为植树造林和森林管理等减排活动提供资金，促进生态碳汇增加。

与欧盟碳市场和美国加州碳市场等发达地区的碳市场设计相比，中国的全国碳市场在设计过程中充分考虑了中国国情。全国碳市场的突出特点之一是，其最初只覆盖了火力发电部门；当体系成熟之后，全国碳市场预计将扩大覆盖到其他主要的排放密集型行业，包括钢铁、水泥、电解铝等。全国碳市场在火电部门的成功运行，将会对未来覆盖多个行业的碳市场发展产生重要影响。

中国的火电部门每年排放约45亿吨的二氧化碳，约占全国碳排放量的40%。电力行业中主要的市场主体是国有企业，超过70%的发电量来自于国有企业，仅五大发电集团就拥有了超过一半的燃煤发电容量。因此，碳市场应该充分调动国有企业在电力行业的优势。

首先，国有企业代表了全体人民的共同利益，秉持履行社会责任的内在价值，因此内部能够建立更严格的碳排放报告和配额履约的合规标准。正如国有企业的监管部门国资委要求，国有企业必须"认真履行企业社会责任，实现企业、社会和环境的全面协调可持续发展"。国有企业参与碳市场交易有助于支持建立准确报告和披露碳排放数据的标准体系，形成及时、足额履约的市场规范，为碳市场的健康运行创造坚实基础。

其次，在碳市场提供碳价信号的条件下，国有企业有能力进行长期投资规划，这对于电力系统低碳转型非常关键。与私营部门相比，国有企业更能接受投资回报期较长的项目，而这样的项目在低碳领域的投资中十分常见。

一个典型的例子是三峡工程——它涉及了巨额的初始投资，建设也跨时多年。但在建成之后，三峡工程显现其具有长期盈利的能力，并已经产生了巨大的社会效益。三峡工程完工后，中国长江三峡集团成功地复制了这一模式，又建造了四个千万千瓦级水电站。同样地，国有企业在建设核电站、大型可再生能源基地和长距离输电通道方面也发挥了关键作用，这对于中国实现"到2030年，非化石能源占一次能源消费比重达到25％左右"的目标至关重要。

碳市场的另一个重要目标是激励低碳技术的研发。研发活动的特质要求投资者对大规模、长回报周期的投资保有耐心。因此，国有企业一直是中国创新生态的重要参与者。许多央企已经建立了科研机构，以加快新型低碳技术的开发和部署，支持产业结构的升级调整。

最后，国有企业可以充分利用碳市场所创造的新商业机会促进共同繁荣。例如，抵消市场将会带来对自愿减排信用的大量新增需求，这些自愿减排信用在中国被称为"中国核证减排量"（CCER）。我们预计植树造林和森林管理将在未来成为CCER的主要供应来源，大幅提升林业部门的价值。由于中国的大部分林地都是国有或集体所有，国有企业参与碳市场将能带动这一增值为全社会共享。

中国林业集团公司作为一家中央企业，也是中国最大的林业企业，已经宣布了颇具雄心的大规模新增造林项目规划。这些造林项目的收入将提升当地农村社群的福利。2015年自中共中央、国务院关于打赢脱贫攻坚战的决定发布以来，实现共同富裕一直是国有企业一项重要的社会责任。

有别于西方经济体，中国的全国碳市场采用基于市场的碳定价政策，是一个具有强烈的中国特色的交易机制。国有企业作为中国特色社会主义市场经济的主体支柱，可以支持、推动中国碳市场稳步向前发展。

（此文首发于2022年3月16日中国日报中国观察智库）

保护生物多样性：早一天行动，少一分损失

牛志明

亚洲开发银行驻中国代表处高级项目官员

生物多样性丧失和生态系统恶化在社会上至今尚未引起广泛重视。2021年10月，联合国《生物多样性公约》第15次缔约方大会将在昆明召开，旨在达成新的全球生物多样性框架，激励变革性行动，需要人们加强对生物多样性保护的意识，充分重视生态系统提供的服务和产品的价值，同时要求各国优化配置资源，积极参与到行动之中。

政府间气候变化专门委员会的最新报告明确指出，气候变化已经是一场全球危机。这一事实已被媒体广泛报道，并为社会所接受。然而，生物多样性丧失和生态系统恶化的程度其实同样严重，令人十分担忧，但相关信息并没有引起广泛重视。

根据生物多样性和生态系统服务政府间科学政策平台（IPBES）2020年的评估，过去50年自然界经历的变化速度之快，是人类历史上前所未有的。

正是在这种背景下，联合国《生物多样性公约》第15次缔约方大会于2021年10月在中国昆明召开。论坛旨在达成2020年后全球生物多样性框架，以推动各方紧急采取变革行动，实现影响深远的生

物多样性保护成果，但实施这一框架具有挑战性。

首先，要大力提高对生物多样性保护的认识，要意识到所有经济活动都依赖于大自然，影响着大自然，而生物多样性和生态系统正是大自然的具体体现。据估计，每年全球有44万亿美元的经济价值——超过全球GDP的一半——都中度或高度依赖于大自然。

大自然对人类的贡献，大部分是不可完全替代的，有些甚至是完全不可替代的。例如，全球约75%的粮食作物，包括一些最重要的经济作物，依赖动物授粉。由于栖息地破坏和农业化学品造成的传粉动物减少，每年可能导致全球农作物产值降低2350亿至5770亿美元。此外，海岸栖息地和珊瑚礁的消失，令鱼类资源减少，也令海岸失去了保护，增加了洪水和飓风对数亿人生命和财产的威胁。

第二，对于生物多样性和生态系统所能提供的产品和服务的价值，必须予以充分评估以改善对其的保护。它们是自然资本的一部分，造福人类社会。充分评估生态系统提供的产品和服务的价值，可以更有效地利用资源，保护和维持生物多样性和生态系统功能。例如，亚洲开发银行发起的"区域自然资本实验室"项目重点关注自然资本核算，以及如何与相关协同政策一起，促成更合理的投资决策，以实现对大自然的正面效益。其他评估生态系统服务价值的倡议还有新西兰的"生活标准框架"和中国的"生态系统生产总值"等，后者由亚洲开发银行帮助构思。这些努力有助于制定出一套全球自然资本核算系统，并应该被各国所采用。

第三，要确保资源优化配置。据不完全统计，每年各国发放对生物多样性有害的直接补贴高达5000亿美元。在此背景下，新的全球生物多样性框架将呼吁各国政府承诺，每年至少改革或削减5000亿美元不利于生物多样性的补贴项目，把这笔资金改作他用。与此同时，该框架下每年用于生物多样性保护的资金要新增至少2000亿美元，其中用于发展中国家的资金将大幅提升。

第四，国家积极参与对框架的成功实施至关重要。框架将主要由国家一级的行动推动，进而延伸至区域、次区域，乃至全球行动。因此，政府的作用对此至关重要。中国在推进生态文明建设方面的经验值得其他国家借鉴。跨国的区域性生物多样性保护倡议也很重要。亚洲开发银行资助的"候鸟迁徙通道计划"就是一个很好的例子。该计划旨在恢复和保护东亚—大洋洲候鸟迁徙通道上的关键栖息地，保护湿地生态系统，让它们能够每年为数百万候鸟提供更好的服务。

最后，协同效应对结果很重要。生物多样性和生态系统的功能和服务是"联合国可持续发展目标"中关于清洁饮用水和卫生设施、气候行动、水下和陆地生物等目标的核心。然而，生物多样性的丧失和生态系统的破坏，令我们在减少贫困、促进健康、清洁饮用水和城市发展等方面的进展出现倒退。此外，生物多样性丧失与气候变化有着不可分割的联系，必须一同应对。为此，必须在缓解气候变化和保护生物多样性之间求得平衡，这是一项挑战，因为一些气候变化缓解和适应性措施，比如生物能源和可再生能源基础设施的大规模扩张，包括修建大坝和海堤，可能破坏生物栖息地，进而对生物多样性产生负面影响。

虽然框架的目标对企业没有约束力，但它象征着全球保护生物多样性的雄心，把防止生物多样性损失的关键活动放在了优先位置。早一天行动，就少一分损失。

（此文首发于2021年9月7日中国日报中国观察智库）

北京冬奥遗产：全民体育新风尚，绿色低碳向未来

杜晖贤（Frederick C. Dubee）

罗马俱乐部成员、中国生物多样性保护与绿色发展基金会国际工作顾问

2022年北京冬奥会秉持"绿色、共享、开放、廉洁"的理念，致力于将奥运会与区域发展相结合，激励更多民众广泛参与体育运动，推动绿色低碳转型。这是对2008年北京奥运会遗产的传承与发展，这一宝贵的精神遗产不仅将令北京、令中国，也将令全世界长期受益。

联合国前秘书长科菲·安南曾说，他最喜欢的奥运时刻是运动员们站在起点听候发令枪响的瞬间。因为那一刻，所有参赛者都是完全平等的，不存在任何形式的歧视。这一深刻见解正是反映出了奥运会的巨大潜力。

2008年北京奥运会和残奥会为世界留下了丰厚的奥运遗产，比如，这是一届具有高度包容性的奥运会，场馆中应用了许多环保技术和无障碍设施，还有先进的城市交通系统被沿用至今并不断完善、拓展。这些奥运遗产使中国人民对体育运动的重要性和价值意义产生了新的认识，让数亿国人参与到更多的体育活动中来。

2022年北京冬奥会传承了2008年北京奥运会及残奥会的遗产，

并制定了极具挑战性的目标。中国致力于将奥运会的价值从单纯的争金夺银，转向追求一个更具包容性的目标，那就是通过举办冬奥会，激励数亿中国人投身冰雪项目，以此吸引世界各地不同年龄的人们，尽可能地参与到体育运动当中。

"健全的心智寓于健康的身体"——在世界各地的不同语言中，都有类似含义的谚语，而个人身体的健康，某种程度上又与其所处的环境息息相关。自工业革命以来，水和空气质量的恶化不断加剧，从隐隐约约到肉眼可见，从偶然事件到长期现象，不知不觉间，环境污染已然成为了人们日常生活的一部分。这种以自然环境为代价的发展模式导致了许多人生活质量的降低，这种发展模式不仅破坏了自然环境，给人类在气候、水、营养和生物多样性领域带来诸多问题，引发公共卫生危机，还抑制了人们进行体育活动的意愿，许多人甚至连最低水平的体育运动都从不参与。

此外，尽管媒体上连篇累牍地报道新冠肺炎疫情或人工智能技术如何给人类带来威胁，但人类面临的真正威胁却是缺乏体育锻炼。国际奥委会医疗和科学委员会成员雅尼斯·匹兹拉迪斯表示，在新冠肺炎疫情肆虐之前，全球仅有不到30%的人口达到世界卫生组织建议的最低体育锻炼水平。而为防控新冠疫情，"非必要不出门"等防疫举措进一步限制了人们进行体育锻炼，使得这一数据进一步下降，世界人口体育运动现状堪忧。

在北京随国际奥委会医疗和科学委员会开展工作期间，匹兹拉迪斯表示："中国通过'冬奥遗产战略计划'，鼓励民众广泛参与体育运动，展示了奥运遗产的真正价值，也是将奥运投资收益最大化的最佳方法。"

2019年2月19日，北京冬奥组委发布《北京2022年冬奥会和冬残奥会遗产战略计划》。该计划旨在通过筹办北京冬奥会，努力创造体育、经济、社会、文化、环境、城市发展和区域发展7个方面的丰厚遗产，为主办城市和区域长远发展留下宝贵财富，惠及广大人民群众，实现奥林匹克运动与城市发展的双赢。

在这些背景下，中国和中国人民共同承诺，在2008年北京奥运会的基础上，落实"绿色、共享、开放、廉洁"的理念，办好冬奥会以及冬残奥会。北京冬奥会的竞赛场馆全部采用了绿色技术，100%使用绿色能源，体现出中国以冬奥会为契机，积极引导人民群众开启绿色低碳生活模式，树立绿色低碳文明观，助力中国在2030年前实现碳达峰，在2060年前实现碳中和的宏伟目标的实现。

北京2022年冬奥会和冬残奥会遗产战略计划聚焦以下三个目标：环境保护、区域发展和惠及大众。

/ 环境保护 /

在交通运输方面，冬奥会的交通工具全面采用可再生能源，几乎完全由电力、天然气和氢燃料驱动，同时采用了智能交通管理系统。在场馆方面，冬奥组委采用清洁的天然二氧化碳制冷技术，取代了传统的氢氟碳制冷技术。中国还实施了植树造林工程，累计造林4.7万公顷、绿地3.3万公顷，累计碳汇量100多万吨。

/ 区域发展 /

在冬奥会筹备工作的助推下，一套便捷省时、节能环保的交通网络加速建成。与此同时，区域性体育、旅游和文化带的开发和城市翻新项目正在进行中。

/ 惠及大众 /

借北京冬奥会举办的良机，相关社区在住房、就业、教育领域进行结构性调整，让居民充分实现工作与生活的平衡。全民健身和冬季体育运动的参与热情不断高涨，让"三亿人民上冰雪"的愿景成为现实。

当然，对主办国家和城市而言，每一届奥运会和残奥会不仅是巨大的机遇，也是严峻的挑战。但无论如何，奥林匹克带来的更多是长期的、可持续的好处。2022年北京冬奥会正在进行，随着奥运圣火从北京传递到巴黎、再到米兰，2022年北京冬奥会和冬残奥会的奥运遗产将令北京、令中国、令全世界长期受益。

（此文首发于2022年2月17日中国日报中国观察智库）

〔 第三章 〕
可持续发展的责任与担当

统筹兼顾：推动实现全球气候与生物多样性双重目标

朱力
保尔森基金会生态保护项目主任
牛红卫
保尔森基金会生态保护项目总监
唐瑞（Terry Townshend）
保尔森基金会顾问

若要形容做事缺乏统筹、顾此失彼，用"头疼医头，脚疼医脚"这一说法，再贴切不过了。当医生诊疗病人时，只有从整体上对症下药，而不是拘囿于局部症状，才能药到病除。与此类似，解决我们当下面临的全球气候变化和生物多样性丧失的双重威胁也需要统筹兼顾，协同一致。

人们日渐认识到气候变化和生物多样性危机之间有着错综复杂的联系：气候变化加剧了生物多样性的丧失，削弱了自然生态系统吸收和储存碳的能力，进而又加速了气候变化。只有齐头并进地积极应对双重挑战，才能打破上述恶性循环，有效解决危机。

近年来，统筹应对气候变化和生物多样性危机正逐渐成为科学家、政府决策者和金融界人士的共识。然而，这一共识尚未在相关投入资金量上有所体现。从全球来看，应对气候变化和保护生物多样性两个领域的资金量相去甚远。据相关统计，2019年/2020年，全球气候融资额已高达6320亿美元，而生物多样性融资总额却仅为1240至1430亿美元。

这一反差在绿色金融资金的投向上也有所体现。支持气候变化相关项目的资金远超支持生物多样性保护和修复的资金。根据国际开发性金融俱乐部的研究，其成员在2020年作出了总计1850亿美元的绿色金融承诺，其中1790亿美元（96%）用于支持应对气候变化，而用于生物多样性保护和修复的资金只有54亿美元（3%）。

在中国，绿色债券的资金投向也凸显了二者之间的显著差异。根据《2020年中国绿色债券市场报告》，2020年中国各机构共发行了440亿美元的绿色债券，募集的资金中只有约5%用于生物多样性或生态保护相关领域，其余大部分资金则流向了与应对气候变化相关的项目。

造成二者在资金规模上产生悬殊差距的原因有很多。

首先，在气候变化领域，不同类型的温室气体排放都可以转化为二氧化碳当量，因此可以准确地量化不同温室气体排放对气候变化的贡献度。这一标准化、普适性高的核算方法使得开发、资助和监测各类气候变化项目成为可能。相比之下，从生物量和经济价值量的角度出发，核算生物多样性或生态系统服务都极其困难。因此，对于依靠量化结果进行决策的投资者而言，其投资意愿不可避免地大打折扣。

　　其次，多国已出台了针对碳排放的监管政策，推动了碳排放外部成本的内部化。因此，应对气候变化的项目（如可再生能源开发和能源效率提升）已经能产生明确的现金流，并吸引到了来自私营部门数量可观的投资。相比之下，尽管生物多样性为人类社会创造了多种效益，但将其转化为经济收益的机制仍不成熟。除了可持续林业、生态旅游、缓解银行等少数例子外，可投资性高的生物多样性项目屈指可数。正因如此，生物多样性保护的资金仍然主要靠公共财政投入。

　　再者，生物多样性通常具有极强的地域性。因此，一个地方的生物多样性保护项目和实施方案很难在其他地方进行规模化复制。一般而言，生物多样性保护项目往往规模适中、性质各异，因此难以跟强调标准化和规模经济的现代金融市场和金融产品相匹配。因此，生物多样性保护和修复项目要充分利用现代金融市场的效率、网络和资金资源还任重而道远。

　　尽管存在着诸多挑战，增加生物多样性保护融资、提升应对气候变化和生物多样性之间的协同性仍大有可为。

　　首先，应尽量避免应对气候变化和保护生物多样性的措施间的相互冲突。例如，一些清洁能源基础设施对土地的占用量高达传统能源项目的12倍。因此，新能源开发项目的选址和规划至关重要。如果不谨慎规划，清洁能源基础设施建设可能会危及生物多样性，也会增加日后修复生物多样性的财政负担。

　　其次，我们应积极探索"基于自然的气候解决方案"的应用，以应对气候变化和生物多样性双重危机。例如，修复红树林可带来多重效益。红树林是鱼类的"育苗场"、固碳储碳的天然碳库，也是防风消浪的天然屏障。

　　令人欣慰的是，中国政府结合保尔森基金会及其合作伙伴共同发布了一项战略性研究，即《红树林保护修复专项行动计划》，旨在大力修复红树林生态系统。行动计划以2020年到2025年为行动周期，明确了工作目标，即到2025年营造和修复红树林18800公顷。

此外，2021年7月，中国碳排放权交易系统上线，覆盖了8个高碳排放行业部门。该系统允许基于生态系统的相关项目所产生的信用额用以抵消碳排放，具有扩大"基于自然的气候解决方案"的应用面的潜力。同时，专家呼吁进行碳排放配额拍卖，并将部分所得收益用于生态系统的保护和修复，此举有助于促进生物多样性的融资。

通过创新机制搭建生物多样性融资和现有金融市场之间的桥梁也是当务之急。例如，将多个相似度高、可复制的项目进行整合，或将多个差异较大的项目进行打包，将其设计成更易为现有金融市场接受的产品，从而释放出大量寻求环境、社会和治理主体投资机会的资金资源。红树林债券是其中一个典型案例，正不断引发中外金融机构的兴趣和关注。

最后，我们还必须探索实现生态服务价值的创新性机制，无论是通过利用现有金融市场，还是通过创造新型市场。例如，纽约证券交易所正在探索一种基于自然的新资产类别，即自然资产公司，其旨在抓取和存储自然的内在生产价值。

当然，要使生物多样性融资实现规模化的增长，还必须解决其他许多方面的挑战。例如，强化政策框架和监管要求以充分体现对自然价值的重视，加强相关机构和人员的能力建设，以及通过各类激励机制降低投资风险，以鼓励私营部门投资生态保护和修复。此外，改革能源、农业和渔业领域的有害补贴，消除商品供应链中生产环节的毁林，这些措施对于实现全球气候变化和生物多样性目标也至关重要。

从根本上讲，全球气候和生物多样性危机反映了人类社会当前的经济活动漠视大自然的现状，那么我们就不得不承担相应的后果。为扭转这一局面，我们必须转型经济体系，承认人类所拥有的自然资本的有限性和重要性。

修复地球生态环境需要时日，也离不开高度协同的应对措施。绿色金融和基于自然的气候解决方案已经显示出其在推动实现全球气候与生物多样性双重目标方面的巨大潜力，我们的当务之急就是提升这些行动的速度和广度。常言道，"时不我待，只争朝夕"，当下尤为如此。

（此文英文原文首发于2022年7月11日中国日报国际版）

从2008奥运到2022冬奥：
"北京蓝"留给世界的启示

艾瑞碧（Rebecca Ivey）

世界经济论坛原大中华区首席代表（2021—2022）

当前全球环境气候形势不容乐观，气候治理动力不足，各国之间缺乏信任，令可持续发展目标难以实现。中国多年来在环保方面付出了巨大努力，尤其是2008年北京奥运会留下了宝贵的"绿色奥运遗产"。"北京蓝"的取得为世界提供了重要经验，那就是全球气候环境治理需要各国加强信任与合作，并为之付出长久努力。

我的办公室位于北京一栋写字楼的18层，透过窗户向外望去，三面远山环绕，在澄澈的蓝天下格外醒目。而与之形成鲜明对比的是，2008年北京奥运会之前，当我第一次造访这座城市时，它还笼罩在雾霾之下。而今，在地缘政治局势紧张以及气候危机愈演愈烈之际，在运动员、体育爱好者和时事评论员们都忙着准备迎接2022年北京冬奥会之时，让我们一起来回顾一下，在净化北京天空的这20年间，我们都收获了哪些经验和教训。

长期以来，中国政府致力于改善空气质量。最终，"北京蓝"成为了新常态。国际奥委会表示，为履行2000年申奥时许下的承诺，中国政府投入了210亿美元用于改善空气质量，6万台燃煤锅炉升级改造，4000多辆公共汽车改用清洁的天然气作为燃料。

联合国环境规划署的一份报告称，中国能够获得国际认可并创造"能够长期传承下去的环境遗产"，靠的是具体行动，而不是华而不实的说辞。过去十年里，任何一个呼吸过北京空气的人都可以证明，通往蓝天的道路从来不是笔直平坦的，瞩目的成就背后是中国的坚持和投入。

空气污染治理的成功预示着中国有能力应对气候变化，也让世界各国相信，一个更加包容、有韧性并且可持续的未来并非遥不可及。习近平主席已经郑重宣布，中国将在2030年前实现碳达峰，在2060年前实现碳中和。这不仅激励了国内各行各业采取行动，也促使其他国家在碳排放问题上加大治理力度。

数据显示，2020年中国的碳强度比2005年下降了48.4%，实现了此前向国际社会作出的承诺，即到2020年碳强度比2005年下降40%到45%。现在"1＋N"政策体系（即顶层设计加上各项具体行动计划），正致力于将可操作的政策落实到位，与习主席最初的承诺相呼应。

2021年底，中美两国在第26届联合国气候变化大会期间签署了《中美关于在21世纪20年代强化气候行动的格拉斯哥联合宣言》，为进一步推动全球气候治理这一艰巨任务注入了动力。此外，两国还就《巴黎协定》下的气候融资和国家自主贡献问题达成了共识。正如世界经济论坛主席布伦德所说，中美两国未来的合作至关重要。"只有认识到我们命运与共，务必携手，我们才能继续前进"。

然而，前景并不乐观。普华永道2021年的净零经济指数显示，为了到2030年将全球碳排放减半、到本世纪中叶实现净零排放，全球碳强度必须以年均12.9%的速度降低，而当前的实际速度尚不及这一数字的五分之一。通过该报告与其他相关研究，我们得出了一个结论：只有对全球经济进行系统性深刻重组，才能实现如此巨大的转变。但各国之间信任的丧失使实现这一目标的前景变得更加渺茫。世界经济论坛在28个国家进行的一项气候研究发现，只有大约四分之一的受访者相信企业关于自身可持续发展的说辞，并且大多数受访者强烈认为目前的环境保护力度远远不够。

为了重建信任，世界经济论坛致力于支持所有利益相关方就可持续发展目标和行动找到共同语言。2020年，世界经济论坛与该领域其他领先机构合作，共同制定了一套综合性的衡量标准，以填补环境、社会和公司治理（ESG）报告标准的空白。一份关于中国企业ESG形势的后续报告指出，一份可衡量的全球可持续发展共识，对中国的利益相关者来说意义非凡，它既符合全球环保投资重点，又能帮助中国企业实现国家环境治理目标。与此同时，"一带一路"倡议的绿色投资原则表明，中国致力于支持发展中国家发展绿色金融、绿色科技，以扩大低碳基础设施规模，借此助力其他国家应对气候问题。

除了气候问题之外，其他的全球性环境问题，如生物多样性问题，都位列中国的优先行动清单之中。世界经济论坛自2020年开始发布《新自然经济报告系列》，该报告利用数据资料为企业和政府提供了向"自然向好"型经济转型的途径。

回顾这两年，全球各国清楚地意识到，合作和信任是人类生存和繁荣不可或缺的重要条件。

窗外万里无云的蓝天给人以永世晴朗的感觉，但我们不应该忘记，蓝天的取得，靠的不是一日之功、一时之效、一人之力。为了确保我们的子孙后代仍能享受大自然的馈赠，我们必须肩负起责任，携手合作，重建信任。

（此文首发于2022年1月17日中国日报中国观察智库）

"绿色发展红利"：中国为全球贡献的又一公共产品

俞子荣

商务部国际贸易经济合作研究院副院长

中国长期重视对其他发展中国家的能源援助与合作。在当前全球能源转型和新冠肺炎疫情压力叠加的背景下，中国低碳绿色发展红利成为可与全球各国分享的公共产品，尤其利于发展中国家发挥"后发优势"，选择适宜本国国情的绿色复苏和可持续发展道路。面对当前疫情条件下发展中国家能源转型的迫切需求和宝贵窗口，中国有针对性地加大绿色能源援助，可提供更大助力。

2021年9月21日，习近平主席出席第76届联合国大会一般性辩论，并就启动"全球发展倡议"作重要讲话，郑重承诺"将大力支持发展中国家能源绿色低碳发展、加大发展资源投入、重点推进绿色发展等领域合作"，展现了中国支持发展中国家绿色复苏和可持续发展的责任担当。

当前，能源短缺已经成为制约广大发展中国家疫情防控和疫后复苏的主要瓶颈之一。中国作为最早控制住疫情的主要经济体之一，正通过分享中国低碳发展经验以及提供绿色能源援助，致力于帮助广大发展中国家在疫情条件下实现能源转型，推进绿色发展。

中国从建国初期开始就深刻认识到能源和电力对国家建设的关键作用。在当时的历史条件下，中国对发展中国家进行的能源援助主要以开发利用化石能源为主。据统计，1956年至1985年间，中国共帮助16个国家建成52个能源项目，总装机容量110万千瓦；援建输变电工程18个，线路总长2400多公里。

在开发利用化石能源的同时，为便利偏远地区生产生活和社会发展，中国还帮助发展中国家建设了一批沼气发电、小水电等因地制宜的离网可再生能源项目，并于1981年同联合开发计划署合作，在国内建设了专注发展中国家间技术合作的小水电研究和培训中心，进行了早期绿色能源援助的有益探索。

随着中国经济飞速发展，中国可再生能源产业获得举世瞩目的成就，为国内能源绿色低碳转型提供强大支撑。中国在能源领域的国际发展合作也随之向现代绿色能源援助转型：在多边层面，中国在南南合作气候基金支持下，持续向发展中国家捐赠光伏照明和发电设备，开展绿色低碳发展的官员和技术人员培训；在双边层面，中国加大了绿色能源援助力度，包括为尼泊尔提供总装机容量1兆瓦的屋顶光伏，通过优惠贷款支持肯尼亚建成东非最大的光伏电站——加里萨50兆瓦光伏电站等。中国快速迭代的能源技术和规模经济效应，使得可再生能源的开发利用成本大大降低。随着与中国的发展合作和商业合作的扩大，更多发展中国家能够分享中国可再生能源发展的利好。

发展中国家一方面面临能源消费需求旺盛与能源供给不足的尖锐矛盾，另一方面也面临全球气候变化条件下控制污染物和温室气体排放的严峻挑战。新冠肺炎疫情无疑进一步加剧了以上难题，致使发展中国家债务负担和主权风险上升，融资成本高企，部分规划当中的可再生能源项目被迫搁置。私营资本缺乏对能源电力基础设施进行长期投资的意愿，甚至在疫情期间扎堆外逃。

但同时，疫情也为发展中国家能源转型提供了一个窗口期。全球经济对化石能源和电力的需求量下降，全球资本对化石能源的投资意愿降低，有利于发展中国家进行能源结构调整。全球主要经济体开始就海外融资退出煤电达成共识，转而寻求支持可再生能源，这有利于发展中国家在可再生能源开发方面引进投资和技术以及降低成本。

面对当前疫情条件下发展中，国家能源转型的迫切需求和宝贵窗口，中国能更有针对性地加大绿色能源援助，帮助发展中国家充分利用可再生能源资源，选择一条符合其国家资源情况和发展规划的能源转型道路，努力实现其后发优势。可以从以下几个方面提供更大助力：

一是对接可再生能源发展规划。中国能源援助应尊重东道国发展议程，回应发展中国家发展需求，对接东道国发展规划，提升能源对外援助项目与东道国能源发展远景的兼容度。

二是分享低碳清洁能源发展解决方案。中国可再生能源设备产能和国内装机已连年稳居全球第一，可再生能源领域比较优势还体现在节能技术、减排技术、绿色金融等领域。例如，对市场机制和营商环境相对良好的国家，可开展绿色金融政策交流和人才培养援助项目；对东道国已落成的化石能源项目，可开展污染物排放改造、综合节能改造和电站灵活性改造援助；对于成本和技术门槛较高、但备受全球关注的新兴技术，例如碳捕捉、利用和封存，也可考虑以援助开展可行性研究或技术培训，撬动后续商业合作。

三是分享中国能源脱贫与能源转型相结合的发展经验。中国在推动14亿人口全民通电和能源转型的过程中，探索了协同推进能源脱贫和能源清洁转型的创新方案，例如，"实施乡村清洁能源建设工程"被纳入了2021年"中央一号文件"，建设高质量乡村能源体系、发展普惠式光伏、实施乡村风电工程等倡议陆续铺开。中国应与其他发展中国家在南南合作框架下加强能力建设合作和政策交流，探讨开展"方案援助"，分享中国经验。

四是以可再生能源助力新冠疫情防控工作。能源电力需求贯穿疫情防控工作的各个环节。在发展中国家偏远地区，可再生能源和分布式电力设施往往比以化石能源驱动的大型集中式电力设施更能满足医疗卫生工作和日常生产生活需求。中国已在应对气候变化的南南合作基金等援助资金项下，多次开展对发展中国家可再生能源物资的赠与。可探讨加强能源部门和卫生部门的跨部门合作，支持发展中国家获得医疗设施必需的供电和照明服务，以及疫苗冷链运输所必需的制冷设备等。

中国低碳绿色发展红利已成为可与全球各国分享的全球公共产品，尤其有利于发展中国家发挥"后发优势"，选择适宜本国国情的绿色复苏和可持续发展道路。

（此文首发于2021年10月20日中国日报中国观察智库）

绿色

多领域齐头并进改革创新

探索

〔 第一章 〕

低碳绿色经济转型：我们不只有承诺

"牛放屁"加剧全球变暖？
畜牧大国巴西这样做

阎甜
永续全球环境研究所（GEI）海外投资、贸易与环境项目官员
龙冬荃
永续全球环境研究所（GEI）对外联络项目官员

　　畜牧业温室气体排放对全球气候变化的影响不容忽视。在这方面，巴西作为一个畜牧大国，已有不少创新实践，包括开发"作物—畜牧—林业体系"，制定碳中和农产品认证标准等。这些实践对中国实现碳达峰碳中和目标具有借鉴意义，中巴两国已经在相关领域开展多层次合作。

　　2021年11月13日，第26届联合国气候变化大会在英国格拉斯哥召开。巴西环境部部长若阿金·莱特代表该国在会上提出了新的国家承诺，以解决温室气体排放以及森林砍伐问题。

承诺内容包括：到2030年，巴西温室气体排放量减半，并于2050年实现碳中和。同时，从现在起到2080年，巴西将彻底禁绝非法砍伐森林的行为。以上诸多举措将有利于保护生物群落，控制全球变暖。

中国和巴西已经建立了多层次的全面伙伴关系。自2014年起，中国公私企业开始在巴西投资农业企业，开展农业基础设施建设。同时，保持经济增长、促进粮食安全也日益成为双边关系的重要纽带。目前，为实现其减排目标，巴西已经建立了相关体制机制，推动了一系列项目落地。这些经验对中国进口持续增长和产业发展具有借鉴意义，对中国实现碳减排目标具有重要价值。

例如，畜牧业的温室气体排放是一项重大挑战。根据联合国政府间气候变化专门委员会的计算，因畜牧业产生的温室气体占人为排放总量的14.5%。而在美国、新西兰和巴西等主要农产品生产国，畜牧业碳排放量的占比更高。

在畜牧业当中，肉牛养殖是甲烷排放的罪魁祸首，而大量排放的甲烷也直接导致了栖息地面貌的改变。牛津大学数据网站"Our World in Data"的统计结果显示，从建设牧场引发的土地使用变化，到最终的食物浪费，在整个牛肉生产周期各环节中所排放的温室气体总量，高于其他反刍动物肉类生产。在养殖阶段实现脱碳，尤其是降低牛的肠道甲烷排放（通俗地说就是"牛放屁"），是应对气候变化的重要一环。

对于因牛肉生产所导致的温室气体排放问题，巴西率先表态并积极采取行动。他们想出的办法是，通过在牧场上植树来中和牛群的甲烷排放，这种办法被称为"畜牧—林业体系"或"作物—畜牧—林业体系"。巴西农业部下属的巴西农牧业研究公司发现，如果在一公顷土地上种植200棵速生树木（如桉树），就能吸收这一公顷土地上11头成年牛一年内所排放的甲烷，而巴西的平均载畜率为1.2头牛/公顷。

这个逻辑就是：在农业系统中多种树，就相当于减少了森林采伐，从而降低碳排放。同时，桉树还能够保持、甚至增加土壤中的有机碳含量。桉树本身又可以用于生产家具等附加值较高的木材产品，延长碳的储存时间，并进一步增加农民收入。

2020年，巴西农牧业研究公司和巴西牛肉行业领军企业马夫瑞集团联合开发的世界上第一条"碳中和牛肉"生产线——"Viva"问世，这是所有公私合作碳减排项目中的明星产品之一。目前这款牛肉已上架巴西圣保罗州的十多家超市。过去5年来，双方在产品概念、生产协议、技术工艺以及认证机制等方面通力合作，投资高达1000万雷亚尔（约合1150万人民币）。

上述这一相当完备的体系是一项智慧农业技术，在其支持下，巴西有望实现该国农业部新确立的减排目标。

中国也开始试图了解并借鉴这一项目，双方企业正通力合作，积极推动碳中和农畜产品创新实践并使巴西享受先发优势。例如，永续全球环境研究所（GEI）近年来从不同角度出发，开展了一系列研究，包括中国巴西贸易投资分析，以及巴西碳中和牛肉产品的标准和市场分析。GEI与巴西马托格罗索州政府有意洽谈签署合作谅解备忘录，并就落地项目展开合作，支持当地创新型智慧农业的发展。

从第26届联合国气候变化大会部长级会议，到机构层面，中巴双方都在就农产品等碳中和软大宗产品未来可能的分销渠道问题进行谈判。这将把低碳、零碳等条件加入到现行的商业标准中，让中巴经贸关系更加"绿色"。同时，巴西的碳中和措施在中国畜牧业的推广和本地化，也与中国的碳达峰碳中和目标相一致，因此也非常符合中方投资者的利益。

在贸易层面，拥有碳中和认证的密封大宗商品对中国企业颇具吸引力。碳中和认证是一种市场导向的实用性方法，且具有工具性功能。中国食品土畜进出口商会的许多成员，对持有与可持续发展相关认证的商品更加青睐，比如他们更倾向于采购"美国大豆可持续保障体系"认证的大豆。

当前，中国的牛肉产品尚无类似认证，而巴西的"碳中和牛肉"认证体系也尚未得到国内认可。中国环境联合认证中心经过分析认为，开发出一套复杂而全面的认证体系是可行的。当然，农民要想获得这一认证，实际难度不小，但认证的本质正是为了提高行业标准，提供一个公平的行业竞争环境。

（此文首发于2022年1月19日中国日报中国观察智库）

多重打击下，小岛屿发展中国家急需援手

石教群

联合国粮农组织亚太区域办公室特别顾问（南南及三方合作）

> 小岛屿发展中国家本就面临气候变化、生物多样性丧失、资源萎缩等多重挑战，新冠肺炎疫情更是令其发展前景雪上加霜。南南合作和三方合作在帮助这些国家解决粮食、环境和健康问题方面，显示出独特的优势和机会。在联合国粮农组织和中国等各方的合作下，相关国家在可持续农业发展方面已有成功实践。

在1992年举办的联合国环境与发展会议上，"小岛屿发展中国家"被确认为一个特殊的国家类别，以反映它们独特的环境和发展需要。这些国家的特点是人口少，环礁众多，分布在加勒比海、太平洋、大西洋、印度洋、地中海等地区。

虽然从单个来看，小岛屿发展中国家的人口比较少，但如果把他们加起来，却能占到了世界人口的1%，即6500万人左右。

由于小岛屿发展中国家固有的脆弱性，包括其国土面积小、地处偏远、气候变化对其生态系统影响巨大、生物多样性的丧失和资源基础的萎缩，这些岛国的居民正面临着独特的社会、经济和环境挑战。

由于耕地有限，许多小岛屿发展中国家只能"靠海吃海"，种植业规模很小。这些国家还严重依赖进口食品，而这些高糖高盐的加工食品往往导致健康问题。联合国粮农组织的统计数据显示，在加勒比和太平洋地区，几乎所有小岛屿发展中国家的粮食进口依赖度都超过60%，其中半数国家进口依赖度超过80%。尽管可以通过进口获得粮食，但小岛屿发展中国家的饥饿水平仍然高达17%，令人震惊。新冠肺炎疫情大流行进一步威胁这些国家的粮食安全、营养和气候韧性。

2020年受新冠肺炎疫情影响，这些国家的整体GDP下降了6.9%，比其他发展中国家的GDP降幅（4.8%）更大。这主要是由于，对许多小岛屿发展中国家至关重要的两个海洋经济部门——沿海旅游业和渔业在全球范围内出现萎缩。经合组织报告显示，对三分之二的小岛屿发展中国家而言，旅游业占其GDP的比重在20%以上。联合国世界旅游组织估计，自疫情发生以来，2020年1月至4月，小岛屿发展中国家接收的国际游客人数下降了47%，并警告称，这些国家的经济复苏之路将是漫长和充满不确定性的。同样，这些国家的渔业部门也受到疫情的严重冲击，对国内就业和居民营养造成不利影响。

在这种严峻挑战之下，南南合作和三方合作恰好有机会介入，发挥出其在解决小岛屿发展中国家的农业、粮食、营养、环境和健康等方面问题的独特优势。通过南南及三方合作，小岛屿发展中国家可以获得并采用其他国家的相关解决方案，这些国家在解决类似社会经济背景和农业生态区的发展问题方面有较新的经验。

联合国粮农组织一直致力于寻找并鼓励发展中国家之间的知识、技能和经验交流，以支持小岛屿发展中国家在农业领域加入气候适应和缓解措施。2013年，粮农组织支持萨摩亚农民协会开展沼气技术可行性研究，包括到中国实地考察。在此基础上，中国农业农村部沼气科学研究所、萨摩亚农民协会在其他合作伙伴的支持下，通过2018—2019年中国援助萨摩亚农业技术合作项目，把中国的可持续动物粪便管理技术带到萨摩亚。21台沼气生产设备运抵萨摩亚并在当地投入使用，22名萨摩亚学员在中方专家指导下提升了技能。该项目为每个家庭每月节省了大约25美元的燃气费用，让许多当地妇女从拾柴的艰苦工作中解脱出来，产生了良好的经济社会效益。

展望未来，为了推动《小岛屿发展中国家粮食安全和营养全球行动计划》，粮农组织还应利用南南及三方合作方式，在小岛屿发展中国家推广本地化的可持续粮农体系。全球许多已经完成或正在进行的南南合作和三方合作项目，通过促进知识和技术交流，巩固了传统的农业生产系统，制定了病虫害防治和水土管理的综合方案，提升了相关国家对根茎作物、芭蕉、面包果等营养丰富的传统粮食作物的种植兴趣。

根据以往的经验和成就，可以进一步为小岛屿发展中国家在后疫情时代利用南南及三方合作促进农业可持续发展，提供如下具体建议。

第一，可以把更多的有效举措整合进"小岛屿发展中国家解决方案平台"，并通过南南合作和三方合作机制，使其他小岛屿发展中国家对相关经验进行分享、交流和实践。例如2021年8月30日至31日，由联合国粮农组织和斐济政府共同主办的小岛屿发展中国家发展对策论坛，就为各国交流经验提供了机会。

在萨摩亚，许多女性农民利用社交媒体，拓宽当地蔬菜、水果和手工艺品市场的渠道。类似项目多由斐济、萨摩亚和瓦努阿图等国家发起，但也有可能通过南南合作和三方合作机制，在其他小岛屿发展中国家培育和壮大。此外，亚洲、非洲和小岛屿发展中国家还开展了很多科技项目，可以促进当地可持续发展，提升粮农系统韧性。

第二，南南合作和三方合作的重点，应与小岛屿发展中国家的发展重点保持一致，以应对小岛屿发展中国家所面临的独特挑战。小岛屿发展中国家对气候变化的责任最小，却受气候变化影响最大。它们也是新冠肺炎疫情面前最脆弱的国家。这些国家经济结构单一，易受外界影响，疫情对其关键经济部门造成了严重干扰。全球所有的小岛屿发展中国家都可从知识和技术的交流中受益匪浅。

第三，作为南南合作和三方合作的全球倡导者和合作伙伴，粮农组织在将多个利益攸关方聚集在一起，促进小岛屿发展中国家粮食和农业可持续发展方面，发挥着独特的作用。据经合组织估计，2020年，粮农组织为应对新冠肺炎疫情危机而向小岛屿发展中国家提供的援助总额，保守估计为28亿美元。粮农组织将积极撬动资金，通过南方伙伴关系，致力于解决小岛屿发展中国家的能力建设和投资问题。此外，它还与岛屿国家政府合作，特别是通过探索公私合作商业模式，让"从农田到餐桌"所有利益攸关方都参与进来，提高粮食价值链每个环节的生产力和生产效率。

（此文首发于2021年9月2日中国日报中国观察智库）

〔 第二章 〕
探索产业低碳转型的中国方案

中国海外投资正变得更"绿"

龙迪（Dimitri de Boer）

克莱恩斯（ClientEarth）欧洲环保协会亚洲区主任、中国环境与发展国际合作委员会特邀顾问

王珂礼（Christoph Nedopil Wang）

复旦泛海国际金融学院经济学副教授，绿色金融与发展中心主任

　　随着"一带一路"建设稳步推进，商务部和生态环境部联合印发《对外投资合作绿色发展工作指引》，为中国企业参与绿色"一带一路"建设提供了新的指导。近年来，中国对"一带一路"沿线可再生能源项目的投资持续增加，通过采取积极行动"绿化"海外投资项目对接《巴黎协定》相关要求。

　　2021年7月16日，中国商务部和生态环境部联合印发《对外投资合作绿色发展工作指引》（以下简称《工作指引》），旨在鼓励

中国企业将绿色发展融入海外投资与合作的全过程。这为加快中国乃至世界的绿色发展提供了助力。

《工作指引》提出，中国企业要在对外投资合作过程中遵循绿色国际规则和标准，鼓励企业按照国际通行惯例开展对外投资项目的环境评估和尽职调查，特别是当东道国环保标准过低时，鼓励企业采用国际组织或多边机构通行标准或中国标准开展投资合作活动。这些都是促进绿色发展的明确举措。该指导方针将污染控制、生态保护和气候变化三个环境方面纳入其中，让中国的海外投资活动与《巴黎协定》的要求相一致。

《工作指引》支持中国企业在太阳能、风能、核能、生物质能等清洁能源领域的对外投资。这是绝对必要的，因为气候变化的风险在世界各地，包括中国，正变得越来越明显。气候变化极大地增加了干旱、热浪和洪水等极端天气的发生概率，所有国家都应该停止建设新的高碳基础设施，并迅速开始减少温室气体排放。

《工作指引》还涉及贸易领域，要求企业加快与全球绿色产业链对接融合，实施绿色采购，优先购买环境友好产品和服务。当前我们的地球仍在遭受严重的森林砍伐，这一要求如果贯彻落实到位，将对生物多样性的保护起到重要作用。

《工作指引》的出台，正值新冠肺炎全球肆虐，世界各国希望尽快实现疫后复苏之际。这些指导方针的公布反映出中国愿意在支持可持续发展方面发挥重要作用。

对于中国国家开发银行、中国进出口银行、中国出口信用保险公司等金融机构而言，这些指导方针有助于推动其环保努力，设定更高目标，采取更严措施。事实上，许多金融机构已经在积极致力于绿色发展。

2021年6月，"一带一路"国际绿色发展联盟、欧洲环保协会、北京绿色金融与可持续发展研究院联合举办了一场为期两天的"一带一路"绿色金融与环境管理专题研讨会，来自"一带一路"沿线国家和地区的多家大型金融机构代表参会。这些机构制定了一系列关键政策，如基于环境风险的项目分类、环境标准要求、影响评估体系、第三方评估机制、信息披露和公众参与、申诉机制、化石燃料替代政策等。当然，这个过程中也遇到了一些困难。同时，在中国人民银行对气候金融的大力支持下，这些机构在发展绿色贷款和债券方面也取得了快速进展。

我们已经可以从当前的投资趋势中看到这种转变。中央财经大学绿色金融国际研究院发布的《2021年上半年中国"一带一路"投资报告》显示，2020年中国在"一带一路"沿线国家的可再生能源投资金额，首次超过对这些国家煤炭行业的投资；实际上在2021年上半年，中国对沿线国家煤炭融资为零。例如，中国工商银行于2021年6月退出对津巴布韦大型燃煤电厂的融资。中国已经开始支持许多"一带一路"国家的能源转型。这种转型不仅具有环境意义，也具有经济意义，例如新增太阳能发电的成本只相当于新增煤炭发电的五分之一。

我们预计这一良好势头将继续下去，中国将越来越积极地参与海外绿色投资。新出台的《工作指引》提出，"推动企业按照境外项目生态环境保护有关要求开展生态环境风险防范工作"。但目前这些相关要求还不存在，这就意味着，它们可能在不久的将来被制定出来。

中国在气候行动和生物多样性保护方面的领导作用，将是推动全球绿色转型的关键一着。

（此文首发于2021年8月10日中国日报中国观察智库）

中国核电为世界低碳转型"充能"

林伯强

厦门大学中国能源政策研究院院长

　　实现碳中和是中国作为一个负责任大国对全人类的承诺，在风电光伏以及水电都面临着不同发展瓶颈的背景下，清洁稳定的核电将成为实现碳中和的一个重要选择。在经历了30多年的发展历程之后，中国核电产业将实现由"引进来"到"走出去"的跨越。中国自主研发的三代核电技术以其安全性、经济性和高效性，将为全世界提供一个有效的低碳解决方案。

　　截至2020年底，包括中国在内的全球27个国家和地区已经提出了各自的碳中和目标，其中23个是发达国家。相较于这些经济发达、工业体系更加成熟的国家和地区，中国的碳中和之路更加复杂和困难。一方面，中国的化石能源消费占一次能源消费总量的85%左右，其中碳强度最高的煤炭更是占据了约58%的比重。另一方面，中国经济还处于中高速发展阶段，经济的增长还会促使能源系统不断扩张。相对耗能的产业结构和不断扩张的能源消费，成为实现碳中和目标进程中需要克服的困难。

/ 替代能源 /

中国也在不断尝试碳排放更低的能源方案，并在风电、水电、太阳能发电等清洁能源领域进行了大量投入。2019年中国风电和光电的总装机容量分别达到了2.1亿千瓦和2亿千瓦，合计占中国电力装机总容量的20.6%。但与高装机容量形成鲜明对比的是这两者的实际发电量，2019年风电和光电的发电总量合计仅占当年发电总量的8%左右。装机利用小时数低、风电光伏自身的不稳定性，以及电网调峰等问题，在很大程度上限制了这两种电力生产方式在碳中和进程中所发挥的作用。而水电则面临着潜能限制和生态环保等多方面的压力。

相较于发达国家核电在能源结构中的占比，中国核电发展空间依然比较大。2019年中国核电装机容量为4874万千瓦，仅占电力装机总量的2%，却占了总发电量的5%，其高效清洁的特征可以为实现碳中和做出重要贡献。

/ 长足进展 /

中国核电技术自20世纪80年代起步以来，经过了30多年不断积累。

1983年，中国首个核电站——秦山核电站破土动工时，它的技术设备，包括反应堆压力容器等都依赖进口，且装机量只有30万千瓦。而到了2015年，"华龙一号"单台机组装机容量达到了116.1万千瓦，它是在国内核电建设经验积累的基础上，结合当前国际核电站最高安全标准及先进的核电站技术，自主设计研发的三代核电技术创新成果。

2011年日本福岛核泄漏事件显然严重影响了中国核电的发展，加之国内电力供需相对宽松，近10年来核电似乎发展速度减缓，但是核电发电量仍然以年均10%的速度增长。目前中国已有5200万千瓦核电装机容量处于商业运行阶段，还有1900万千瓦装机容量处于在建阶段，预计2025年核电总装机容量将达到7000万千瓦。

/ 安全基础 /

核电所有的好处都建立在安全的基础上。

从事核电的人都清楚，核电事故不仅会带来巨大的损失，还将极大地影响核电整体产业的发展。20世纪苏联切尔诺贝利和美国三里岛核电站的严重事故使得美国和欧洲先后出台了URD标准文件和EUR标准文件。这些安全标准对预防核电站严重事故、改善核电站工程安全性方面提出了更高的要求。国际上通常把同时满足这两个标准的核电机组称为"第三代核电机组"。

中国的"华龙一号"是第三代核电机组设计，采用"双层安全壳"技术，并充分吸取福岛核事故的经验，创新性地采用"能动与非能动相结合"的安全系统，真正做到了应对突发事故时安全保障手段的多样性，既符合当前国际最高安全标准，也达到了《核安全与放射性污染防治"十二五"规划及2020年远景目标》《福岛核事故后核电厂改进行动通用技术要求（试行）》和《"十二五"期间新建核电厂安全要求（征求意见稿）》等要求，为核电产业提供了新的安全标杆。

/ 经济高效 /

此外，"华龙一号"还打破了三代核电站"首堆必拖"的怪圈，有效提升了三代核电技术的经济性。

所谓"首堆"指的是采用全新的核电技术建造的首台核电机组。由于新的核电技术在应用过程中往往涉及大量新设备、新工艺，因此一般需要在建设过程中边施工边完善，从而导致工期拖延。比如，采用美国西屋公司第三代核电技术（AP1000）的浙江三门核电站，和由法国负责建造、采用第三代压水反应堆（EPR）技术的广东台山核电站，二者的工期都拖延了4—5年，由此产生了巨大的财务成本。

"华龙一号"首个反应堆——福建福清核电站5号机组的计划工期为72个月，从2015年5月开工到投入商业运行仅用时68个月，成为全球首个如期完工的三代核电站首堆机组，体现了中国核电建设能力和"华龙一号"的经济性，也标志着中国正式进入核电技术先进国家行列。

/ 打破瓶颈 /

中国的碳中和需要发展核电。实现碳中和是中国作为一个负责任大国对全人类的承诺，在风电、光伏以及水电都面临着不同发展瓶颈的背景下，清洁稳定的核电也将成为实现碳中和的一个重要选择。

在国际上，特别是对那些目前面临着电力短缺，且由于可再生能源发展缓慢而无法满足短中期电力需求的国家而言，"华龙一号"以其安全性、经济性和高效性，将可以提供一个有效的低碳解决方案。到目前为止，中国已经得到一些国家的"华龙一号"核电机组订单，标志着中国核电产业将实现由"引进来"到"走出去"的里程碑式跨越。可以预见，随着建设经验的完善和成熟，未来"华龙一号"必将成为更多国家的选择。

全球的碳中和需要发展核电。据估计，在碳中和目标的指引下，全球共有72个国家已经或正在计划发展核电，其中包括41个"一带一路"沿线国家。具备安全性和经济性的"华龙一号"将获得更大的市场，帮助世界实现迫切的绿色转型。

（此文首发于2021年3月3日中国日报中国观察智库）

建筑业对中国实现"碳中和"至关重要

王元丰

中国发展战略学研究会副理事长，中国城市科学研究会可持续土木工程专业
委员会理事长，北京交通大学教授

城市化浪潮推动全球建筑业空前增长，对遏制气候变化的努力构成挑战。中国能否实现2060年"碳中和"目标，建筑行业的角色至关重要。建筑行业实现"碳中和"是可以做到的，但必须在战略规划、政策法规、行业标准、教育培训和社会意识强化等方面付出长期努力。

在2020年9月22日举行的第75届联合国大会一般性辩论上，习近平主席提出中国二氧化碳排放力争2030年前达到峰值，努力争取2060年前实现"碳中和"。在中国朝着这一目标迈进的过程中，建筑行业的角色至关重要。

/ 从何而来 /

建筑业占全球能源和相关二氧化碳排放过程的近40%。根据国际能源署（IEA）和联合国环境规划署（UNEP）发布的《2019年全球建筑和建筑业状况报告》，2017年至2018年，全球建筑行业的

排放量增长了2%，达到历史最高水平。更令人担忧的是，到2060年，全球人口将达到100亿，其中三分之二的人口将生活在城市中。要容纳这些城市人口，就要新增建筑面积2300亿平方米，需将现有建筑存量翻倍。如此巨大的建筑需求，加上城市化程度的不断提高，意味着建筑行业的温室气体排放量将持续上升。

中国建筑行业规模位居世界第一，现有城镇总建筑存量约650亿平方米，这些建筑在使用过程中排放了约21亿吨二氧化碳，约占中国碳排放总量的20%，也占全球建筑总排放量的20%。这部分碳排放被称为"运营碳排放"。

在此基础上，中国每年新增建筑面积约20亿平方米，相当于全球新增建筑总量（61.3亿平方米）的近三分之一。工程建设每年产生的碳排放约占全球总排放量的11%，主要来源于钢铁、水泥、玻璃等建筑材料的生产和运输，以及现场施工过程。这部分排放被称为"内含碳排放"。

/ 双管齐下 /

鉴于建筑行业在全球应对气候变化挑战的重要性，为了在2060年前实现"碳中和"以更好地应对气候变化，中国必须在未来几十年内大幅减少建筑业的碳排放。IEA和UNEP的报告建议，建筑行业应采取适当措施扭转其碳排放上升的趋势，并以每年3%的速度提高建筑的能源效率。但到2050年，现有建筑面积的近三分之二仍将在使用。因此，要建设低碳或"碳中和"的建筑环境，就必须同时解决新建建筑和既有建筑的问题，即内含碳排放和运营碳排放。这就要求到2030年新建建筑应达到净零碳排放。

然而，建筑行业目前的排放水平对中国实现"碳中和"目标构成了挑战。根据中国建筑节能协会能耗统计专委会发布的《中国建筑能耗研究报告（2019）》，中国建筑行业的碳排放将继续增加，达到峰值时间预计为2039年前后——也就是说，在全国碳排放总量达峰之后，建筑行业的碳排放仍将继续增长9年。因此，中国能否在2060年前实现"碳中和"，将在一定程度上取决于建筑业的表现。

能源转型委员会（ETC）2019年发布的一份报告指出，中国的建筑业可以实现碳中和，但要在整个生命周期内实现建筑脱碳，就需要对该行业进行彻底改革。例如，在明确而强有力的政策推动下，建筑业应采取一系列措施，推动"被动式建筑[①]"设计，提升材料效率，推广使用低碳材料、高效隔热建筑围护结构以及照明设备和电器。

/ 努力方向 /

中国的建筑行业要实现"碳中和"，应从以下几个方面进行努力：

首先，建筑行业应该制定具体的"碳中和"时间表和路线图，必须在2060年前达到"碳中和"，以确保中国履行其绿色承诺。

其次，要对建筑行业所有部门的碳排放进行测算，使用生命周期评估方法进行量化。

第三，有必要对建筑行业标准和规范大幅度修改，因为要实现"碳中和"，该行业几乎所有的标准规范都需要整合节能减排

---

① 被动式建筑（passive building）：指通过自然采光、太阳能辐射等被动式节能措施，与建筑外围结构保温隔热节能技术相结合，不使用主动的采暖和空调系统就可维持舒适的室内热环境的建筑。

的相关要求。

第四，应全面、明确地出台促进"碳中和"的政策法规，以及其他相关的经济、财政、金融和自愿标识政策（特别是绿色金融政策）。

第五，要实行包括碳税和碳交易在内的碳定价。碳定价是强制行业及企业二氧化碳减排的有效手段，因此整个行业的碳排放，包括内含碳排放和运营碳排放，应该尽早纳入碳交易市场。

第六，由于政府、开发商、设计单位、承包商和用户等各方对"碳中和"的认识理解不到位，因此政府应担负起更多的"科普"责任，组织培训项目，提高他们对碳中和的认识和相关能力。

第七，应加大宣传力度，帮助人们认识到"碳中和"的重要性，鼓励他们养成环保习惯。大学应该开设以"碳中和"为重点的环境课程和专业，为未来培养人才。同时，在中小学开设此类课程也很重要。

此外，中国还应大力开展国际合作，这不仅将有助于中国的"碳中和"工作早日走上正轨，还将推动全球气候治理。当中国在促进"碳中和"方面获得一些经验时，还可以帮助其他国家达到《巴黎协定》的要求，为全球应对气候变化做出贡献。

总而言之，达到"碳中和"是一项艰巨的任务，但中国建筑业可以实现这一宏大目标。

（此文首发于2020年11月20日中国日报中国观察智库）

健康海洋：通向碳中和未来的"蓝色道路"

谢茜

世界经济论坛北京代表处"海洋行动之友"项目负责人

陈冀俍

创绿研究院高级研究员

2021年"达沃斯议程"对话会在1月27日举办"塑造新的海洋经济"分论坛。海洋对于缓解气候变化、构建碳中和的未来非常重要，但当前海洋生态环境和生物多样性正面临长期风险。中国已经出台多项法律法规，推动海洋经济与海洋生态保护相协调。未来中国可在海洋可再生能源等方面重点发力，抓住"蓝色经济"新机遇，推动经济、社会、环境和气候事业协同发展。

当前新冠肺炎疫情给世界带来的挑战十分紧迫，但同时我们也不应忽视气候变化和生物多样性丧失的长期风险。

越来越多的国家致力于碳中和，一个碳中和的未来，就是人与自然和谐相处的未来。

海洋覆盖了地球表面的70%，是地球的主要特征，对地球气候和生物圈具有重大影响。但目前海洋正受到人类活动和气候变化的威胁，必须采取紧急行动，恢复海洋健康。

/ 利用与保护 /

生态环境部印发的《关于统筹和加强应对气候变化与生态环境保护相关工作的指导意见》，其中明确提出，要推动海洋及海岸带等生态保护修复与适应气候变化协同增效。

过去几十年，中国在海洋科学方面投入了大量资金，并在水域管理方面加强了法律法规建设。

自20世纪80年代以来，中国海洋保护区的数量迅速增加。截至2019年底，中国共建立海洋保护区271处，大部分位于沿海水域，总面积约12.4万平方公里，占领海总面积的4.1%。

中国正在逐步建立以国家公园为基础的保护区体系，但保护区的规模和质量仍有待提高。应进一步加大科技投入，更好地支持国内海洋保护区的认定和管理，同时为国际海洋保护区建设做出贡献。

中国是世界上最大的海产品消费国和加工国，拥有世界上最大规模的水产养殖业。渔业要实现高质量发展，必须进行改革。

中国政府已经出台了更严格的规定，打击非法、不报告和不受管制的捕捞。2020年，在中国境外水域发生了几起针对中国的此类指控，中方做出了坚定回应，表明了遏制此类活动的决心。中国渔政部门对远洋渔船的非法捕捞采取了严厉的惩罚措施。

农业农村部于2020年11月发布《中国远洋渔业履约白皮书2020》，有力阐明了中国在远洋渔业方面的原则、立场、管理政策及其执行效果。同时，中国也正在积极推动《港口国措施协定》的批准。当然，这需要一段时间才能产生明显效果，但起码中国已经走上了正确的轨道。

限制捕捞对于海洋生态系统的质量至关重要。投入品监管、季节性禁渔令和渔业补贴改革是主要手段。《中国远洋渔业履约白皮书2020》呼吁将气候变化影响评估纳入渔业决策，这表明中国正在考虑更多的预防性措施。

/ 挑战与机遇 /

可持续地管理海洋，是制定环保政策、应对气候变化的重要抓手。在以自然为基础的解决方案方面，中国已经是一个先行者，但在利用海洋来缓解气候变化，发掘海洋潜力来弥补碳减排缺口方面，我们仍需要增加关注度，增强信心。

2018年9月，澳大利亚、加拿大、智利等14个国家的领导人联合发起"可持续海洋经济高级别小组"，旨在推动海洋资源的有效保护和可持续利用。该组织于2019年10月发布《海洋：应对气候变化的解决方案》报告，提出为了缓解气候变化，可在以下五个与海洋相关的领域发力：

1. 海洋可再生能源

2. 海洋运输

3. 沿海和海洋生态系统

4. 渔业、水产和饮食方式的转变

5. 海底碳储存

对中国而言，以上五大领域中的海洋可再生能源无疑是重点，而沿海和海洋生态系统以及海底碳储存的相关研究也正在增加。

可持续的"蓝色经济"预示着未来几十年的新机遇和新趋势，包括航运的绿色转型、海洋可再生能源、碳储存、生态旅游、海洋生物资源的利用、可持续的水产养殖和新型海洋食品的开发等。只要建立起明确的政策框架、确保激励措施到位，提高环境和社会标准，那么投资可持续的海洋经济将推动经济、社会、环境和气候事业协同发展。

/ 协调与合作 /

中国是一个快速发展的海洋强国，拥有1.8万公里的海岸线。海洋经济的健康发展对中国尤其重要，海洋经济将在中国实现碳中和的过程中扮演重要角色。

为了进一步发挥海洋在未来碳中和过程中的作用，中国需要健全以科学和预防为基础的国内和国际政策决策机制，同时还需要通过立法和海洋空间规划，在各级更顺利地进行跨部门协调。

《关于统筹和加强应对气候变化与生态环境保护相关工作的指导意见》的发布是一个重大进展，预计未来我们还将看到更多的联合政策和行动。

（此文首发于2021年1月27日中国日报中国观察智库）

按下绿色金融"放大键",
助力"双碳"目标早实现

马骏

中国金融学会绿色金融专业委员会主任,北京绿色金融与可持续发展研究院院长,二十国集团可持续金融工作组共同主席

中国提出的碳达峰碳中和目标对绿色金融提出了更高要求。未来中国需要撬动更多社会资本投入可持续发展领域,完善绿色金融分类标准,加强环境信息披露,加大绿色金融政策激励,建立转型金融框架。

过去几年,中国绿色金融市场发展迅速。截至2021年9月底,中国绿色贷款余额达15.9万亿元,居世界首位。2016年至2021年,中国累计发行绿色债券约2万亿元。2021年,绿色金融市场发展速度加快,同年9月份对此绿色贷款增长28%,绿色债券发行比去年增长约170%,远远高于同期银行贷款和债券发行的总体增长率。

绿色金融是指为支持环境改善、应对气候变化和资源节约高效利用的经济活动所提供的金融服务。长期以来,支持绿色发展一直是中国金融部门的基本政策之一。早在2007年,为了遏制高耗能高污染产业的盲目扩张,环保总局、人民银行、银监会三部门就联合推出了绿色贷款政策。2016年,人民银行牵头七部委发布了《关于

构建绿色金融体系的指导意义》。

2020年9月22日，习近平主席在第75届联合国大会上宣布，中国力争在2030年前二氧化碳排放达到峰值，努力争取在2060年前实现碳中和目标。

"双碳"目标的确立对中国绿色金融提出了更高要求。该目标要求绿色金融市场在未来不断扩大其规模。据中国金融学会绿色金融专业委员会（绿金委）的最新研究估算，从2021到2050年，中国在绿色低碳领域的投资需求总额将达487万亿元（以2018年不变价格计算）。这意味着未来30年，中国需在该领域年均投入16万亿元，其中约90%的资金需要通过金融市场筹集，另有约10%来自政府财政。通过绿色金融体系筹集的资金将主要用于可再生能源开发利用、能源利用效率提升、清洁交通、绿色建筑和低碳制造等领域。

为实现碳达峰和碳中和的"30·60"目标，中国必须按下绿色金融"放大键"：撬动更多的社会资本投入绿色低碳领域，完善绿色金融分类标准，开展环境信息强制性披露，加大绿色金融政策激励，建立转型金融框架。

撬动民间资本参与绿色金融是达成"双碳"目标的关键。绿金委的分析认为，碳中和背景下绿色金融发展的核心是通过完善标准体系、激励机制和产品创新，用有限的公共资金，撬动数倍乃至十几倍的社会资本投入到绿色低碳产业，支持"双碳"目标实现。完善绿色金融体系的几个主要任务包括：

一是完善绿色金融分类，推动绿色分类标准"国内统一，国际趋同"。借鉴欧盟"无重大损害"原则，确保所有绿色金融支持的项目能实现一定的环境效益，而不对环境、气候和生物多样性等任何可持续发展目标造成损害。

二是参考气候相关财务信息披露工作组的建议，逐步建立针对企业和金融机构的强制性环境信息披露体系，要求寻求融资的机构公开ESG相关信息。其中一个关键内容是企业和金融机构其经营活动的碳强度（碳足迹）。

三是加大政策激励，提高绿色低碳项目的预期收益。这些激励政策的选项包括央行提供的低成本资金、地方政府提供的贴息和担保，以及碳排放交易机制对低碳活动产生的激励。

四是鼓励包括绿色信贷、绿色债券、碳排放权质押贷款、绿色供应链融资等绿色金融产品的创新与发展。

五是建立支持转型金融的政策框架，支持和鼓励金融机构向有明确碳减排路径的企业和项目提供融资。这一政策框架的内容应包括转型活动分类目录、转型风险信息披露要求、相关金融工具以及气候转型相关激励机制。

目前，中国已经在部分上述领域开展了多项试点工作。在环境信息披露领域，中英绿色金融工作组在20家中英金融企业中组建了环境信息披露试点，其经验为中国人民银行制定的环境信息强制性披露要求提供了重要依据。在完善相关激励机制领域，几个月前中国人民银行推出了碳减排支持工具，这一结构性货币政策工具将向金融机构提供低成本资金，引导金融机构在自主决策、自担风险的前提下，向碳减排重点领域的企业和项目提供碳减排贷款，从而降低脱碳项目等绿色项目的融资成本。为保障碳减排支持工具的精准性和直达性，人民银行要求金融机构公开披露碳减排贷款的情况以及贷款带动的碳减排数量等信息，并由第三方专业机构对这些信息进行核实验证。在转型金融领域，浙江省湖州市正在编制政策文件，明确转型金融支持的经济活动范围。

随着碳中和政策的实施，煤炭开采、燃煤发电、钢铁、水泥和石化等高排放高污染产业将会面临成本增加或利润减少的压力。这些行业中不能成功实现低碳转型的企业将会面临财务状况恶化、拖欠银行贷款和企业估值或股价下跌等问题，最终可能转化为银行和投资机构的金融风险。因而，除了动员和激励更多社会资本参与绿色投入，绿色金融的另一大任务就是在低碳转型过程中，防止金融体系出现系统性的"转型风险"。

中国人民银行明确指出，要"增强金融体系管理气候变化相关风险的能力"。最近，中国人民银行要求21家主要银行针对其在燃煤发电、钢铁和水泥行业的资产风险敞口进行气候风险压力测试，这仅仅是在量化和管理气候风险方面进行更加系统化尝试的开端。从长远来看，进行气候风险分析的机构范围还应当逐步扩大，还应该考虑除碳价变化之外的更多情景和因素，包括各类政策冲击或技术冲击。监管部门也应要求其他类型的金融公司（如资产管理公司）进行此类分析。一旦明确了气候风险敞口，金融机构就需要制定应对策略，包括采取具体措施管理好风险敞口，协助高碳企业脱碳，以及使用碳风险对冲工具。

"双碳"目标给中国金融业既带来了巨大的机遇，也带来了重大的挑战。金融界和企业界各层面要通力合作，共同努力，抓住机遇，迎接挑战。好消息是，金融市场从业者们对于参与到"双碳"事业表现出高涨的热情。2021年9月，超过40万人（主要通过线上形式）参加了以"金融支持碳中和"为主题的2021中国金融学会绿色金融委员会年会。2022年1月，绿金委又发起了五个工作组（研究组），组织成员大力推动环境信息披露、转型金融、产品创新、国际合作和生物多样性融资等领域的研究、创新与试点。

（此文首发于2022年2月7日中国日报中国观察智库）

电力系统脱碳：挑战与策略

周勤

落基山研究所（RMI）中国高级研究员

刘雨菁

落基山研究所（RMI）中国部门总监

占中国碳排放总量四成的电力系统脱碳，是中国实现"双碳"目标的关键。针对中国电力系统的特点，为构建适合中国国情的新型电力系统，需重点关注四个方面：一是确保可再生能源的可持续发展，二是明确煤电转型的节奏与速度，三是电网规划与系统调度运行与时俱进，四是实现电力需求弹性化。

中国已经做出在2030年前实现碳达峰、2060年前实现碳中和的坚定承诺。电力部门碳排放大约占中国碳排放总量的40%，因此，电力系统脱碳是中国实现"双碳"目标的重点领域。

要实现脱碳目标，我们首先必须分析中国现有电力系统的特点，认识到其脱碳挑战，进而探索并构建符合中国国情的新电力系统。

虽然全世界的电力系统遵循的物理规律是普遍相同的，但每个电力系统的特点可能具有很大的区别。中国电力行业的特点是高度依赖燃煤发电，可再生能源发电资源与主要负荷中心距离遥远，且终端电力用户无法感知到价格信号。

中国电力系统的这些特点和正在推进的工业化、城市化进程，意味着电力需求将继续增长，因此，中国将不可避免地面临一些关键挑战。一是为了取代现有的燃煤电厂，同时也为了满足未来额外的电力需求增长，必须大规模开发可再生能源。二是为了平衡电力供需双侧的波动性，电力系统需要更高的灵活性，但在煤电转型时期，传统上由燃煤电厂提供的灵活供电能力缺乏短期替代方案。三是由于可再生能源与负荷中心距离遥远，需要大力开发远距离可再生能源输送能力。此外，还需要加快电力市场改革，以实现电力生产、输送与消费的资源优化配置。

为了克服这些挑战，构建适合中国国情的新型电力系统，需要重点关注以下四个方面：一是确保可再生能源的可持续发展，二是明确煤电转型的节奏与速度，三是电网规划与系统调度运行与时俱进，四是实现电力需求弹性化。

/ 可再生能源的可持续发展 /

虽然风电与光伏发电的平准化发电成本已大幅下降，但在政府补贴退坡带来成本回收不确定的情况下，可再生能源开发商依然对未来投资抱有疑虑。因此，需要利用长期合同或拍卖机制等形式，为可再生能源投资提供更强的确定性。此外，在一些仍处于早期阶段，尚未具备经济可行性，但具有广阔发展前景的可再生能源（如海上风电、太阳能热发电等）技术方面，政府的激励性措施依然发挥着非常重要的作用。

由于距离中国东部地区主要负荷中心较近，海上风电应该成为下一个重点关注的主要可再生能源技术，应给予优惠政策和激励。

/ 煤电转型的节奏 /

2021年的电力短缺危机突显了一个问题，即在为确保气候安全而淘汰煤电的同时，确保可靠的电力供应也同样重要。为了支持系统的灵活性，一定数量的燃煤电厂将继续发挥作用。而在大规模淘汰燃煤电厂之前，必须大规模开发多样化的储能技术，以满足日常和季节性的系统灵活性需求。

此外，碳捕集、利用与储存技术应该在保留部分燃煤电厂继续服役的过程中发挥重要作用，以保证系统的灵活性与备用容量需求。

/ 电网规划与系统调度 /

中国的电网公司已经具备了全球最先进的技术能力。然而，要显著提高可再生能源在中国发电组合中的比例，电网规划和运营能力必须进一步提升，以适应不断变化的动态形势。基于市场信号的经济电力调度，最终应成为系统运行的规范。此外，现有的大规模可再生能源"西电东送"模式的可持续性也需要被重新审视。开发大规模的海上风电以及分布式可再生能源可能成为一种可行的替代方案，因为这些资源距离负荷中心更近，可以避免昂贵的长距离电力输送。

/ 电力需求弹性化 /

只有让需求侧资源也参与电力平衡，一个低碳、高效的电力系统才能够真正成为现实。

要实现需求侧的可控性，就要大规模发展微电网、虚拟电厂等多种技术解决方案，从而使电网运营商可以通过调整供需两侧的资源来实现实时的电力平衡。

同时，电力市场改革应重点关注实时价格信号对需求侧的传导，以促使电力用户调整其用电行为，并促进购电方能够利用长期合同购买绿色电力。

综上所述，尽管中国已具备强烈的意愿和多样化的实践尝试，但在电力系统实现真正的脱碳之前，整个行业对于如何全面应对挑战的策略仍然缺乏共识。因此，我们迫切需要汇集电力行业的决策者、顶级行业专家与政策设计者来探讨理念、推广最佳实践，共同规划以可再生能源为主体的中国新型电力系统路线图。

（此文首发于2022年2月10日中国日报中国观察智库）

多边

探索低碳绿色发展无国界

合作

〔第一章〕

倡导对话，"天下一家"

全球升温1度，后果已然很严重，现在正朝着2.7度发展

尼古拉斯·斯特恩（Nicholas Stern）

伦敦政经学院政治经济学帕特尔（IG Patel）讲席教授、格兰瑟姆气候变化和环境研究所主席

邹骥

能源基金会首席执行官兼中国区总裁

  中共中央国务院印发的《关于完整准确全面贯彻新发展理念做好碳达峰碳中和工作的意见》于2021年10月24日发布。随着全球从新冠疫情中逐步恢复，人们有机会追求可持续经济增长的新模式，有效应对气候变化、生物多样性丧失等问题。中国已在气候变化问题上显示出全球领导力，向全世界展现一个庞大经济体如何实现能源转型。

  世界已经迈入了一个关键的历史时刻。在我们正从新冠肺炎疫

情大流行中恢复之际，我们有机会通过追求可持续、包容和有韧性的经济发展和增长新模式，来创造一个更安全、更繁荣的世界。

通过强有力的投资和创新，这种新的增长形式有望把全球经济变得更加清洁高效。我们将能够借此有效地应对气候变化、生物多样性丧失和环境退化等全球威胁。

在开发和部署未来新科技的过程中，我们将开辟出新的产品和公共服务市场，创造新的就业岗位。至关重要的一点是，我们将推动能源系统转型，摆脱化石燃料高能耗、高污染的能源生产与消费模式。

我们可以使用替代能源来推动经济增长，避免气候变化和空气污染给我们的生命健康和生计带来危害。

世界卫生组织估计，全球每年有700多万人死于当地的空气污染。而造成空气污染的主要原因在于生物质和化石燃料燃烧后产生的有毒有害气体。在全球发展中国家和新兴市场国家当中，许多发展迅速的城市正承受着沉重的社会和经济负担，许多人因空气污染而生病甚至死亡。

2021年8月，政府间气候变化专门委员会发布了最新的气候变化科学评估报告，指出大气层中二氧化碳和其他温室气体浓度的上升正在影响世界的每一个角落，导致全球极端天气事件愈发频繁和强烈。

2021年夏天，我们目睹了全球各地的热浪、洪水和野火——全球气温仅上升1摄氏度，就能导致气候问题变得如此严重。数百万人的生命和生计遭到破坏和毁灭，即使再富有的国家也不能独善其身，更不要说那些在天灾面前最无力保护自己的穷人了。

英国已根据"在本世纪末把全球温度上升幅度控制在1.5摄氏度以内"的总体目标，制定出了本国的行动目标。政府间气候变化专门委员会指出，超过这一幅度的升温将令灾难性后果的风险大大增加，例如极地冰盖的气候将变得不稳定，喜马拉雅山脉和季风季节的河流流量将受到严重干扰等。

要把全球升温控制在1.5摄氏度以内，那么全球主要温室气体二氧化碳净排放必须在本世纪中叶之前"归零"。许多国家现在已经制定了净零排放的目标，通过植树造林或直接空气捕捉等技术增加碳吸收量，同时减少温室气体排放量，最终使二者达到相当的水平。

但COP26会议本身并不能确保万无一失。发达国家曾承诺，每年筹集1000亿美元公共和私人资金，用以支持发展中国家采取气候行动，但这一承诺迟迟没有兑现。他们必须在本次会议召开前证明各自信守了承诺，制定了规划，在今后几年增加财政支持。例如，他们可以承诺到2025年，每年通过双边渠道提供600亿美元，从多边渠道提供900亿美元。

但根据联合国的说法，各国在本次气候大会之前提交的2030年减排新承诺总体上太过薄弱。按照目前的承诺水平，到本世纪末全球升温幅度将达2.7摄氏度，这将给地球带来灾难。

中国已经在气候变化问题上展现出全球领导力。2020年9月，习近平主席在第75届联合国大会上历史性地宣布，中国将努力争取在2060年前实现碳中和。在第76届联合国大会上，习近平主席再次做出重要承诺，中国将不再新建境外煤电项目。

中国还可以向其他国家展示，一个庞大的经济体如何摆脱化石燃料，实现能源转型。尽管中国国内能源供给仍严重依赖煤炭，但中国正在加快开发可再生能源等替代能源，并大力投资新型交通，如清洁能源驱动的电动汽车等。在实现转型的同时，中国还将受益于能源多样化，中期来看可以降低市场危机爆发的可能性。

习近平主席还表示，中国将控制国内煤电的发展，并将严格监管高能耗、高排放项目。随着新技术成本的下降，碳达峰和碳中和领导小组加强了政府间的协调行动，中国必定会加快向可持续增长模式转型。

如果中国加快向强大、可持续和有弹性的经济模式转型，使二氧化碳排放达峰时间从2030年提前到"十四五"时期内，那么这将有力推动整个世界的繁荣与和平。

（此文首发于2021年10月25日中国日报中国观察智库）

会也开了，技术也有了，为何环境问题越来越严重？圭亚那前总统一语中的

唐纳德·拉莫塔（Donald Ramotar）

圭亚那前总统，人民进步党前总书记

几十年来，人们对于气候环境问题的重要性和紧迫性的认识日渐清晰，应对方案和技术路线也很明确，但问题依然日渐恶化。究其原因，根本上在于当今全球社会经济体系被大型跨国企业所把持，而企业的首要目标是逐利，因此当环境保护和获取利润相矛盾时，他们往往会选择后者，导致相关承诺最终沦为空谈。要真正解决问题，不能光靠开会讨论，更需要切实行动，转变经济运行模式。

气候变化是当前最紧迫的全球性问题之一，也是每个人都关心的问题。这个问题非常重要，关乎地球生命的生死存亡，因此需要立即采取行动，而不仅仅是空谈。

真正悲剧的地方在于：几十年来，我们一直被警告，却从未做出改变。自20世纪60年代末70年代初以来，科学家们一直在大声疾呼：如果我们不改变与自然的关系，就要大难临头。

世界领导人也曾多次会晤。自1995年以来，联合国已经召开了25次这样的气候大会，2021年是第26次。关于气候问题的讲话有一

大堆，说得头头是道，把问题的原因和应对措施分析得明明白白，然而情况继续恶化，自然灾害的频率和强度不断增加。看到这些现象造成的苦难，让人心碎。

会也开了，承诺也做了，但问题是承诺没有落实，或只是落实了一部分。

究其原因，根本上在于人类的经济活动和对财富的追求是不可持续的，这对全球生态造成了严重破坏。在我们过度开发地球资源的同时，储存在森林、海洋和地球中的碳正在被释放出来。

此外，人类还在工业化进程中向大气中排放了巨量的有毒气体。

当然，解决方案也很清楚。我们必须保护大自然，这样地球才能继续支撑人类活动。我们必须了解自然规律，与大自然和谐共存。

有人很可能会问，既然我们知道问题原因和解决办法，为什么仍然没能制止这种情况呢？

在我看来，这是因为我们只提出了技术解决方案来处理这个问题。我们听到了相关问题的讨论，也看到了新技术手段的实施，比如太阳能、风能、地热、核能等多种新技术被用于发电。当然这对我们的生存是必不可少的，因为我们确实需要清洁能源发电。

科学家们还发明了新能源汽车等交通工具，减少了大气污染。这也是非常积极的举措，这些成就和持续的努力应该得到赞扬。

但是，尽管这些技术进步都很了不起，情况却正在迅速恶化。

技术方案固然很重要，但仅靠技术本身并不能解决问题。在我们的历史上从未有过如此多的神奇技术可供我们支配，然而，全球环境状况却比以往任何时候都要糟糕。

这并不是贬低技术方案的重要性——它们是至关重要的，但它们并没有解决主要问题。

主要问题在哪里？在于主导我们这个世界运转的社会经济关系

体系。从根本上说，这套体系被非常强大的跨国企业所控制，而这些企业的主要目标是利润最大化。他们总是口头上说环境问题，但是一旦他们认为环境保护会触及他们的底线，环境问题就会立即被忽略。主宰和控制我们这个世界的体系，本质上就是这样的。

100多年前，马克思在《资本论》中援引英国经济学家邓宁的话写道："资本逃避动乱和纷争，它的本性是胆怯的。这是真的，但还不是全部真理。资本害怕没有利润或利润太少，就像自然界害怕真空一样。一旦有适当的利润，资本就胆大起来。如果有10%的利润，它就保证到处被使用；有20%的利润，它就活跃起来；有50%的利润，它就铤而走险；为了100%的利润，它就敢践踏一切人间法律；有300%的利润，它就敢犯任何罪行，甚至冒绞首的危险。如果动乱和纷争能带来利润，它就会鼓励动乱和纷争。"

我们从自己的亲身经历中也可以知道，确实是这么回事。例如，美国雷诺兹公司、罗瑞拉德公司、菲利普莫里斯公司等烟草巨头跟美国司法部打了几十年官司，才终于在2017年"认罪"，就吸烟的危害在大众媒体上做出说明。烟草公司明知香烟是导致肺癌和胃癌等多种癌症的主要原因，然而他们却在这方面撒了谎，还大肆推销自己的产品。烟草行业的利润非常高，因此他们雇佣了最好的律师来为他们做说客。对他们来说，烟民的生命健康无关紧要。

再如，我们都知道石油是气候变化的主要原因之一，给地球带来了危险。其实石油公司早在40多年前就知道这一点了，但他们没有试图寻找解决办法来纠正它，而是花了数十亿美元来聘请说客，质疑最先提出警告的科学家，他们还资助竞选活动，对一些政党进行了大量投资。直到今天，他们仍在更广泛的油气资源勘探和开发领域进行着大量投资，也就是说，他们并无意遵守任何约束。

对于这些巨大的盈利组织来说，没有什么比赚钱更重要了。

人的生命对他们来说毫无意义。20世纪七八十年代，艺名"大麻雀"（Mighty Sparrow）的加勒比地区著名歌手斯林格·弗朗西斯科（Slinger Francisco）有一首经典歌曲《资本主义疯掉啦》（Capitalism Gone Mad），讽刺那些为赚钱不顾一切的资本家们。歌中所描绘的情况正在我们眼前上演。

Capitalism Gone Mad 歌词节选

You got to be a millionaire	在我们国家
Or some kind of petit-bourgeoisie	要想活得下去
Any time you living here	你要么得是个百万富翁
In this country	要么起码是个"小资"
You got to be in skullduggery	在我们国家
Making your money illicitly	要想过得体面
To live like somebody	你得会钻营使诈
In this country	靠不法手段赚钱
It's outrageous and insane	说来真是荒唐，天下奇闻
Them crazy prices in Port of Spain	在我国首都，物价飞涨
And like the merchants going out dey brain	那帮商人，脑子全都坏掉啦！
And the working man, like he only toiling in vain	那些工人，全都白辛苦啦！
Where you ever hear, a television for seven thousand	一台电视，卖七千块
Quarter million for lil piece of land	一小块地，二十五万
A pair of sneakers, two hundred dollars	一双球鞋，要价两百
Eighty, ninety thousand for motor cars	买辆汽车，得八九万
[Chorus]	（副歌）
At last here in Trinidad	在特立尼达
We see capitalism gone mad	资本主义疯掉啦
It's sad and getting more bad	民生困苦，越来越糟
Because, doudou, capitalism gone mad!	因为，哎呀呀，资本主义疯掉啦！

117

　　因此这就出现了一对根本性矛盾：一方面，对利润的追求促使企业忽视环境，过度开发资源；另一方面，为了减缓和扭转气候变化，我们需要更多的反思和行动来保护自然。当前的环境危机告诉我们，我们长期以来身处其中的国际经济体系已经失灵，为了地球上的生命，它必须做出改变。

　　毫无疑问，召开气候大会是好事一件，但仅靠开会不能解决问题。要真正解决问题，需要切实采取大规模行动，还需要经济模式的转变。

（此文首发于2021年11月8日中国日报中国观察智库）

绿色赋能：中国的脱贫经验可用以引领气候治理

埃里克·索尔海姆（Erik Solheim）

"一带一路"绿色发展国际研究院联合主席、联合国环境署前执行主任

2020年9月中国明确提出了碳达峰和碳中和目标，随后世界多个主要经济体提出了各自的气候目标，全球绿色转型进程取得重大进展。解决气候环境问题是有利于环境、经济和社会的"三赢"之举。在绿色转型过程中，中国要协调各部门进行整体动员；要考虑到社会公平，照顾到各地区发展水平不均；充分发挥领导者作用，开展国际合作。

历史就是这样：有时在几十年中，似乎什么都没有发生，有时在几个星期中，变革之剧烈仿佛是过去了几十年。

我们在气候环境问题上的进展也是这样：在经历了长期的缓慢进度后，在新冠疫情这几年取得的巨大进展下，全球好像一下子"快进"了几十年。2020年9月，中国国家主席习近平在第75届联合国大会上宣布，中国将力争在2030年之前达到二氧化碳排放峰值，并努力争取在2060年之前实现碳中和。随后，一股"绿色冲击波"席卷了整个国际社会。

抗疫过程中，全球在生态环境治理事业的赛道上更加斗志昂扬。在中国提出"双碳"目标不到一个月的时间里，时任韩国总统文在寅和时任日本首相菅义伟分别宣布了各自国家的碳中和目标。美国总统拜登致力于推动一项雄心勃勃的国际气候融资计划[1]，尽管其通过气候立法的努力在国会接连受挫。欧盟正在推出"绿色新政"和绿色分类标准[2]，将绿色发展制定为欧洲一体化的中心议题。在印度，莫迪总理正逐个叫停燃煤电厂，朝着全球领先的太阳能和绿氢生产国方向迈进。

绿水青山就是金山银山，这一科学论断由时任浙江省委书记的习近平在考察浙江省安吉县余村时首次提出。为了建设"美丽中国"，助力全球低碳经济，中国应践行这一理念。应对气候变化、保护自然环境不是人类"付出的代价"，而是创造就业、实现繁荣和改善民生的大好机会，是有利于环境、经济和社会的"三赢"之举。有趣的是，拜登在竞选期间也提出了惠及全体美国公民的环境气候计划。在这一问题上，中美双方处在同一"频道"：气候变化既是一个亟待解决的问题，更是一个值得拥抱的机遇。

在相互尊重与平等互利的基础上，中国气候变化事务特使解振华和美国总统气候问题特使约翰·克里多次会面并最终发表了《中美应对气候危机联合声明》[3]，推动两国就气候治理达成友好合作。该声明在第26届联合国气候变化大会上公布。中美在共同应对气候变化问题上为世界作出表率，也成了缓解地缘政治紧张局势的范

---

[1] https://www.state.gov/translations/chinese/ 概述：美国国际气候融资计划 /

[2] https://cn.climatebonds.net/cn.climatebonds.net/resources/Taxonomy_UK%20PACT

[3] http://www.xinhuanet.com/world/2021-04-18/c_1127342714.htm

例。由此可见，中美在其他领域也应开展广泛合作。

今天，推动全球环境议程的不再是联合国气候谈判，而是政治经济学考量。太阳能的价格在过去10年内下降了90％，风能的价格下降了60％，电池成本下降了85％。中国是一个极富创新精神的国家，中国经济的庞大体量意味着更大的生产规模和更低的创新成本。同样，我们也看到全球许多其他国家，在解决环境问题方面，商界已经跑在了政界的前头，而这一切都与创新和规模有关。

西方企业已经对绿色议程做出了强有力的承诺：美国微软承诺到2030年实现碳中和，甚至提出要通过负碳排放抵消掉公司历史上的所有碳排放；印度尼西亚最大的造纸和纸浆企业，即亚太资源集团，做出了森林零砍伐的承诺[1]，并同意帮助印尼政府实现这一关键目标；瑞典宜家的循环经济策略也令人惊叹。

在中国，也有同样的趋势。腾讯、阿里巴巴和华为等企业正在制订自己的绿色议程；华为助力光伏电站提质增效，凭借其智能光伏技术为环境保护作出重要贡献；宁德时代在几年内跃居全球最大动力电池企业，在行业内遥遥领先。不过，企业绿色发展的步伐还应继续加快，范围还应继续扩大。"先污染后治理"的发展模式已经走到头了。

/ 制度优势 /

中国用最短的时间实现了最多人口的脱贫，成就人类历史上前所未有的创举。韩国、越南和新加坡等其他亚洲国家在减贫实践方

---

[1]　https://www.eco-business.com/news/april-rge-finally-commit-to-zero-deforestation/

面同样表现不俗。

中国在抗击疫情过程中所展现的执行能力，也可以用来应对21世纪最大的挑战——保护地球母亲。生态环境部已经开始推动立法，加速中国碳排放达峰，并为地方各省市和企业设定目标。中国环境保护部、外交部、国家发展改革委、商务部四部门联合发布了《关于推进绿色"一带一路"建设的指导意见》[①]，让"一带一路"成为促进绿色发展的助推器。这些是以目标为导向的战略，侧重于问责和量化。中国人民银行也正在制定绿色金融标准，以及银行和金融机构披露环境信息的指导意见。低碳绿色战略融入到了"十四五"规划的方方面面，各省（市）和企业需要制定自己的绿色发展目标。如果中国要在2030年前实现碳达峰，部分发达省市需要更早达峰。

/ 社会公平 /

对于世界各国的绝大多数人来说，绿色转型的影响是正面的：它将创造新的就业机会，形成更好的社会习惯，产生更少的污染。然而，对部分人来说，转型更为不易。例如在中国，同样是绿色转型，由于不同地区的经济结构存在差异，广东、江苏的转型可能比辽宁、山西更加容易，像深圳、苏州这样的高科技产业密集型城市的转型可能比北方重工业地区更加容易。转型的过程必须确保社会公平，其实欧美也面临着同样的问题，若与中国交流最佳实践的经验，必定受益匪浅。

转型过程中的社会公平至关重要，因为这将大大降低转型难

---

① http://www.gov.cn/xinwen/2017-05/27/content_5197523.htm

度。照顾到的人越多，障碍和阻力也就越小。我在拜访中国网约车企业滴滴时，有一件事令我印象深刻。他们告诉我，滴滴和煤炭企业签署了战略合作协议，帮助下岗煤矿工人改行当网约车司机，实现再就业，在转型的过程中促进了社会公平。

/ 引领作用 /

最后，也是最重要的是，中国应该承担起领导世界的责任。当然，仅靠中国一己之力是不行的，但中国可以与美国、欧洲和其他国家合作，分享其独特的思路和经验。例如，在城市空气污染防治、西北地区沙漠绿化、长江禁渔、公园城市建设、杭广等地绿色发展的落实等方面，中国已经取得了巨大进步，积累了丰富经验，总结制定出了许多行之有效的科学方法和制度安排。通过向世界展示后疫情时代绿色复苏的可能性，中国有望成为全球绿色转型的领导者。

没有人能全面、明确地告诉我们下一步需要怎么做，明智的做法是遵循中国前领导人邓小平的建议："摸着石头过河。"在这种求真务实思想的指导下，我相信，到2060年，我们将回顾中国在保护地球环境方面取得的成功，正如我们现在回顾过去几十年里中国让数亿人摆脱贫困一样。

（此文英文原文首发于2020年12月29日中国日报国际版）

〔 第二章 〕
"碳中和"的实现路径在哪？

从碳达峰到碳中和，英国要走将近80年，中国如何30年走完？

尼古拉斯·斯特恩（Nicholas Stern）

伦敦政经学院政治经济学帕特尔（IG Patel）讲席教授、格兰瑟姆气候变化和环境研究所主席

齐晔

香港科技大学（广州）碳中和与气候变化学域署理主任、清华大学公共管理学院教授

　　中国迫切需要一种新的城市发展模式，从对高碳行业大规模投资，向低碳、可持续发展转型，这对于中国实现2060年碳中和目标至关重要。一些城市已经开始行动并走在了前列。"十四五"时期，在全国范围内加快推进城市可持续发展，将为经济增长注入新的活力，让中国更加坚定地走上生态文明之路。

2020年，中国在抗击新冠肺炎疫情和重启经济方面成绩斐然，成为世界经济的复苏的"领头羊"。现在中国正面临一个重要的机遇期，向全世界展示，如何朝着更可持续、更具韧性的经济增长转型——尤其是在城市。

最新数据显示，2020年中国经济增长2.3%。尽管这与前几年的增长率相比大幅度下降，但是与其他许多国家相比，包括发达经济体的经济收缩情况，已经是很好的表现了。尤其是在2020年四季度，中国GDP增长了6.5%，高于2019年全年增长率。

但2020年中国经济快速复苏的负面影响就是二氧化碳排放量的持续增加。2020年中国煤炭、石油和天然气消耗量分别增加了0.6%、3.3%和7.2%。

这提醒我们，在通往生态文明的道路上仍会面临不小的挑战。

/ 模式转型 /

近几十年来，经济增长帮助数亿中国人脱贫，带动了全国各地生活水平提升。这一经济奇迹之所以出现，主要是由于城市经济的高速增长，吸引了大量农民工进城就业。

但是这种城市发展模式在很大程度上造成了污染、浪费和效率低下。在刚刚结束的全国两会上通过的"十四五"规划纲要，为中国实现以可持续发展为中心、更高质量的城市经济增长提供了机会。

在中国的许多地区，尤其是沿海地区，城市不断扩张，地方政府希望通过向外扩张来增加收入，例如卖地收入。

这种发展模式的代价，是牺牲了周边农村耕地、自然生态系统和生物多样性。同时，因为许多工人的通勤时间延长，能源和化石燃料的消耗增加，也构成了效率低下和污染严重的问题。

城市转型联盟（Coalition for Urban Transitions）近期研究指出，中国未来应重点发展"CCC城市"，即生态良好（Clean）、规模紧凑（Compact）、彼此紧密相连（Connected）的中小城市，在这样的城市里，交通更便利，空气更清洁，工作更高效。

随着对高碳行业的大规模投资渐行渐远，中国迫切需要这种新的城市发展模式。更有效的空间规划政策，以及能源、建筑、材料和运输部门的改革将为这种发展模式提供支撑。

中国的一些城市已经在清洁能源、高效资源利用和科技、金融、政策创新的驱动下，开始向更可持续的发展模式转型。

深圳就是一个积极实践低碳发展、产业绿色转型的例子。相比狭隘地专注于增长速度，深圳以创新和工业现代化为核心，更注重经济发展质量。深圳碳市场于2013年6月启动，是全国首批碳排放权交易试点之一。

可持续的城市发展提升了深圳的国内国际竞争力，这个宝贵案例值得中国其他城市借鉴。

/ 主导作用 /

中国拥有庞大且不断增长的城市人口，在推动绿色金融发展方面占据主导地位，这意味着中国未来在全世界，包括"一带一路"沿线国家的城市可持续发展方面将发挥尤为重要的作用。

城市可持续发展对于实现中国的碳中和目标至关重要。

在2020年9月的第75届联合国大会上，中国宣布"二氧化碳排放力争于2030年前达到峰值，努力争取2060年前实现碳中和"。也就是说，中国将努力用30年时间，从碳达峰走到碳中和，比其他国家计划用时短得多。

例如，英国早在1972年就已实现本土碳排放达峰，而它计划的碳中和时间为2050年。

"十四五"时期，应加快推进城市的可持续发展，使中国在经济振兴的同时，稳步走上生态文明的道路。

比如说，如果中国很多城市的碳排放能够在"十四五"期间，也就是2025年之前达峰，那么中国整体碳达峰时间可能提前到2025年，这样就为2060年实现碳中和目标留出了更多时间。

再比如说，如果中国在更新后的《巴黎协定》国家自主贡献承诺中包含2025年碳排放达峰的目标，那么就可能对美国政府造成压力，作为回应，美国也不得不作出更大的承诺。

作为世界上最大的两个碳排放国，中美现在携手领导全球碳减排行动比以往任何时候都更需要。联合国近期发布报告称，全球气候变化峰会将于2021年11月在英国格拉斯哥举行，目前已有部分国家提交了更新后的碳排放计划，但这些计划仍无法实现全球升温幅度控制在2摄氏度以内的目标。

在过去的一年里，气候变化带来的持续影响已经让我们付出了沉重代价，包括森林大火、洪水和风暴，2020年还是欧洲和亚洲有史以来最热的一年。

最重要的是，城市可持续发展将展示世界是如何受益于中国的国际领导力，来共同应对疫情、生物多样性丧失和气候变化等全球性威胁。

（此文首发于2021年3月18日中国日报中国观察智库）

有效碳定价：中国减排新探索

黄杰夫

芝加哥气候交易所前副总裁，AEX控股公司创始合伙人

2022年3月，首个底层资产是国际碳配额期货的交易所交易基金（ETF）在港交所上市，它追踪美国洲际交易所（ICE）交易的欧盟碳排放配额（EUA）期货指数，该指数主要计量一篮子长仓欧盟碳配额期货合约。

2021年8月至2022年4月，生态环境部向纳入全国碳排放交易市场（ETS）的2200多家发电企业发放的碳配额累计交易量达1.89亿吨，价值82亿元人民币。

参考欧盟和美国加州的经验，交易所内受监管的碳配额期货和场外衍生品交易对于一个有效的"总量控制加交易"（cap and trade）的碳市场至关重要，因为控排企业可以在这些合规的期货市场中对冲其配额价格的远期风险敞口。例如，2021年在美国洲际交易所成交的各国碳配额达180亿吨（名义金额相当于1万亿美元），其中152亿吨交易来自欧盟、24亿吨来自美国加州、2.55亿吨来自英国、3.46亿吨来自美国区域温室气体倡议（RGGI）覆盖的区域。

欧盟和美国加州的电力企业先在电力市场里总结出一套交易和风险管理的"工具箱"，多年后直接将这套"工具箱"应用于碳配额交易。相比之下，中国的电力企业一开始就必须同时面对电力、

配额两个市场交易的挑战。未来中国的配额发放将收紧、免费配额逐步削减，配额市场反映真实供需的价格波动将会出现，如同当下的省级电力现货市场的交易价格。尽管风电、光伏等新能源企业正在尝试抓住现货市场的交易机会、将其风险转移给金融机构，更大的挑战来自于建立规范的风险管理体系、培养相关人才和团队。当然，熟练掌握了交易、风控能力的电力企业，同时也获得了经营层面的竞争优势。

以山西为例，其电力现货市场在全国范围内率先实现连续平稳试运行一周年。目前山西约40%的电力消纳来自可再生的风能和太阳能。然而，在2021年一整年里，可再生能源发电的现货结算价格一直低于全省平均价格。

为帮助山西企业缩小在交易和风险管理中的技术差距，AEX控股公司联合四家中国合作伙伴成立了"中国碳电场外模拟交易实验室"，旨在通过模拟全周期场外交易，帮助煤炭和新能源发电厂商以及电力零售商体验全周期的交易和风险管理流程。

大宗商品期货有效定价的关键在于较高的机构参与度，碳期货和电力期货也不例外。期货持仓量（OI）是用来衡量机构参与度的一个很好的指标。截至2021年7月底，中国五家期货交易所的持仓数为2990万手，只占全球11亿手合约总量的2.7%，相比之下，中国GDP约占全球总量的17%。同时，在我国期货交易所上市的90多个期货品种中，拥有一年以上远期价格曲线的寥寥无几。

有效定价的底线在于：期货交易所是需要培育12个月以上长期合约的流动性，从一开始就吸引更多的机构参与者。这对电力及碳期货合约同样适用。较高的机构参与度是定义中国"大宗商品交易2.0版"的关键点。

在过去30年里，中国的商品期货交易实践已经取得了长足进步。2022年4月，全国人大常委会刚刚通过了《中华人民共和国期货和衍生品法》，标志着商品期货交易步入新阶段。在过去的几年里，几个省级试点市场尝试了碳配额场外远期交易，但交易的流动性并未显现。《中华人民共和国期货和衍生品法》首次提出了场外衍生品交易的监管框架，同时为"中国碳电场外模拟交易实验室"等市场主体自下而上的探索和实践打开了大门。

欧美高效的碳排放交易定价体系的运行经验充分说明，应当建设中立、透明、有竞争力的期货交易所生态。相比之下，我国期货和衍生品法中"期货交易所的高管由监管部门任免"的规定，仍然属于计划经济到市场经济过渡期的制度安排，已经难以适应市场发展的需要。

2008年，芝加哥气候交易所（CCX）来到天津，帮助中国探索建立碳排放总量控制和交易体系。今天，中国的电力企业和金融机构可以引进国际最佳实践实现高效的碳定价，助力我国"2030碳达峰"及之后能源转型目标的实现。

（此文英文原文首发于2022年4月22日中国日报国际版）

应对气候变化是门"好生意"

戴青丽（Deborah Lehr）

保尔森基金会副主席兼总裁

　　当前各国政府和企业都在积极参与应对气候变化的进程，绿色低碳转型发展意味着巨大商机。绿色金融已经进入主流商业领域，成为全球领先金融机构的优先事项。中国以其巨大的碳排放规模，以及领先的绿色金融和清洁技术，将在这一股"气候商业"浪潮中占据核心地位。

　　当前我们正迎来三十年一遇的技术创新热潮，这次的重大机遇与气候相关。从政府到企业，都正在一起寻求创新方法，以帮助世界实现碳中和转型。

　　在世界各地，应对这一挑战的政治意愿正在不断增强：中国和欧盟已成为绿色金融的领先者，中东、拉美和非洲也相继跟进，美国总统拜登甚至将应对气候变化上升为"国策"。

　　政府的政策、良好治理和监管架构都是政治意愿的重要组成部分，对于制定成功的绿色金融框架及支持碳中和转型十分必要。但我们都很清楚，这还不够，我们需要调动私人资本。

　　好消息是，私人资本正在跃跃欲试，绿色金融已经从一种慈善活动转变为一种主流商业活动。

新冠肺炎疫情和越来越直观的气候灾害表明了长期韧性的重要性。金融机构已经意识到气候风险对金融稳定构成的巨大威胁。

世界各主要投资银行、对冲基金和其他金融机构已将绿色转型作为一个日益重要的优先事项，利用其平台的力量成为支持绿色转型的倡导者。

简而言之，应对气候变化现已成为一门"好生意"。根据彭博新能源财经的数据，2020年，为能源转型投入的资金达到了创纪录的5010亿美元。

除了企业把净零排放转型发展作为自身发展优先考虑之外，我们还看到了自20世纪90年代技术热潮以来从未见过的投资机会。

气候投资不再只涉及可再生能源和基础设施，而是正在向主流化发展。最典型的例子是特斯拉：2020年特斯拉股票飙升了740%，其市值现已超过老牌车企通用。

与气候变化相关的新技术研发和商业化对我们实现碳中和至关重要，支持这些技术落地符合我们所有人的利益。但与此同时，我们必须确保生意不会变成冲突。我们已经看到，新能源汽车、太阳能电池板和锂电池领域竞争激烈。良性竞争是好的，可以推动成本下降，但如果是因为国家安全以外的原因，让竞争限制了技术进步，将不符合任何人的利益。

客户的需求也在增加。2020年年底，全球可持续基金的资产总额达1.65万亿美元，比上一季度增长29%，创历史新高。

例如，大型美国私募股权公司德太投资正在推出一只全球气候基金，投资于技术和解决方案，以帮助绿色股权投资增加，平衡绿色债券的大幅增长。

贝莱德等世界上最大的资产管理公司正在将可持续发展确定为重要优先事项，推动它们所持股的公司增加气候信息披露，并利用它们自有的资金平台来鼓励变革。

这是一个不可逆转的浪潮。

中国将成为这一气候商业热潮的核心，这不仅是因为中国的碳排放规模创造了机会，还因为中国正在成为创新绿色金融和清洁技术的领导者。

以环境产品和服务为例，中国已开始向外国企业进一步开放。高盛最近的一项研究预计，这个行业的潜在市场价值高达16万亿美元，到2060年可创造多达4000万个就业机会。这是一门好生意。

2021年6月底正式启动的中国碳交易市场也将创造新的机会。尽管首批只纳入发电行业，但其规模将达到中国碳排放量的45%及全球碳排放总量的14%。当水泥、电解铝等其他八个重点排放行业被逐步纳入后，中国碳市场将有可能覆盖全球30%的碳排放量。

碳可能成为新的"货币"，而中国将可能掌握条款、标准的制定权和定价权。

因此，我们需要继续这样的讨论，以便我们能够了解一些可能出现的爆发点，并希望找到正确的架构，处理未来不可避免的分歧。

（此文首发于2021年6月8日中国日报中国观察智库）

〔 第三章 〕
携手合作，共创绿色未来

中美合作牵头，低碳转型可能比想象的更快

杰弗里·萨克斯（Jeffrey Sachs）

美国哥伦比亚大学可持续发展中心主任、经济学教授

开展气候行动，推动低碳转型已成为各主要经济体的共识。中美气候合作可以为两国在其他领域的合作开个好头，也有利于促进世界合作共赢。

2021年4月，中美双方发表的《中美应对气候危机联合声明》无疑是一个可喜的进展。回想2015年，中美合作对于《巴黎协定》谈判的成功至关重要；而如今，中美再次携手对于顺利贯彻《巴黎协定》亦不可或缺。

较之2015年，今天的气候变化形势更加严峻，气候危机持续深化，并大有加速之势。地球平均气温过去每十年上升约0.2摄氏度，但在最近的一二十年间，升温趋势加剧，差不多每十年升温约0.3摄氏度。地球现在的气温要比工业化前水平高出1.2摄氏度，并且可能

在未来几年内跨过1.5摄氏度的门槛。

开展应对气候问题的全球行动势在必行。幸运的是，当今世界上大多数主要经济体都已认识到了这一基本事实。中国、欧盟、日本、韩国、美国等方最近纷纷做出承诺，要在本世纪中叶前后实现温室气体净零排放，其中中国的目标是在2060年前。

/ 加快脱碳步伐 /

我相信各主要国家不久就将认识到，世界可以而且应当加快实现零排放目标，起码可以提前到2050年。为什么说这一步伐很可能加快呢？主要原因有二：第一，气候威胁远比大多数人想象的更加凶险；第二，实现净零排放的技术手段也远比大多数人想象的更加丰富。

气候变化引发了多种自然灾害，飓风、干旱、洪水、热浪以及森林火灾正变得越来越严重，越来越危险。尤其令人不安的是，由于格陵兰和南极冰盖部分脱落，全球海平面可能会整体上升数米。如此大规模的海平面上升对世界各地的沿海城市而言无疑是灭顶之灾。

与此同时，实现温室气体零碳排放其实并不像人们一直以来认为的那样困难。在本世纪中叶之前，技术进步将推动世界资源结构由化石燃料向零碳能源过渡，和国民收入相比，这一能源转型的成本并不算高。问题的关键在于，所有主要经济体都应当规划出一条明确的零碳能源过渡路径。

全球要实现碳减排，关键要走好以下六步：

第一，所有新建发电设施应当基于零碳能源，如太阳能、风能、水力、核能、地热等新型能源，而依靠化石燃料的传统发电厂应逐步淘汰。

第二，交通运输应电气化，用电动车替代燃油车。

第三，取暖和做饭也应从烧煤、烧气改为用电。

第四，清洁电能应当被用于生产其他用于工业用途的绿色能源，例如氢能。

第五，应发展智能电网等数字技术，以节约能源。

第六，人们应改变饮食结构，多摄入植物蛋白，少摄入动物蛋白，这不仅有利于身体健康，也可以减少环境压力。

/ 转型成功经验 /

《中美应对气候危机联合声明》中最重要的内容之一，就是中美双方共同承诺，在格拉斯哥联合国气候公约第26次缔约方大会之前，制定各自旨在实现碳中和的长期战略。根据《巴黎协定》，各国应提交不同于短期国家自主贡献方案的"长期"发展战略，并且应说明他们如何实现零排放的具体工作路径。

未来几个月，中美两国政府将制定各自的长期战略，它们很可能会得出两个主要结论：首先，电力部门实现零排放并不像现在所设想的那么难。其次，转型的速度也将比现在所设想的要更快。中国承诺将在2060年之前实现零排放，但我相信，专家进一步分析后便会发现，2050年之前实现零排放也是可行的，而且对中国和世界都是有益的。

中国处于向零排放模式快速转型的有利位置，因为它在一系列重要领域拥有强大的技术水平和制造能力，如光伏、风电、水电、远距离高压输电网、5G、人工智能、电动汽车、电池等。另外，在"十四五"期间，中国还将加大关键技术领域的资源投入，这将使其能够以更低成本，更快实现低碳转型。

诚然，如何让那些对碳能源依赖过高的地区和劳动力实现低碳转型，是中美两国均面临的难题。然而要说转型，世界上恐怕没有哪个国家比中国的成功经验还多。中国在兼顾包容性发展的同时实现了快速的结构性转型，在城市化和劳动力市场的重大结构转变过程中，中国的极端贫困发生率在过去30多年间从80%一路下降，最终成功实现"清零"。

/ 扩大合作共赢 /

另一件令我欣慰的事就是，最新的中美联合声明表明，两国将合力助推2021年10月在昆明举办的生物多样性大会成功举办。美国目前还不是《生物多样性公约》的缔约国，我希望拜登总统能将这份公约送交美国参议院审议，让美国成为该公约的正式成员。《生物多样性公约》所倡导的土地可持续利用，不但对保护生物多样性非常重要，而且与实现零排放密切相关，因为不可持续的土地开发是导致温室气体排放的主要因素之一。

中美在应对气候危机方面的共同承诺，应当为两国在其他多个领域的积极合作开个好头。中美也好，世界也罢，合则两利，斗则俱伤。中美携手共进，世界合作共赢，其结果必是功在当代，利在千秋。

（此文首发于2021年4月22日中国日报中国观察智库）

COP26将把世界带向哪里，关键看中美欧

芮悟峰（Wolfgang Röhr）

同济大学德国研究中心特聘研究员，德国前驻上海总领事

　　第26届联合国气候变化大会于2021年10月31日在英国格拉斯哥开幕。作为世界上最大的温室气体排放者，中国、美国和欧盟是这次会议最重要的参与方。中国低碳技术进步惊人，未来逐渐摆脱煤炭依赖值得期待；美国近年来将气候问题政治化，态度反复无常；欧盟整体气候政策是一贯的，但各成员国在具体问题上存在分歧。广泛的国际合作，尤其是中美欧三方合作，对于实现全球气候目标至关重要。

　　中国、美国和欧盟是第26届联合国气候变化大会最重要的参与方，理由很简单：全球温室气体排放总量中，中美欧加起来占了约一半。目前，中国的排放量占28%，美国占15%，欧盟占8%。然而如果把时间线拉长，计算历史累积排放量的话，情况就不一样了：美国占了29%，欧盟占了22%，中国则仅占13%。

　　中美欧三方都为自身设定了未来十年，乃至更加长远的雄心勃勃的减排目标。习近平主席在2020年联合国大会上宣布，中国将力争在2030年前实现碳排放达峰，努力争取在2060年前实现碳中和。美国总统拜登承诺，美国将在2030年前减少50%的排放量，在2050年前实现碳中和。欧盟则承诺将在2030年前减排55%，并在2050年

前实现碳中和。

在过去几年里，中国的低碳技术取得了惊人的进步。如今，全球45％的风电机组和72％的太阳能电池板均为"中国制造"。但是，尽管中国在可再生能源领域处于世界领先地位，中国仍然需要依赖煤炭能源。习主席在2021年联合国大会上表示，中国将停止新建海外燃煤发电项目，这无疑是一项重大进展。然而对于中国来说，煤炭依旧十分重要。2020年，中国的煤炭发电量是世界其他国家总和的三倍多。随着"生态文明"被庄严地写入中国宪法，以及2021年5月在昆明召开的联合国生物多样性大会上，习近平主席再次强调了这一理念，我们期待中国未来将逐渐摆脱煤炭依赖。

美国在特朗普时期退出了《巴黎协定》，这使得人们对美国应对气候变化的诚意心生疑虑。拜登上台后，很快表示要重回《巴黎协定》，并对外宣布了大手笔的气候计划。美国的问题在于，气候政策变成了一个党派色彩浓厚的政治问题：民主党人雄心勃勃地要大砍大减，而共和党人则非常不愿意大幅削减温室气体排放。现在距离美国中期选举只有一年的时间了，而下届总统选举将在2024年举行，我们很难预测美国未来几十年的气候政策会出现何种变故。然而，要想让其他国家履行减排承诺，美国必须首先作出表率。

相比之下，欧盟的气候政策是一贯的。2021年6月28日，欧洲理事会发表公报称，欧盟国家最终通过了《欧洲气候法案》，把遵守减排目标列为了一项法律义务。然而，最令欧盟头疼的难题是，其内部27个成员国之间存在意见分歧。比如德国等一些国家支持更大幅度的碳减排，但另一些国家——尤其是中欧国家，则更为谨慎。德国认为核能已经过时，并计划在2022年前关闭所有剩余的核反应堆，而法国则不这样想。目前法国共有50多座核反应堆，核电占该国发电总量七成以上。法国总统马克龙近期还宣布了一项新的能源政策，可能会在未来几年大批量修建小型模块化反应堆。

长期以来，欧盟和中国在气候问题上达成了一定程度的合作。从2005年《中欧气候变化联合声明》到2018年《中欧领导人气候变化和清洁能源联合声明》，这些曾经的努力都为双方深入合作奠定了良好的基础。中美应该以2021年4月发表的《中美应对气候危机联合声明》为起点，进一步推进双边合作。欧盟和美国在2021年也发表了联合声明，承诺在应对气候危机上加强合作。

这样的国际合作是必要的，有助于解决一些有争议的议题，比如"碳边界调整机制"。这个机制是欧盟提出来的，希望通过阻止"碳泄漏"来避免气候政策有效性受到破坏。从本质上说，这是一种针对进口商品的新型税收，凡是对温室气体排放管制不那么严格的国家，今后向欧盟出口商品时都要额外交这么一笔钱。中国已经明确表示，不赞成引入那些可能阻碍贸易的新型调控手段。美国对此也不怎么感冒。

然而，更大的挑战正在降临。国际能源署发布的《世界能源展望》报告显示，全球能源相关排放在因新冠疫情大流行而短暂下降后，2021年将会重新上升，净增长量将是2010年以来的最大值。即使各国政府都能够落实其减排承诺，到2030年，世界各国对天然气和石油的需求量，也将远高于零排放所限定的使用量。因此，各国政府需要做更多的工作来完全兑现他们的承诺。

国际社会为自己设定的目标虽高，但只有通过制定更严格的国家政策，更坚定地履行承诺，更密切地相互合作——特别是在气候政策上尤为重要的中美欧三方合作，这些目标才能实现。应对气候变化需要全面的团队协作：如果在其他问题上都存在竞争甚至敌意，那我们更别指望能在气候问题上达成合作了。

（此文英文原文首发于2021年10月28日中国日报国际版）

如"约"而"植"　植树造林没有定法，
关键是广泛参与、因地制宜

费翰思（Hans Friederich）

国际竹藤（INBAR）前总干事

巴西、加拿大、中国、刚果（金）、印度尼西亚、俄罗斯和美国等国共同签署了《关于森林和土地利用的格拉斯哥领导人宣言》，承诺到2030年停止砍伐森林，积极应对土地退化问题。植树造林需要城市与农村共同发力，需要人人参与。

2021年在英国格拉斯哥召开的《联合国气候变化框架公约》第26次缔约方会议（COP26）的重要成果之一，是巴西、加拿大、中国、刚果（金）、印度尼西亚、俄罗斯和美国等国共同签署了《关于森林和土地利用的格拉斯哥领导人宣言》（以下简称《宣言》），承诺到2030年停止砍伐森林，扭转土地退化状况。这些国家拥有的森林面积约占全球85%。

保护这些天然森林资源的益处之多不言而喻，因此《宣言》的签署意义重大。原生林为人类提供了诸多服务，例如水源供给和土壤保护，为濒危动植物提供庇护，以及至关重要的碳汇功能。

多国实践证明，"先伐天然林，后补人工林"是一种有害无益的做法，这一做法有望在《宣言》框架下得到遏制。但有些地方的天然林已经遭到砍伐，残破林不断退化，土地侵蚀日益严重，在这些地方开展植树造林是帮助当地恢复自然生态的重要手段。

《巴黎协定》的科学咨询机构——联合国政府间气候变化专门委员会（IPCC）明确指出，植树是有效减少二氧化碳排放的措施。鉴于此，多国已经开始着手进行植树造林运动。

然而，仅仅通过植树来增加的碳汇，远不足以抵消目前的碳排放，碳抵消应是在尽最大努力减少当前碳排放之后的补救措施。未来几年内实现碳中和，其实远不足以实现将全球变暖控制在1.5摄氏度以内的目标，因为碳中和意味着当前的碳排放并没有怎么降低，而只是通过碳抵消措施被"平衡"掉了。

对植树增汇持批评态度的人还指出，人工造林地往往是单种栽培的纯林，因此对其环境价值严重存疑。科学研究表明，纯林比混交林更易受病虫害的影响，生物多样性的效益也更低。

树种的选择亦引发关切。桉树是世界上广泛种植的一种速生树种，但桉树并非没有害处：由于桉叶有毒，因此其落叶无助于土壤肥力的增强。同理，鲜有树种可以与桉树间作。因此，除了用作建筑材料和木柴外，桉树人工林的作用有限。

地方对新植林地的所有权问题常存争议。当地人的参与对新植林地的存续至关重要，如果没有他们的积极参与，新植林地恐怕很难搞得好。在公共用地上植树造林的一大关键挑战在于林地维护，因为幼树可能会被食草动物啃食，或被侵入者连根拔起，且幼树在初生的若干年内通常需要灌溉。很多造林计划都由于树木未能存活而无法善始善终。

不过，植树造林之功不止在于碳减排。比如中国在20世纪90年代启动的"退耕还林还草"计划，涉及25个省区市1897个县的1.24亿人口。截至2010年，实现退耕还林还草面积约1500万公顷，还使

1700万公顷的荒山变绿林。

其中的一些林地以竹子为主，而中国竹业的发展也领先世界。根据中国国家林业和草原局的数据，目前中国的竹林地面积超过700万公顷，其中一半专用于人们的生活和工业生产。竹子生长速度快，气候适应力强，根系发达，能够在不利于其他作物生长的土壤条件下茁壮成长，为年产值约500亿美元的中国竹产业奠定了基础。该产业覆盖食品、家具、建筑和装修材料、纺织品、纸浆、纸张等多种由竹和竹纤维制成的产品。

要将造林和还林置于更宏观的土地结构背景下进行考量。现代土地利用体系多由自然保护区、农业用地和包括基础设施及村庄在内的其他农村开发用地构成。人工林地可以成为多样化的土地结构中的一部分，在不同地区选用不同树种，为整体生态环境的改善做出贡献。

植树造林不应只限于农村。许多新近研究表明，树木对人类的健康福祉大有裨益，能为城市提供荫蔽，使街道保持清凉。

在近年来的城市化进程中，中国提出了"海绵城市"概念，其他一些国家也纷纷效仿。发展海绵城市有赖于湿地和绿地的建设或恢复，以保障城市在强降水期间的排水和吸水能力。随着气候变化导致的极端天气情况增加，"海绵城市"建设的重要性凸显，对地势低洼的城市而言尤甚。

树木还可用以助力"棕地"（通常指工矿企业或市政设施关闭搬迁后遗留下来，因环境污染而被闲置或遗弃的场地）修复和受污土地的再生。现有的森林必须得到尽可能的保护，但同时，退化地的森林恢复和皆伐地的重新造林也必不可少。

总之，植树无定法，树种的选择要因时制宜、因地制宜，但无论采取何种措施，当地居民的参与都是立林之本、茂林之要。

（此文英文原文首发于2021年12月22日中国日报国际版）

发展中国家恐成气候变化受害者，《全球发展倡议》助力发展中国家实现绿色过渡

杨力超

北京师范大学社会学院副教授

罗伯特·沃克（Robert Walker）

北京师范大学社会学院教授，牛津大学格林坦普尔顿学院名誉研究员

今年，中国、巴基斯坦和欧洲分别遭遇了干旱、洪涝和森林大火，反映出应对气候变化时不我待。虽然第27届联合国气候变化大会 (COP27) 即将于今年11月在埃及沙姆沙伊赫举行，但在应对气候变化方面取得的进展却微乎其微。

新冠疫情打乱了应对气候变化工作的节奏，近期天然气价格也出现大幅上涨。考虑到这些因素，重开燃煤电厂或开发新油气田导致碳排放增加，使减排进程出现倒退的风险切实存在。若这一假设成真，那么将开创只顾眼前不管长远、牺牲后代利益满足当代人需求的危险先例。即使这中倒退可能只是暂时的，要想实现碳减排目标，各国也必须加快转型脚步，甚至可能要以更强硬的态度大力推进。

在气候变化亟待解决的背景下，国际上对于"公正转型"的讨论有很多。根据国际劳工组织的描述，"公正转型"重点关注那些

为了实现零碳排放而被削减的高碳工作岗位，强调要对对受影响的人和社区进行实质性补偿。这也提醒政策制定者，若处理不当，转型可能将造成长期损害。

在欧洲和北美，很多地方早在40多年前就关停了高碳排放产业，但直到今天，那些地区仍饱受贫困之苦。而在中国，如果完全关闭重工业，国企员工可能受影响不大，因为他们可以转岗，社保金也比较高，但私企员工会受多大影响就不那么明朗了。

而且，在全球向低碳经济转型的过程中，面临公平问题的并非只是受到直接影响的个人，"分配公正"问题显然也很重要，也就是谁获得收益，谁承担损失；哪些人或机构的做法值得提倡，哪些又需要改进。另外还有"程序公正"问题，也就是谁来参与决策，以及如何参与。最后我们还要看到权力不对称以及制度性歧视和压迫现象的存在。

2021年在英国格拉斯哥召开的第26届联合国气候变化大会（COP26），为我们生动展示了什么叫"程序不公正"——由于工业巨头们实力强大，谴责它们长期以来肆无忌惮地开采和利用资源的声音被淹没了。化石燃料游说团体共有503名代表参会，比任何国家的与会代表都多；而除了全体会议之外，最大的会议室只有144个座位，根本坐不下《巴黎协定》的所有缔约方。各国曾希望在2100年将气温上升幅度控制在1.5℃以内，但大会后最乐观的预计是1.8℃。

中国代表团高级顾问王毅指出，"如果将目标设为1.5℃而非2℃，就必须增加资金。"虽然发达国家曾承诺共同投资1000亿美元，用来支持发展中国家气候变化减适工作，但在大会上它们却翻脸不认账。目前，至少有11个非洲国家在适应气候变化方面的支出超过其医疗卫生支出。此外，对各国损失进行补偿的相关协议也尚未达成。据估计，仅美国的温室气体排放就给其他国家造成了1.9万亿美元的损失。

与这次大会令人大失所望形成鲜明对比的是，习近平主席在同年召开的第76届联合国大会一般性辩论上提出了全球发展倡议，主张构建"相互尊重、公平正义、合作共赢的新型国际关系"。习主席的讲话提醒世界各国领导人，应对气候变化是更广泛的全球议程中的一项内容，事关17项联合国可持续发展目标能否在2030年实现。

在2022年1月的全球发展倡议之友小组启动会议上，中国常驻联合国代表张军再次强调了发展的重要性，并表示，全球发展倡议的八大优先事项，是从解决发展中国家面临的最紧迫问题入手，以重点领域带动实现所有17个可持续发展目标。其中，气候变化、减贫和粮食安全反映了绿色转型的挑战，而工业化、数字经济和互联互通是促进绿色转型的手段。他还指出，全球发展倡议以人民为中心，以发展为优先，在发展中保障和改善民生，保护和促进人权。

一些西方批评家提出了质疑，他们要么认为人权与发展无法结合，要么无法理解为何要共同发展、共同繁荣。前者的观点忽视了渐进式发展的核心原则：一个国家能否采取适当措施，遵守义务，关键要看它手上有多少可利用的财政和其他资源，发展是充分实现人权的根本前提。而后者则忽视了公正转型原则，即在政策的制定、实施和执行过程中，应公平对待所有人。对公司股东有利而对工人或失业者不利的政策显然是不公平的；同样，牺牲发展中国家利益，只为让发达国家更加富裕的做法也是不公平的。如果不能使所有人从转型中受益，那么至少应该将损失降到最低，并由所有人公平分担。

公正原则不同于其他类型的道德关切，因为其确立了（或者说应当确立）正当可执行的预期及权利。因此，在发达地区，污染环境要受到惩罚，而化石燃料的消费者也无法得到绿色能源补贴。然而，至于程序正义有没有贯彻执行，底层民众是否过多地承担了转型带来的不利影响，就不太清楚了。

由于缺乏资源、投资以及获得技术专长的机会，发展中国家的绿色转型十分艰难。再加上对发达国家的债务负担，公正转型的可能性更是微乎其微。在联合国气候变化大会框架下，应对气候变化和促进绿色转型的国家义务目前看仍无法执行，本质上难言公正。这种情况在沙姆沙伊赫也不会改变，发展中国家依然得不到足够的国际支持。但是，全球发展倡议通过提供资金和技术援助的方式，为发展中国家实现向绿色经济的公正转型提供了一个至关重要的新手段。

（此文英文原文首发于2022年9月22日中国日报国际版）

The Imperative Action

The Global Significance and Challenges of the Dual Carbon Goals

Ⅰ Fostering Mutual Trust through Multilateral Dialogue for Global Environmental Risk Mitigation

Pathways to a green recovery

By ZHUANG JUZHONG

There is huge potential for Belt and Road countries to cooperate with each other to promote sustainable development

The countries participating in the Belt and Road Initiative have intensified their efforts to promote a green transition in recent years, by improving energy efficiency, investing in renewable energies, reducing carbon dioxide emissions intensity, controlling pollution and protecting biodiversity.

China is leading by example. Renewable energies accounted for 29 percent of China's power generation in 2019, up from 17 percent in 2000. China now aims to peak its carbon emissions before 2030 and achieve carbon neutrality before 2060. Other Belt and Road countries also have carbon neutrality targets, including Hungary (2050), Slovakia (2050) and Singapore (in the second half of 21st century).

But despite the progress, Belt and Road countries still have a long way to go to realize a green transition. For instance, their energy consumption per unit of GDP is still 40 percent to 50 percent higher than OECD average and their CO2 emissions per unit of GDP is 80 percent higher.

According to the International Energy Agency's "sustainable development scenario", the share of fossil fuels in total primary energy consumption globally has to be reduced to 56 percent by 2040, and the share of power generation by fossil fuels reduced to 24 percent. But the share of fossil fuels in the total primary energy consumption of the Belt and Road countries is as high as 89 percent, and fossil fuels still account for more than 70 percent of their power generation.

Among the 60 countries with the most serious PM2.5 air pollution globally, about half are Belt and Road countries. Further, considering Belt and Road countries' need for future economic development, without changing the growth model, their CO2 emissions and other pollutions will continue to rise rapidly. To further promote their green transition and development, Belt and Road countries should strengthen policies in the following areas.

First, they should change their growth models to improve the quality of growth. The most important is to shift from resources-driven growth to innovation-driven growth. Belt and Road countries should also promote the circular economy and raise the efficiency of resources utilization.

According to the fifth assessment report of the Intergovernmental Panel on Climate Change, to achieve the Paris Agreement's goal of keeping the global temperature rise "well below 2 C above pre-industrial levels and pursuing efforts to limit the temperature increase to 1.5 C above pre-industrial levels", CO2 emissions have to be reduced by 40 percent to 70 percent from the 2010 levels by 2050, and all countries should achieve carbon neutrality before the end of this century. Global sustainable development therefore requires all the Belt and Road countries to set appropriate carbon neutrality targets.

The second is to strengthen environmental protection legislation and control pollutions and emissions, and not to repeat the old way of "polluting first and cleaning later". Most Belt and Road countries have environmental protection legislation. The key is to ensure the laws are effectively enforced.

The third is to use market mechanisms to protect the environment. Market mechanisms can also make emissions reduction cost-effective. One important measure is to eliminate fossil fuel subsidies. According to data from the IEA, among the 25 countries with the highest fossil fuel subsidies in 2019, 18 were Belt and Road countries. Saved fiscal resources from eliminating fossil fuel subsidies can be used to subsidize renewable energies.

Despite the significant reduction in the cost of renewable energies over the last 10 years (for example, the long-term unit cost of solar power declined by 80 percent and wind power by 30 percent to 40 percent), these new energy sources require very high initial investment, and hence need government support.

Another way of using market mechanisms is to introduce a carbon tax. More and more countries are developing carbon markets, including Belt and Road countries such as China, India, Thailand and Kazakhstan. Several Southeast Asian countries are also planning to develop or are in the process of developing carbon markets, such as Indonesia, the Philippines and Vietnam. But overall, the development is still in its nascent stage in most Belt and Road countries.

The fourth is to promote green investment. According to a simple extrapolation of an Asian Development Bank study, over the next 10 years, Belt and Road countries' annual infrastructure investment needs will amount to $2.3 trillion. It is critical to ensure these investments promote green transition and development. This requires investing in renewable energies, green transport, green agriculture and green technologies.

The fifth is to develop green finance. In most Belt and Road countries, public resources are insufficient to meet their needs. Developing green finance is an important way to attract private funding for green development. Green finance has developed rapidly in China in recent years. China became the world's largest green bond issuer in 2018 and 2019. But in many Belt and Road countries, green finance is still in an early stage.

The last is to strengthen international cooperation. Most Belt and Road countries are developing countries that may have not contributed a lot to global CO2 emissions historically, but will be affected disproportionately by climate change. Developed countries have an obligation to support them in their green transition. The Paris Agreement envisages annual funding support for climate mitigation and adaptation in developing countries to reach $100 billion by 2020 and a higher level by 2025. Developed countries should fulfill their pledges despite the difficulties due to the pandemic.

There is huge potential for Belt and Road countries to cooperate with each other in green development. China, as the initiating country of the Belt and Road Initiative and the world's second-largest economy, has an important role to play in promoting the green transition and development of Belt and Road countries, through policy dialogue, knowledge sharing, better infrastructure connectivity, capital flows and trade and technological cooperation.

December 14, 2020 China Daily global edition

Torchbearer for climate governance

By ZHANG JIANYU

'Beautiful China' goals should maintain domestic focus on green growth but also promote the building of a global ecological civilization

The incorporation of ecological protection into China's goal of building a moderately prosperous society in all respects has been the major driver of the country's efforts to realize our ecological civilization since the 18th National Congress of the Communist Party of China in 2012. As the country is set to realize the goal of building a moderately prosperous society in all respects in 2020, achieving the "Beautiful China" goals by 2035 will become the next priority task. Different from the goal of building a moderately prosperous society, the Beautiful China 2035 goals need to be developed from a perspective of global ecological civilization.

Facing the threat of climate change, a well-functioning global environmental governance system is needed by 2035 to ensure a smooth transition from the Paris Agreement's 2030 goals to its 2050 long-term low-emission development goals.

Under the Paris Agreement countries are expected to submit their Nationally Determined Contributions outlining their commitments to reduce greenhouse gas emissions and strengthen resilience to climate change by 2030.While countries that have signed the agreement are stepping up efforts to hold true to their NDCs, action plans with even greater commitments by 2035 have already been unveiled.

The European Union plans more ambitious 2035 climate targets under the framework of the European Green Deal. A number of European countries have also unveiled action plans with goals to be achieved by 2035. For instance, Germany was inclined to bring forward its deadline to fully phase out the use of coal from 2038 to 2035; the United Kingdom plans to end the sale of new diesel and gasoline cars by 2035 and Finland has vowed to become carbon neutral by 2035 and carbon negative soon after that.

China is expected to be the world's largest economy by 2035, with even greater economic power and therefore a bigger responsibility in global environmental governance. China's pursuit of an ecological civilization is not just important for its own sustainable development, it will also exert an impact on the progress of sustainable development worldwide. Since its ecological civilization cannot be separated from the rest of the world, China needs to work more closely with countries, regions and organizations to address the grave environmental and climate challenges facing the whole of humanity.

On Sept 22, 2020, President Xi Jinping stated in his speech at the general debate of the 75th session of the United Nations General Assembly that China aims to "achieve carbon neutrality by 2060". As the world's largest developing country, this commitment reflects China's international responsibility to address climate change and also China's unwavering determination to follow the path of green and low-carbon development. However, how to achieve this goal? That is a question needed to be considered by China and it also attracts global attention.

The goal of 2035, which connects the CO_2 emissions peak and carbon neutrality, will determine to what extent the speed and path of China's greenhouse gas control in the future. By 2030, China needs to fulfill two major climate commitments-bringing national carbon emissions to a peak, as stated in the Paris Agreement, and the UN Sustainable Development Goals. The 2035 "Beautiful China" goals will exert a great impact on their implementation path and progress. The "Beautiful China" goals will also decide which path the country can take to fulfill its carbon neutral pledge. After the peak of CO_2 emissions, how China will align its domestic goal of a "Beautiful China" with its international commitment of carbon neutrality, and how to position itself to play a leading role in the international climate governance system. The goal-setting of 2035 "Beautiful China" will give an answer.

China has made notable progress in ecological and environmental protection, making concerted efforts to realize an ecological civilization. From the development concept of "Lucid waters and lush mountains are invaluable assets" to the idea of building a shared future for all life on Earth with a holistic approach to conserving the mountains, rivers, forests, farmlands, lakes and grasslands, China's vision of an ecological civilization has shifted from being merely an abstract concept to practical actions to realize it.

Indeed, the construction of China's ecological civilization for 2035 should be planned from the perspective of strengthening global endeavors to form an ecological civilization for humanity, with broadened scope and integrated solutions for both domestic and global environmental issues.

Domestically, the 2035 "Beautiful China" environmental protection goals should be set to match China's social and economic development goals. The quality of the ecological environment should be substantially improved with stricter environmental standards from the perspective of safeguarding health.

Internationally, China should have sustainable development goals and emissions control targets matched with China's development level. China should ensure a smooth transition from the 2030 climate goals to the 2050 and sustainable development goals and become a torchbearer for global climate governance.

The key to formulating the "Beautiful China" goals lies in upholding the concept of green development and maintaining a strategic focus of green growth in the face of the complex international political landscape. China needs to use the concept of "Lucid waters and lush mountains are invaluable assets" to guide its climate actions, turn the "burden" of emissions reduction into a precious opportunity to enhance its competitiveness in green development and make climate actions benefit sharing rather than cost sharing as before. These will ensure that China formulates ambitious 2035 "Beautiful China" goals.

The COVID-19 pandemic and rise of anti-globalization sentiment have brought about great uncertainties to the construction of a global ecological civilization, but also created opportunities. We are currently seeing a rapid acceleration in the development pace of 5G communications technology and other digital technology and their application, which has quickened the process of digitalization of the Chinese economy and provided new momentum for the green and low-carbon transformation of energy and manufacturing sectors. Since May, China has introduced a dual-circulation development pattern, in which the domestic market takes a dominant role while the domestic and global markets boost each other. Beefing up investment on green infrastructure, adjusting the global industrial chain and promoting green consumption domestically when fighting against the pandemic and restoring economic growth will help China lay a solid foundation to formulate and achieve more ambitious "Beautiful China" goals.

October 26, 2020 China Daily global edition

More dynamism for energy transition

QIU BAOXING/ANDREAS KUHLMANN

Cooperation on a green recovery provides a clear direction for getting out of the current global recession

Economic collapse caused by the novel coronavirus outbreak must be followed by a green new beginning: sustainable economic packages involving international and supranational cooperation that add further momentum to the energy transition. The novel coronavirus outbreak has changed the world. In every country, people are fighting against this crisis in the most effective ways possible. But the approaches to solve the problem sometimes seem as manifold as the challenges themselves. One key fact has emerged though: in an interconnected world such as ours today, global answers must be found to global crises.

Even if the crisis is unprecedented, we are not starting from scratch in this respect. There are time-tested forms of international collaboration. In matters of the energy transition and climate protection, for example, China and Germany have cooperated with one another for many years and done some successful work. Both countries can build on this.

The pandemic and the climate crisis may be different, but they also have points in common. The effects of both are not limited to individual countries and both are truly global challenges. We will only make progress in overcoming them through solidarity and cooperation rather than by isolating ourselves and pursuing individual paths. As a consequence of the worldwide lockdowns, a global recession of historic proportions is staring us in the face. Solutions for this exceptional situation must be found quickly, but not mindlessly. The way out of the crisis needs to have a clear direction.

Around the world, governments are being asked to plan the rebound after the pandemic in accordance with sustainability targets. The Sustainable Development Goals issued in 2015 provide a good point of orientation here. Now it's a question of exploiting the present momentum and ambitiously directing economic programs at investment for the future.

A well planned "green recovery" could progress cross-sectoral transformation in line with the integrated energy transition with greater urgency and impact. The energy transition needs dynamism. It can make a decisive contribution to a zero-carbon economy geared toward climate protection. It creates jobs and prospects. By contrast, funding the traditional fossil industry structures misses the target.

Objectives must, therefore, be set here and now, to create the conditions for good living on a transnational basis, through good standards and economic incentives. For more than 10 years, the Deutsche Energie-Agentur (the German Energy Agency) has been developing and implementing collaborative projects in China in the fields of energy-efficient construction, sustainable urban development, energy efficiency in industry, renewable energy sources, smart energy systems and air pollution control. The practical, trusting and successful collaborations with partners such as the Centre of Science and Technology of Construction or the Chinese Society for Urban Studies are evidence of the degree to which Germany and China are driving the green transformation processes forward together.

This cooperation is imbued with the spirit of sustainability, which has grown up alongside society's development with regard to global climate protection. From its initial projects in the field of energy-efficient construction, other exciting projects have emerged over time, such as German-Chinese Eco-Cities and integrated urban districts.

In particular, the project for constructing energy-efficient houses with passive house technologies, begun in 2008, has achieved outstanding results and has now been rolled out all over China. These collaborative successes and the mutual trust built up between China and Germany form a good basis for further boosting the cooperation between both countries in the area of climate protection.

Both countries have some good approaches. Current discussions are focusing on plus-energy houses as well as urban district refurbishment and the future of cities. Innovative procedures such as the serial refurbishment of residential buildings could be developed and promoted in both countries as well.

The energy transition and climate protection offer the most diverse approaches for future cooperative agreements in line with sustainable industry objectives. Topics such as digitalization and research into new, application-focused technologies such as hydrogen are becoming ever more important.

Both countries are active in these fields and can support one another reciprocally. Green financial schemes are playing an increasingly important role internationally as a lever for greater climate protection. China and the European Union are the pioneers here and must remain in dialogue with one another regarding questions of detail, such as drawing up taxonomies.

In particular, it should be remembered that investments in climate protection are not just an investment in the future, but also an investment in solving many of today's pressing problems. For example, the energy-efficient refitting of a large number of existing buildings could create millions of jobs at a stroke and more or less solve the problem of air pollution caused by using fossil fuels for heating.

Let us, therefore, use the crisis as an opportunity for more cooperation, not less an opportunity to transform to sustainability in industry and to develop common fundamental innovation and modernization processes, in order to overcome the recession that is just emerging and simultaneously relieve the burden we are putting on the environment and the climate. We have already set the targets through international agreements. We already have many possibilities at our fingertips, and we can develop others. By cooperating with one another, we can initiate a great many things.

July 17, 2020 China Daily global edition

II Green Development Aligns with Global Trends

Energy evolution or extinction

By BEATE TRANKMANN

As COP 26 draws to a close, humanity stands at a critical crossroads. The path we have travelled until now cannot continue much further, for it ends in extinction for millions of species-and, ultimately, humankind. Yet, another path remains open, to a lasting future for us and our planet-if we take it in time.

"Climate change is nature's alarm bell," President Xi Jinping said. It rings especially loud for Asia, home to 80 percent of the people globally who will be worst-affected. The year of 2021, we saw massive flooding in Central China's Henan province, while Indonesia's South Kalimantan province also experienced its worst flood in decades. These were just two of the extreme climate-related events that have occurred around the world, which also include severe droughts and catastrophic wildfires across Europe and the United States.

A sustainable path is our only road to survival. It requires a steeper climb than we have ever undertaken. To avert climate catastrophe, the Paris Agreement aims to limit temperature rises to 1.5 C above preindustrial levels, which requires the world to cut annual greenhouse gas emissions by half over the next eight years. Yet, going into the COP 26, the world was not on track to meet this target. Instead, we face the prospect of a disastrous 2.7 C of warming by the end of the century. With the latest commitments made by countries over the last week, we are moving closer toward 2 C, but we must be even more ambitious. Unless we stay within 1.5 C, the consequences will still be severe.

Fossil fuels, namely coal, oil and gas, are the biggest culprits, creating three-fourths of the global greenhouse gas emissions. Yet the world spends $423 billion annually to subsidize them-an amount that could vaccinate every person on earth against COVID-19, or three times what is needed every year to end extreme poverty globally. Such investments must urgently be redirected toward people and planet, instead of undermining both. Administrator of the United Nations Development Programme Achim Steiner said, "If we cannot decouple economic growth globally from emissions, we are doomed."

China is well-positioned to enable the necessary transformation. It is a leader in renewable technologies such as solar and wind, along with green finance. China's two consecutive announcements at the UN General Assembly: to peak CO2 emissions before 2030 and achieve net zero before 2060, as well as to stop building overseas coal power plants-have reinforced its commitment to combating climate change. Given that China is currently the world's largest carbon emitter, these are game changers. However, they must be underpinned by concrete plans.

The two most important policy documents supporting these—the Guidance for Carbon Peaking and Carbon Neutrality, together with the Action Plan for Carbon Peaking before 2030—were recently released by the State Council, China's Cabinet, providing a clearer and more concrete road map for China to lower carbon emissions. In particular, they put forward specific emissions targets for key sectors including steel, energy and transport, which will be vital in achieving the goal of net zero.

This is an opportunity to accelerate action, so 1.5 C remains within reach.

It requires peaking emissions ideally well before 2030 and reducing the consumption of fossil fuels, particularly coal, as early as possible. Investments should be channeled toward innovating and developing green technologies, which hold the key to limiting climate change. Such areas should be viewed as investments in our future, not costs, because the costs of inaction, to people, planet and prosperity, would be infinitely higher.

While transitioning to a green, low-carbon economy is essential, it must be done in a just way, given how it affects energy security and livelihoods. So this is also an opportunity to create better jobs to last and open up new growth areas, thereby reducing inequality. Green sectors are already among the fastest growing in China, with renewables now creating more jobs than fossil fuels. Across all sectors, just, green transitions could create 395 million jobs globally by 2030 and $10 trillion in economic value annually.

Admittedly, a just and manageable transition to a low-carbon and eventually net-zero economy in China and elsewhere requires considerable investment. To achieve net-zero emissions globally by 2050, an annual investment of $4.4 trillion in clean energy and energy efficiency is needed. However, the issue is not a shortage of capital, but rather where capital is being directed. According to the Atlantic Council think tank, $9 trillion was spent on quantitative easing in the pandemic response over the last 18 months. So, the finance we need to save our planet already exists. The solution lies in aligning it with nature, across public and private sectors, as well as financial markets.

Five actions can help to facilitate this: First, prices of renewables and fossil fuels must be reset by ending fossil fuel subsidies and taxing emissions. This would create the necessary fiscal space to buffer any unintended consequences of the low carbon transition on people's livelihoods, particularly those most vulnerable. Second, public spending must be directed toward investments that protect the climate and nature, rather than destroying it. This would also encourage private sector participation in the necessary transitions, as costs and risks would be lowered. Third, countries should mandate climate-related information disclosures, so climate change counts in every financial decision. Two of China's largest banks-the Industrial and Commercial Bank of China and the Bank of China-have already joined the Taskforce for Climate-Related Financial Disclosures and we look forward to more doing so. Fourth, climate action Key Performance Indicators for high-emission companies and investors must be set to give a clear direction toward net zero. Finally, policies must create opportunities for everyone in tomorrow's economy. This includes reskilling workers whose livelihoods may be impacted, which could be financed by nature-positive public budgets and revamped carbon pricing.

The UNDP supports countries, including China, in shifting from fossil fuels through a phased approach that is fair and equitable. We stand ready to deepen our cooperation in this vital area.

There is only one path to our shared future: the uphill road to sustainability. All countries must step forward. China has the scale, resources and opportunity to act now, as well as help others move in the right direction. We have one last, collective chance to take that crucial path now. We must seize it.

November 12, 2021 China Daily global edition

Bills to pay

By GRZEGORZ W. KOŁODKO

The current times require intensely working together to address common challenges, by identifying and implementing shared, coordinated and equitable responses. This requires vision, dialogue, mutual understanding, and a profound awareness of our common global responsibilities. We also need to look beyond the COVID-19 crisis, toward a rapid economic recovery that addresses people's needs. This implies a focus on reducing inequalities, on women's empowerment, on the younger generations and on protecting the most vulnerable. It means promoting the creation of new jobs, social protection and food security. This was the message from the 2021 G20 Summit held in Rome in October, 2021.

The G20 forum is definitely more representative of humanity and the world economy than the meetings of the leaders of rich countries, the G7, which focus mainly on their own interests, or the BRICS group, whose members have little in common. The G20-or more precisely the G43, because it includes 19 countries plus the European Union, which, apart from the three largest countries already included in the group, Germany, France and Italy, includes 24 other countries has become an additional, apart from international organizations, mechanism for global policy coordination. Such coordination in the face of a volatile world is especially needed. As always, the expectations for the summit were enormous, and it delivered-also as always-less than anticipated. However, the little it has delivered is of importance.

The G20, whose rotating host country in 2021 was Italy, was held under the slogan 3P: People, Planet, Prosperity. Although a seemingly minor decision, the summit's resolution to apply a minimum taxation of company profits at the level of 15 percent is noteworthy. This should stop the development-damaging race to the bottom tax competition. Much more important, however, was the decision to provide less developed countries, especially the poorest, with COVID-19 vaccines free of charge. China has done this already, without the blessing of the other G20 members, and more than any other country. Let us recall here that it was President Xi Jinping, who, more than a year ago when no vaccines had been developed-was the first to say that the vaccines must be a global public good. It is a pity that the action, which requires good coordination on a global scale, did not start earlier and has not moved faster.

In the third decade of the 21st century, it is already obvious that the greatest existential threat to humanity is climate change, largely caused by human economic activity. This aspect of the summit, headed in a pragmatic manner by Italian Prime Minister Mario Draghi, was the most important. The more so as the participants of the G20 meeting went directly from Rome to the United Nations conference on climate change, COP 26, in Glasgow, Scotland.

Correct targeting of actions to counteract the continuation of disastrous climate trends requires not only knowledge of what can be done on the technological side to accelerate the shift to renewable sources of energy, but also a strong political commitment to act and clear decisions about who and to what extent is responsible for the current state of affairs. The distribution of the costs of actions to be undertaken in the following years by individual countries and by integration groups must be based on this assessment. Not the one who currently is, but the one who was in the past the greatest polluter should bear the greatest burden for the fight to limit the global temperature rise.

Most often, the answer is deceptive-and at the same time highly politicizing-that the worst contributor to the climate crisis is the one who emits the most greenhouse gases, especially carbon dioxide. And it is known that China is currently the largest emitter of carbon dioxide, so attempts are being made to direct world public opinion against it. This, which is by no means conducive to inclusive globalization, makes the mood of Sinophobia even stronger in certain countries. Yes, China sends into the atmosphere about 28 percent of the total volume of global CO_2 emissions, twice as much as the United States, which emits about 15 percent, but per capita, which is a more appropriate measure, the Chinese release just half of what people in the US do, respectively 8.1 and 15.5 metric tons annually. Starting the counting from 1750, China's entire emissions of CO_2, huge amounts of which still exist in the atmosphere surrounding the Earth, contributing to its heating, amounts to 13.7 percent, while the US' historical contribution to this global furnace is almost twice this, as much as 25.5 percent. The countries of the European Union plus the United Kingdom, account for 22.7 percent, India 3.2 percent, Africa 2.9 percent and South America 2.6 percent. The sinking islands of Oceania only 1.2 percent.

When one looks at the issue from this perspective, it is hardly surprising that poorer countries request greater sacrifice from the wealthy of this world. Historical bills must be paid fairly. It is therefore not surprising that at the COP 26, Indian Prime Minister Narendra Modi declared his country's intention to achieve net zero carbon emissions only in 2070.

President Xi proclaimed China would make effort to achieve carbon neutrality before 2060, while developed countries declared their target was by 2050, although they would attempt to achieve it earlier. Net zero represents a situation where greenhouse gases emitted to the atmosphere are counterbalanced by their removal. Further social pressure should therefore force not so much to shorten the period to reach net zero in all countries, but to accelerate the transition to such a desired state in the richest countries. After all, they have contributed the most to bringing us all to a verge of cataclysm.

November 5, 2021 China Daily global edition

Profusion of all species

By XIE YI

China is striving to strike a balance between economic development and biodiversity conservation

When it comes to biodiversity conservation, how to strike a balance between ecological protection and local community development is a common challenge facing the world, which has a bearing on realizing the United Nations 2030 Sustainable Development Goals. Communities with rich biodiversity mostly have weak economic foundations, a mono development model and lack of growth impetus. The resource and environmental constraints imposed on communities with rich biodiversity give rise to the "biodiversity curse", trapping them in the mire of economic backwardness.

With the Kunming Declaration, adopted at the 15th meeting of the Conference of Parties to the UN Convention on Biological Diversity held in October, "Building a shared future for all life on earth" has become a global consensus.

Having embarked on a path of green and sustainable development, China has made remarkable progress in coordinating ecological protection and community development.

The country has put in place a strict system for ecological and environmental protection, having built a protected areas system with national parks as the mainstay. So far, the country has established more than 10,000 natural protected areas of all types, covering about 18 percent of its land area. The well-planned protected areas system has brought 90 percent of terrestrial ecosystem types, 85 percent of wildlife species and 65 percent of higher plants species under protection, and has sheltered more than 300 different wild animal species and over 130 wild plant species under State protection.

There are several aspects to the country's efforts to seek a balance between biodiversity protection and local community development.

First, seeking new economic growth drivers for areas with rich biodiversity and enabling local communities to share the benefits of the protection of local biodiversity and economic development. By adhering to the path of innovative development, China supports local communities to use natural resources in a sustainable and efficient way, and break away from the traditional path of over-exploiting nature, thus forming a green economic pattern. For example, Longli county in Southwest China's Guizhou province boasts a typical karst landform, a unique ecological system and rich biodiversity. It used to be a poverty-stricken county. In recent years, by developing the chestnut rose industry and combining farming with ecotourism, the county has pulled 7,100 people out of poverty and got rid of local people's dependence on logging for a living, realizing common prosperity and coordinated development between urban and rural areas.

Second, coordinating ecological protection and economic development through targeted poverty alleviation policies, infrastructure building, skills training, development of leisure agriculture and the forest-based non-timber economy to increase the added value of products and boost the incomes of local residents. By aligning poverty alleviation efforts with the protection of the local ecosystems, the government offers local people jobs in forest cultivation and management, and wildlife protection to increase their incomes. Higher subsidies have been granted to households that return their farmland to forest, grassland or wetland. In addition, people that have lost ability to work have been covered by social security systems through government transfer payments.

Third, letting the market play a decisive role in resources allocation and improving the utilization of natural resources in areas with rich biodiversity, and boosting the incomes of local residents while promoting natural protection. Yangxian county in Shaanxi province, which is known for its rich biodiversity, was once a poverty-stricken county. In 1981, seven crested ibis, which were thought to be the world's only wild population of the species, were spotted in Yangxian after the species was declared extinct in Japan and other range states. To conserve the endangered birds, which forage in rice paddy fields, locals began cultivating organic rice free of chemical fertilizers and pesticides, and used biological technologies to control pests and fertilize the soil, which offset the decline in incomes caused by lower yields. Locals also developed homestay and tourism businesses based on birdwatching to raise incomes. Thanks to the decades of conservation efforts, the population of crested ibis has surged from seven to more than 5,000, making it a shining example of protecting endangered species while maintaining local economic development.

Fourth, raising public awareness of ecological protection and mobilizing resources from the whole society for biodiversity conservation. In the Northeast China Tiger and Leopard National Park, the Sanjiangyuan National Park and the Wuyishan National Park, there are volunteers that participate in science popularization, the patrolling and monitoring of protected areas, as well as in the development of local communities, becoming an important complement to professional conservationists and social workers. Yunnan province is one of the areas in the world with the richest biodiversity and home to China's only sanctuaries for Asian elephants. To protect the habitats of the animals, local conservation organizations launched an online crowd-funding program to widely engage all those who care about the fate of elephants, with the funds raised larger than expected.

With such efforts the richness of the country's biodiversity and local economies are both on a steady rise.

December 29, 2021 China Daily global edition

Ⅲ Building a Fair, Reasonable, and Cooperative Global Climate Governance System

Plan for a zero-carbon society

By JEREMY RIFKIN

China can lead the world to a sustainable future in less than a generation by implementing its smart digital infrastructure initiative

We are facing a global emergency. Our scientists tell us that human-induced climate change brought on by the burning of fossil fuels has precipitated the sixth mass extinction of life on Earth.

According to the famed Harvard biologist Edward O. Wilson, "the extinction of species by human activity continues to accelerate, fast enough to eliminate more than half of all species by the end of this century"—by the time today's toddlers are senior citizens. The last time the Earth experienced an extinction event of this magnitude was 65 million years ago.

While the global climate crisis has become a lightning rod in the political sphere, there is a parallel movement within the business community that will shake the very foundation of the global economy in coming years. Key sectors of the economy are beginning to decouple from fossil fuels in favor of ever cheaper solar and wind energies and the accompanying clean technologies, green business practices, and processes of circularity and resilience that are the central features of sustainable development.

The levelized costs of utility-scale solar and wind installations have plummeted and are now below the cost of nuclear power, oil, coal and natural gas, leaving the conventional energies and accompanying technologies behind. New studies are sounding the alarm that upwards of trillions of dollars in stranded fossil fuel assets could create a carbon bubble likely to burst by 2028, causing the collapse of the fossil fuel civilization. To date, over $11 trillion of investments in the fossil fuel industry have either been divested or are in the process of being divested. "Stranded assets" are all the fossil fuels that remain in the ground because of falling demand as well as the abandonment of pipelines, ocean platforms, storage facilities, energy generation plants, backup power plants, petrochemical processing facilities, gasoline stations, auto service centers and the myriad industries tightly coupled to the fossil fuel culture.

The leading oil-producing nations will be caught in the cross-hairs between the plummeting price of solar and wind and the fallout from peak oil demand and accumulating stranded assets in the oil industry. Other nations-including China-that rely heavily on fossil fuels will face a similar economic and social crisis. The marketplace is speaking, and governments everywhere will need to quickly adapt if they are to survive and prosper.

It's clear that China and the world need a new economic vision and accompanying deployment plan for instituting a zero-carbon society that can be implemented quickly in less than a generation. To understand the historic moment we are in as we exit the 200 years of a fossil fuel civilization and enter into a new era of renewable energies to manage the economy and daily life, we need to step back and ask the question of how the great economic transitions in history occurred. If we know how they occurred, we can get a roadmap for countries around the world and chart a new course into what we call the Green New Deal in the West, and what China calls an Ecological Civilization.

Every major economic infrastructure transformation in world history has required three elements, each of which interacts with the others to enable the system to operate as a whole: a new communication medium, a new power source and a new transportation mechanism to "manage", "power" and "move" society. Infrastructure paradigms also create new kinds of human habitats and are accompanied by new economic systems and new forms of governance to manage them.

In the 19th century, steam-powered printing and the telegraph, abundant coal, and locomotives on national rail systems meshed in a common infrastructure to manage, power and move society, giving birth to the First Industrial Revolution and the rise of urban habitats, capitalist economies and national markets overseen by nation-state governance.

In the 20th century, centralized electricity, the telephone, radio and television, cheap oil, and internal combustion vehicles on national road systems converged to create an infrastructure for the Second Industrial Revolution and the rise of suburban habitats, globalization and global governing institutions.

We are on the cusp of a Third Industrial Revolution. The digitized broadband communication internet is converging with a digitized continental electricity internet, powered by solar and wind electricity, and a digitized mobility and logistics internet made up of autonomous electric and fuel-cell vehicles, powered by green energy from the electricity internet. These three internets are continuously being fed data from sensors embedded across society that are monitoring activity of all kinds in real time, from ecosystems, agricultural fields, warehouses, road systems, factory production lines, retail stores, and especially from the residential, commercial, and institutional building stock, allowing humanity to more efficiently manage, power, and move day-to-day economic activity and social life from where they work and live. This is the internet of things (IoT).

In the coming era, buildings will be retrofitted for energy efficiency and climate resilience and embedded with IoT infrastructure. They will also be equipped with edge data centers, giving the public the ability to share data more quickly in managing communication, energy generation, and mobility and logistics. Smart buildings will also serve as green micro power-generating plants, energy storage sites, and transport and logistics hubs for electric and fuel cell vehicles in a more distributed zero-carbon society.

Buildings in the Third Industrial Revolution will no longer be passive, walled-off private spaces but, rather, potentially actively engaged nodal entities sharing their renewable energies, energy efficiencies, energy storage, electric mobility and a wide range of other economic and social activity with one another at the discretion of their occupants.

Connecting everything and everyone via the Ecological Civilization infrastructure offers substantial economic benefits. In this expanded digital economy, individuals, families and enterprises will be able to connect in their homes and workplaces to the IoT and access big data flowing across the world wide web that affects their supply chains, production and services, and every aspect of their social lives. They can then mine that big data with their own analytics and create their own algorithms and apps to increase their aggregate efficiency and performance, reduce their carbon footprint, and lower the marginal cost of producing, distributing, and consuming goods and services and recycling waste, making their businesses and homes greener and more self-resilient in a zero-carbon society.

The massive scale-up and deployment of the digital 3.0 infrastructure will involve virtually every Chinese sector and industry and will create millions of new jobs. Moreover, every dollar invested in the infrastructure is projected to return $3.3 in

GDP between 2020 and 2040. In addition, over the 20-year deployment, China will save trillions of dollars from improvement in public health and the mitigation of climate disruptions in the economy.

What we are learning from climate change is that everything that each of us does in our own communities, regions and nation-states spills over political boundaries and affects every other human being on Earth, as well as our fellow species and the biomes and ecosystems that sustain all of life. The real question at hand is whether all of humanity can come together in time to forestall the mass extinction of life on Earth? This is the new dawning reality that gives impetus to China's vision of an Ecological Civilization and the European Union's comparable vision of the Global New Green Deal. China can lead the world into a zero-carbon society by introducing a seamless smart digital Third Industrial Revolution infrastructure in its 14th Five-Year Plan (2021-2025) that can take the country and, hopefully, the human race into an Ecological Civilization.

July 24, 2020 China Daily global edition

Action planned

By VLADIMIR NOROV

With the adoption of the Green Belt Program, the SCO countries will seek to accelerate their emission reduction by sharing their experience in the use of environmentally friendly technologies

Reducing carbon emissions and achieving a state of carbon neutrality can only be achieved through the use of advanced technologies. As such, this has become the focus of attention for the entire world community due to the every more acute problems caused by climate change.

Experts agree that it is human activity—the burning of oil, gas and coal—that is generating the greenhouse effect that is resulting in a seemingly inexorable rise in the average global temperature, which leads to many negative consequences for humanity, in particular, the deteriorating ecological situation that is accelerating biodiversity loss and the emergence of many zoonotic diseases.

According to the World Health Organization, 2 billion people suffer from infectious diseases every year, of which 14 million die.

According to the United Nations, in recent decades, due to climate change, there has been an acceleration of the rate of desertification worldwide.

At the moment, more than 2 billion hectares of productive land has been degraded worldwide by desertification, and an additional 12 million hectares is being degraded annually.

Problems related to desertification and land degradation, water scarcity and food security affect the entire Shanghai Cooperation Organization region, mostly Central Asia, which is the core area of the organization.

Socioeconomic stability in this region is of key importance for all the SCO members.

In this context, we are talking about the drying up of the Aral Sea, once the fourth-largest closed sea in the world, an environmental disaster, which has been of not only regional, but also global significance.

The declaration of the heads of the SCO member states, adopted at the end of the Bishkek Summit in 2019, stressed that the growing cross-border security challenges and threats, including climate change and the shortage of drinking water, require special attention, close coordination and constructive interaction with the rest of the international community.

Based on the importance of preserving the ecological balance within the SCO region, restoring biodiversity, ensuring favorable conditions for people's well-being and sustainable development, and in order to implement the concept of cooperation in the field of environmental protection of the SCO member states and the action plan for its practical implementation at the Moscow SCO Summit last year, President of Uzbekistan Shavkat Mirziyoyev proposed to develop and adopt the "SCO Green Belt Program" within the organization.

This program is aimed at promoting the use and implementation of technologies with low greenhouse gas emissions in many sectors of the economy, and increasing the share of renewable and low-emissions energy in order to reduce greenhouse gas emissions.

Currently, the SCO Green Belt Program is being discussed by experts of the SCO countries and it is due to be adopted at the SCO anniversary summit to be held in Dushanbe on Sep 16 to 17 this year.

Today, all the SCO member states are striving to significantly reduce their carbon emissions and achieve a state of carbon neutrality, which, in turn, will lead to a number of significant, far-reaching positive effects on people's well-being, by helping to ensure food security, preventing natural disasters and strengthening energy independence.

Good news for both China and the SCO countries, as well as the global fight against climate change, was the adoption by Chinese President Xi Jinping at the 2020 UN General Assembly of commitments to achieve carbon neutrality before 2060.

For the world, China's acceptance of these commitments brings the world community closer to achieving the goals of the Paris Agreement to limit global warming to less than 2 C.

The implementation of an active program to combat climate change will bring tangible economic benefits to China.

According to available calculations, the program to achieve the goal of 1.5 C will increase the country's GDP by 2 percent to 3 percent, reduce the demand for fossil fuels by about 80 percent, and reduce emissions by 75 percent to 85 percent for the period up to 2050.

China's decarbonization initiatives create huge opportunities to accelerate technological innovation and modernize production, which will further strengthen the country's economy.

We should also not forget that China is a global manufacturing and innovation center, and by setting emissions reduction goals for itself, it is on the way to becoming the largest supplier of decarbonization technologies for other countries striving to achieve net zero greenhouse gas emissions.

September 14, 2021 China Daily global edition

Powering forward

By YUAN JIAHAI

China's leadership in renewable energy is fueling the global green transition

Official data showed that the total renewable energy generating capacity in China had reached 1,002 gigawatts by the end of October 2021, passing the milestone of 1,000 GW. This is a critical milestone for the green energy transition in China, and good news for the global energy transition.

Renewables now account for 43.5 percent of China's total generation capacity, up by 10.2 percentage points from 2015. Among the renewables, the capacity of hydropower (including pumped-storage), wind, solar and biomass is 385 GW, 299 GW, 282 GW and 35.34 GW, respectively, by the end of October 2021, all of which rank the first in the world.

Actually, China has been the leader in hydropower development since 2004 and in wind and solar power since 2012.

Looking back to the end of 2005, when China passed its Renewable Energy Law, wind and solar power capacity was just 1,060 MW. Afterward, in just 15 years, the total capacity of wind and solar power skyrocketed to 590 GW.

Both benefited from the Renewable Energy Law, the ambitious development planning for renewables, the facilitating of feed-in tariffs and effective rollout.

Observed from the perspective of meeting the needs of electricity consumption growth, the contribution of wind and solar power is also on the rise, from 2.7 percent during 2006-2010 to 11.7 percent during 2011-2015, then to 27 percent during 2016-2020. These figures highlight the government's determination to advance the energy transition and actively cope with climate change.

The development of China's renewable energy industry has been an eye-catching process that started from scratch, first as a follower, then gradually moving forward as a parallel runner and then striding forward as a frontrunner. Since 2017, China has been the leading manufacturer of renewable energy technologies, and it has formed the most complete renewable industry chains and supply chains in the world, and it is now striving to become a key global renewable technology innovation hub.

Seven Chinese companies are among the global top 10 wind turbine manufacturers, six among the global top 10 solar photovoltaic manufacturers and seven among the global top 10 battery manufacturers.

But although China has made great achievements in developing its renewable energy industry, the share of renewables in primary energy consumption is still low. In 2020, non-fossil energy accounted for 15.9 percent of the country's energy consumption, and excluding nuclear power, the share of renewable is 13.7 percent. And rather than looking at the great progress China is making in its green energy transition, international observers still tend to focus on its coal use data.

In 2020, the added annual capacity of wind and solar PV in China was 119 GW, approximating an annual electricity generation of 190 terawatt hours, which accounted for only 1.1 percent of China's primary energy consumption. In the same year, China's primary energy consumption was 4,980 million metric tons of coal equivalent. But is the figure of 119 GW a small one? Let's look at two pioneering nations in the global energy transition. For Germany, the total renewable capacity was 131.74 GW by the end of 2020, while for the United Kingdom the figure was 48 GW.

As the most populous developing country and the world's factory, China has an immense energy demand, which renders the rise of the share of renewable in primary energy consumption a challenging process. However, policymakers have already delineated a definitive ending for this process with the commitment to peak carbon emissions before 2030 and reach carbon neutrality before 2060.

The gradual implementation of the means to realize China's carbon neutrality target will open infinite space for renewable energy development. According to the top-level design, non-fossil energy will account for at least 80 percent of China's energy consumption by 2060, among which, a small portion will come from nuclear power while the majority will be from renewable sources.

The implication is that the deployment of renewable is accelerating in China. It is expected that during the 2021-2025 period, the annual addition of wind and solar will reach 120 GW, then 140 GW during 2026-2030, and 160 GW during 2031-2035. With these, we can expect that the second 1,000 GW from renewables will happen by 2028.

In becoming the center of global renewable manufacturing, innovation and industry services, China is also playing a big role in facilitating the global energy transition.

China's powerful manufacturing capability is a key factor behind the rapidly falling costs of renewables worldwide. In the future China's innovation capability will further fuel improvement of the renewable energy sector. China is the leading global renewable equipment exporter and is directly driving the rapid renewable deployment globally. China accounts for 28 percent of global solar panel exports and 13 percent of global wind turbine exports. Renewable energy also plays an important role in China's foreign power projects. According to data from the Global Development Policy Center at Boston University, during 2000 to 2021, hydropower, wind and PV projects accounted for 36.6 percent of Chinese overseas power investment.

In recent years, China has formulated stricter green outbound investment guidelines and the Belt and Road Initiative green project development guide. President Xi Jinping announced at the United Nations General Assembly in September that China will stop building coal-fired power plants overseas. With these encouraging changes, the priority for China's overseas power projects has already shifted to renewable energy. In 2020, renewable projects exceeded more than 50 percent of the total. We are quite confident that the experience and lessons that China has learned in renewable manufacturing, technology innovation, market deployment and system integration can be replicable best practices for developing countries participating in the Belt and Road Initiative as they build their power infrastructure.

December 10, 2021 China Daily global edition

China Steps Up

Deeds, Not Words

I Contributing Chinese Wisdom to Global Climate Governance

Turning a harmful tide

By SHI JIANBIN and WANG WENQING

With a nationwide program to restore its mangroves, China can lead the way in restoring, safeguarding these vital ecosystems

Known as the "guardians of the seashore" and "ocean forests", mangroves are one of the most productive ecosystems on earth, providing many important services, including prevention of coastal erosion, protection from storm surges and sea-level rise, water purification, carbon sequestration, habitat for unique biodiversity, and provision of local livelihoods.

It is estimated that mangrove ecosystem services are worth $33,000 to $57,000 per hectare per year.

Yet despite their incredible values, mangrove forests are being destroyed and degraded as a result of human activities, exacerbated by climate change. About half of the world's mangroves have been lost just in the past half century and, at this rate, mangroves could be gone altogether within this century unless we take action now to turn the tide.

A joint study recently released by the Paulson Institute, Laoniu Foundation and Shenzhen Mangrove Conservation Foundation concludes that despite the global trend, China has made substantial achievements in mangrove conservation and restoration in recent decades. China has put in place a set of laws and regulations such as the Forest Law, the Marine Environmental Protection Law and the National Wetland Conservation and Restoration Scheme, all of which include provisions to protect mangroves.

At the same time, China has enhanced its efforts to restore mangroves, including the National Mangrove Forest Conservation Program initiated in 2001 and the National Plan for Construction of Coastal Shelterbelt System (2016-2025). These initiatives have helped China's mangrove forest area increase from 22,000 hectares in 2000 to around 29,000 hectares in 2019, making the country one of the few in the world to log a net increase. Thirty-eight mangrove-oriented protected areas have been established on the Chinese mainland, and over 50 percent of natural mangrove forests are under protection, far exceeding the world's average level of 25 percent.

However, as the joint study reveals, many challenges and issues remain to improve the protection, restoration and management of mangroves in China.

There has been substantial degradation of mangroves in some places, caused by pollution from aquaculture, exotic invasive species, and construction of sea walls which block the connection between mangroves and inland ecosystems.

The rise in mangrove forest area in China has been mostly attributed to artificial plantation of mangroves on mudflats over the past two decades. The success rate of artificial plantation is low because of inappropriate siting and unsuitable conditions, as well as a lack of post-plantation maintenance, and the costs are high. Artificial plantation could even cause ecological damage if using a limited number of mangrove species or even alien invasive mangroves for afforestation. Furthermore, mangrove plantation on intertidal mudflats sometimes destroys or occupies important habitats for other wildlife, such as migratory waterbirds and benthic animals. More efforts are needed to encourage natural restoration and restoration of the entire mangrove wetland ecosystem, rather than mangrove forest only.

Returning fish ponds to mangrove forests is a more effective way of restoring mangrove ecosystem functions. A large number of fish ponds in China's coastal area could be returned to mangrove forests. However, the funding needed to compensate fish pond owners and the lack of specific standards and technical guidance for returning fish ponds to mangroves have prevented this restoration from being widely adopted.

Mangrove forests account for only a small percentage of the total forest area in China, but they have attracted the attention of Chinese leaders. On April 19, 2017, President Xi Jinping urged protection of mangrove forests while inspecting the Golden Gulf Mangrove Ecological Protection Zone in Beihai city in the Guangxi Zhuang autonomous region. And, on June 8, 2020, the theme of World Oceans Day in China was set as "Protecting mangroves, Protecting Ocean Ecosystems", indicating the government's efforts to increase public recognition of the valuable functions of mangroves. A social climate conducive to the conservation and restoration of mangroves is emerging in China.

The Ministry of Natural Resources and National Forestry and Grassland Administration jointly conducted a comprehensive and detailed inventory of mangrove forests and coastal areas suitable for mangrove restoration in 2019, and a nationwide mangrove restoration program is being developed.

China recently released its comprehensive Overall Plan for Protection and Restoration of Important Ecosystems (2021-2035). One of the targets is to safeguard at least 35 percent of the country's natural coastlines and prevent the marine ecological condition from worsening through various key projects, including protection and restoration of mangrove ecosystems.

With all these in mind, we are confident that a golden opportunity for mangrove conservation and restoration is coming in China. As recommended by the joint study, to strengthen the health of mangrove ecosystems, the following measures and actions should be adopted and undertaken:

First, treat mangroves as an entire wetland ecosystem, rather than a simple forest, and shift restoration to cover the entire mangrove wetland ecosystem and its functions, including habitats for other wildlife such as birds, benthic organisms and fish.

Second, modify and formulate standards and evaluation systems for mangrove restoration which focus on natural recovery, with artificial recovery as a supplementary means, and improve the income of surrounding residents while restoring mangrove forests.

Third, artificial plantation on the intertidal mudflats should be carried out only on those mudflats that are assessed to be suitable for mangrove afforestation and avoid negative impacts on important intertidal habitats for sea grasses and waterbirds.

Fourth, develop technical guidelines and standards to facilitate returning fish ponds to mangroves.

Fifth, establish community-based models and mechanisms for the protection, ecological restoration and management of mangroves, whereby local communities are encouraged to actively participate in and benefit from the protection and restoration of mangrove ecosystems.

During the course of mangrove conservation and restoration, China must learn experience and lessons from other countries, but what's equally important, given that research on mangroves in China ranks among the best in the world, is to export its knowledge and successful case studies. It is hoped that mangrove conservation and restoration can become a new bridge to link China with other countries, particularly those involved in the Belt and Road Initiative.

July 3, 2020 China Daily global edition

Hungry for change

By REBECCA CARTER and YU TIAN

Transformative adaptation in agriculture is imperative to ensure food security in the face of climate change

Climate change is already undermining food systems worldwide, contributing to a rise in global hunger and threatening the livelihoods of millions of farmers, herders, and fishers.

According to the United Nations Food and Agriculture Organization report, 690 million people—60 million more than in 2014—are already going hungry, in part due to climate change. Farmers, herders and other rural people make up a large proportion of the 100 million people that climate change threatens to pull below the poverty line.

Agriculture in China has also been severely impacted by climate change. Drought has had the greatest influence, followed by floods and hailstorm disasters. Changes in temperature and precipitation patterns caused by climate change in the future will continue to reduce crop yields directly or indirectly. It is expected that by 2030, seasonal droughts will reduce the yield of China's three major staple food crops (rice, wheat and corn) by 8 percent.

It's becoming clearer that agriculture as we know it will not be able to thrive in a warming world—especially in hotspots such as coasts, semi—arid and arid areas, and in farming regions fed by glaciers and snowpack. Incremental adaptation alone won't be enough in these places. Agricultural systems will need to be fundamentally transformed to survive.

A new World Resources Institute report, Food Systems at Risk: Transformative Adaptation for Long-Term Food Security, underscores the need for transformative adaptation in agriculture and lays out what is needed to make it happen.

The Intergovernmental Panel on Climate Change defines transformative adaptation as being that in which the focus is on larger, more profound system changes, in contrast to incremental measures that aim at maintaining existing systems by taking relatively minor measures, such as introducing more drought-resistant varieties of crops or using more efficient irrigation means.

Transformative adaptation, in relation to agriculture, intends to change the fundamental attributes of agricultural systems in response to actual or expected climate change and its effects, often at a scale and ambition greater than incremental activities. Our research shows that there are often three key types of actions associated with transformative adaptation in agriculture.

First, shifting the geographical locations where specific types of crops and livestock are produced, processed, and marketed. For example, some Costa Rican coffee farmers in areas that are becoming too warm for coffee production are switching to citrus fruits instead. In Ethiopia, cultivation of staple crops such as wheat and teff are shifting to higher, cooler elevations as temperatures rise. In their place, farmers are now growing maize more widely.

The second key aspect of transformative adaptation is aligning agricultural production with changing ecosystems and available water and arable land. For example, in China, 400,000 hectares of saline-alkali land nationwide have been obtained for commercial production of a saline-alkali tolerant type of rice called seawater rice, which was developed through cross-breeding and other technologies to grow in tidal flats or other areas with heavy salt concentrations. Compared to conventional rice, seawater rice has a deeper root system and taller plants, so it can be more resistant to dislodging and won't be easily submerged completely by rising seawater. Even if submerged by seawater, it still grows fine after the tide is out. Therefore, in areas where sea levels are rising due to climate change, seawater rice is a good choice. In June 2019, experts from China and the United Arab Emirates observed the yield of this rice, planted in the deserts of Dubai, reaching 9,435 kilograms per hectare. Chinese experts say the yield is on par with the advanced level of international rice planting in desert areas and saline-alkali soil.

The third aspect of transformative adaptation is new methodologies and technologies being applied at a scale that substantially changes the types of agricultural products, and the way existing ones are produced and processed, in a particular area. For example, in parts of India, vegetable farmers have started using low-cost polyhouses (plastic greenhouses) to protect their produce from more severe storms. They discovered that the polyhouses also enable them to produce a wider range of vegetables and conserve increasingly scarce water resources.

China has already seen successful examples of transformative adaptation in agriculture locally, but more work needs to be done to ensure that it is prepared to undertake systemic changes as climate change impacts become more severe. In the examples above, it is wealthier farmers who have greater access to key resources such as credit, information and land that are leading these types of transformations; poorer farmers will need additional support to ensure that they are not left behind. For example, more investment will be needed to teach local farmers the technical knowhow required to produce unfamiliar types of crops and livestock. More financial resources and policy support are also required to encourage less wealthy farmers and communities to make these transformative changes-especially to make sure that those most vulnerable to climate change impacts, including smallholders, women and children-are able to make such changes.

Who can drive the action to create transformative changes in food systems?

Implementing transformative adaptation is difficult if not impossible for most farmers and communities to carry out on their own. Without focused action, food system shifts tend to occur on medium- to long-term timelines. It takes time to alter fundamental components of existing systems, as well as markets and institutional arrangements. Supporting and expanding transformative adaptation in food systems will therefore require action from policymakers, funders and research organizations, who must work collaboratively to enhance food security, minimize losses and damages, and reduce the risk of displacements and conflicts.

Perhaps the most important opportunity that transformative approaches to adaptation offer is time and space for those most affected by climate change to have greater decision-making power about which solutions are best for them. Meaningful inclusion in participatory planning processes is far more likely with advanced planning, rather than after extreme climate events have already pushed existing systems beyond their tipping points. Vulnerable communities also need better access to evidence about which adaptation options will work in their context, as well as longer-term, predictable funding to help them enact the solutions they choose.

The UN is convening a Food Systems Summit as part of the Decade of Action to achieve the Sustainable Development Goals by 2030, which aims to awaken the world to work together to transform the way the world produces, consumes and thinks about food. We need more ambitious actions to deliver progress on all 17 SDGs, each of which relies to some degree on healthier, more sustainable, and equitable food systems-and to include transformative adaptation as a powerful solution.

July 13, 2021 China Daily global edition

Ⅱ New Policies and Resolutions for Green and Low-Carbon Development

Decarbonizing, the Chinese way

By ZHANG DA and HUANG JUNLING

Leveraging the strengths of State-owned enterprises to foster the country's nascent emissions trading scheme

China, the world's largest carbon emitter, officially launched its national emissions trading scheme on July 16, 2021, marking a significant step toward peaking carbon emissions before 2030 and achieving carbon neutrality before 2060, a pledge President Xi Jinping made in September 2020.

The Emissions Trading System (ETS) allows companies that are covered under it to trade their emissions permits and incentivizes emissions abatement activities where the cost is the lowest. Companies that face higher costs to reduce their own emissions can purchase permits either from companies with surpluses or from an "offsets" market that is connected to the ETS.

The ETS arrangement will encourage companies with lower abatement costs to reduce their emissions so that they can sell surplus permits for revenue.

Consequently, the ETS is expected to help industries with high emission to upgrade production technology, increase the share of non-fossil energy consumption, and enhance low-carbon research and development capacity. The offsets market, which grants emissions reduction activities, such as afforestation and forest management, can also promote the increase of carbon sinks in the ecosystem.

Compared to the ETS design in developed regions, such as the European Union ETS and the California ETS, China's national ETS needs to incorporate China's own characteristics in its design. One of its prominent features is that it initially only covers the thermal power sector. Once the system matures, it is expected to expand to other major emissions-intensive industries, including iron and steel, cement, aluminum, and so on. The successful operation of the ETS in the thermal power sector is critical for a full-fledged ETS in the future.

China's thermal power sector is responsible for about 4.5 billion metric tons of carbon dioxide emissions annually, accounting for about 40 percent of the country's total CO_2 emissions. State-owned enterprises are dominant players in the power sector. More than 70 percent of power generation is from the SOEs, and the five largest State-owned power generation companies alone hold more than half of the total coal-fired generation capacity assets. Therefore, the ETS should leverage the strengths of these State-owned Enterprises (SOEs) in the power sector.

First, SOEs can help set up high standards in emissions reporting and permit compliance, as they represent public interests and hold intrinsic values for fulfilling social responsibilities. As stated by the State-owned Assets Supervision and Administration Commission, the central government body responsible for supervising SOEs, the latter are required to "earnestly fulfill corporate social responsibilities to realize the coordinated and sustainable development of enterprises, society and environment in all respects".

When participating in the ETS, SOEs can help establish a norm of accurately reporting and disclosing their emissions data and submitting adequate permits for compliance, laying a solid foundation for a healthy ETS.

Second, SOEs are well-positioned to make long-term investments critical for decarbonizing the power system with the carbon price signal from the ETS. Compared to private investors, SOEs have a higher tolerance for projects with longer payback periods, which are common in the field of investment in low-carbon industries. A prime example is the China Three Gorges Dam project. It involved enormous investment and years of construction. However once built, its long-term profitability and social benefits have been proved. After the dam was built, China Three Gorges Corp successfully replicated the model and built four additional 10 gigawatt-level hydropower plants. Similarly, SOEs have played pivotal roles in building nuclear power plants, large-scale renewable energy bases, and long-distance transmission lines, all of which are important for China to achieve the target of increasing the share of non-fossil fuels in primary energy consumption to 25 percent by 2030.

Incentivizing research and development of low-carbon technologies is another important objective of the ETS. The nature of R&D also requires investors to be patient with the long payback cycle of massive investments. Hence, SOEs have been important players in China's innovation ecosystem. Many centrally administered SOEs have set up research institutes to accelerate the development and deployment of new low-carbon technologies, supporting the upgrading and restructuring of industries.

Finally, SOEs can promote common prosperity with new business opportunities created by the ETS.For example, the offset market will present a growing demand for voluntary emissions reduction credits, which are called China Certified Emissions Reductions in China's context. We anticipate afforestation and forest management will be major suppliers of CCERs in the future, raising the value of the forestry industry substantially. As most forested land in China is State-owned or collectively owned, the value appreciation would also be enjoyed by the whole society through SOEs' participation in the ETS.

China Forestry Group Corp, a centrally administered SOE and the largest forest enterprise in China, has already announced an ambitious plan of developing new large-scale afforestation projects. The revenue will improve the welfare of local communities in rural areas, which has been a key social responsibility of SOEs since 2015 when the central government stepped up its nationwide campaign to eliminate poverty.

Unlike ETS operated in Western economies, China's national ETS is a market-based carbon pricing policy with strong Chinese characteristics. SOEs, as a key pillar of China's socialist market economy, are expected to steadily foster the development of China's ETS.

March 15, 2022 China Daily global edition

Act before it's too late

By NIU ZHIMING

Conference in Kunming must promote urgent and transformative actions to enhance biodiversity and ecosystem protection

The Intergovernmental Panel on Climate Change's latest report makes it clear that climate change is already a global crisis. This message has been broadly reported and accepted by society. However, a similar message on critical biodiversity loss and ecosystem deterioration has not resonated as widely. But the facts are alarming.

According to the 2020 assessment of the Intergovernmental Science-Policy Platform on Biodiversity and Ecosystem Services, the rate of global change nature underwent during the past five decades is unprecedented in human history.

It is against this background that the 15th meeting of the Conference of Parties to the Convention on Biological Diversity is due to be held in Kunming in Southwest China's Yunnan province, in October 2021. The forum aims at reaching an ambitious Post-2020 Global Biodiversity Framework to galvanize urgent and transformative actions to achieve far-reaching biodiversity conservation outcomes. But implementing the framework will be challenging.

First, awareness and knowledge of biodiversity needs to be strengthened significantly to show that all economic activities depend on and affect nature, which embodies biodiversity and ecosystems. This is illustrated by the fact that an estimated $44 trillion of economic value generation-over half of the global GDP-is moderately or highly dependent on nature.

Most of nature's contributions to people are not fully replaceable, and some are irreplaceable. For example, about 75 percent of global food crops, including some of the most important cash crops, rely on animal pollination. Pollinator loss due to habitat destruction and agriculture chemicals risks global crop output shortfalls in the range of $235 billion to $577 billion per year. Loss of coastal habitats and coral reefs adds to this by reducing fish stocks and coastal protection, increasing the risk from floods and hurricanes to life and property for hundreds of millions of people.

Second, goods and services provided by biodiversity and ecosystems must be valued adequately to enhance their protection. They are part of natural capital and benefit human society. Valuing the goods and services provided by ecosystems can leverage resources more effectively to conserve and sustain biodiversity and ecosystem functions. For example, the Regional Natural Capital Lab, an initiative of the Asian Development Bank (ADB), will focus on natural capital accounting and how that, along with synergized policies, can lead to informed investment decision-making for nature-positive benefits. There are also other initiatives to value ecosystem services, such as New Zealand's Living Standards Framework and China's Gross Ecosystem Products that the ADB helped conceptualize. These efforts can contribute to developing a global natural capital accounting system that should be adopted by countries.

Third, it is important to ensure the optimal allocation of resources. Available estimates suggest that direct subsidies that are harmful to biodiversity amount to $500 billion per year. Against this backdrop, the new framework will trigger governments' commitments to redirect, reform or eliminate incentives that are harmful to biodiversity by at least $500 billion per year. Side-by-side, the framework targets increased global financial resources to at least $200 billion annually, with sizable increases devoted to developing countries.

Fourth, country ownership and engagement are essential to successfully implement the framework, which will be driven by actions at the national level that spill over to the subnational, regional and global levels. Therefore, the role of government is critical to these efforts. In this regard, China's experiences in promoting its ecological civilization agenda offer worthy lessons for other countries. Regional initiatives for cross-boundary biodiversity conservation are also important. The ADB-supported Regional Flyway Initiative, which aims to restore and protect the critical habitat of the East Asian-Australasian Flyway to preserve the wetland ecosystems and the services that they provide to millions of migrant birds every year is a good example.

Last, synergies are important for impact. Biodiversity and ecosystem functions and services are at the core of the Sustainable Development Goals (SDGs) on water and sanitation, climate action, life below water and on land. However, biodiversity loss and damaged ecosystems will undermine progress toward the SDGs on poverty, hunger, health, water, and cities. Moreover, biodiversity loss and climate change are inextricably connected, and must be addressed jointly. To that end, resolving the trade-offs between climate change and biodiversity is a challenge, as some climate change mitigation and adaptation actions may negatively affect biodiversity through damage to habitats. Large-scale expansion of bioenergy and renewable energy infrastructure, including big dams and sea walls, illustrate the challenge.

While the targets of the framework, such as the Paris Agreement, are not binding for businesses, they signal vital global ambitions and the prioritization of key activities to fight biodiversity loss. Reversing biodiversity loss now will be less costly than delaying these efforts. Actions should be taken before it is too late.

September 2, 2021 China Daily global edition

Sustainable legacy

By FREDERICK C. DUBEE

Former United Nations secretary-general Kofi Annan once shared the observation that his favorite Olympic moment is when the athletes are in their starting positions at the precise instant when the start signal is given, as at that moment all the contestants are perfectly equal, and there is no discrimination of any kind. This offers an insight into the powerful potential of the Games.

The Beijing 2008 Olympics and Paralympics left an important legacy which included inclusivity, accessible and dynamically environmentally friendly venues and an advanced updatable and expandable urban transportation system in the Chinese capital that is still in use and still being improved upon today. They also brought a new understanding of the importance and value of recreational physical activity and sports to the people of China which induced and supported an expanding array of recreational activities involving hundreds of millions of Chinese.

Dovetailing with the legacy of the 2008 Olympics and Paralympic games, challenging aims were set and committed to for the 2022 Beijing Winter Games. In a critical and fundamental decision, China refocused the value of the games, from a unidimensional interest in medals to a more inclusive goal to ensure that the Games motivated hundreds of millions of Chinese to engage in winter sports. And through this example to gently entice the young and elderly around the world, regardless of their age, but respecting their abilities, to become more physically active.

Despite the media headlines, the biggest threat to the future of humanity is not COVID-19 or artificial intelligence as many suggest, but a lack of physical activity. Yannis Pitsiladis, a member of the International Olympic Committee Medical and Scientific Commission, says that prior to the COVID-19 pandemic, less than 30 percent of the world's population met the minimal levels of physical activity recommended by the World Health Organization. And as each of us knows too well, the restrictions imposed to try and control the novel coronavirus have made and continue to make this statistic even worse.

On landing in Beijing and rushing to start his work with the IOC Medical and Scientific Commission, Pitsiladis said: "With its Olympic legacy program to increase sports participation, China is demonstrating the real legacy value of the games. This is the most prudent way to recoup and maximize the major investment in the Games."

Since the dawn of humanity, our ancestors have repeated in every language the mantra "a healthy mind in a healthy body". As we matured as a species, we increasingly understood that in some way or other our physical health was somehow related to the health of our immediate environment. As the Industrial Revolution gathered steam, it was noticed that the local water and air were not as clean as they used to be and that progressively the deterioration in quality became more pronounced and what was occasional became persistent and imperceptibly embedded in people's daily lives. This assault against nature resulted in a reduction in the quality of life for many. And while development has affected the quality of our environment and presented humanity with existential climate, water, nutrition, biodiversity and health emergencies, this same development has reduced the desire and incentives for physical activity for a great proportion of the global population. At the same time, environmental degradation has acted as a disincentive for many to engage even in minimal levels of physical activity.

In this context and building on the legacy of the 2008 Games, China and the Chinese people have undertaken to deliver a "green, inclusive, open and clean" Winter Olympics and Paralympics. The venues are applying green technologies and are wholly powered by green energy, viewing the Games as a good opportunity to guide the Chinese public to low-carbon practices and to spotlight China's commitment to peak carbon emissions before 2030 and achieve carbon neutrality before 2060. The 2022 Beijing Sustainability Plan focused on three themes designed to support the development of the legacy of the Games: a positive environmental impact, new development for the region and a better life for the people.

In terms of environmental conservation, the Games are being powered totally by renewable energy; transportation is being supplied almost exclusively by electric, gas and hydrogen vehicles and supported by intelligent traffic management systems; natural carbon dioxide refrigeration systems have replaced the traditional hydrofluorocarbon approach; afforestation projects have provided 47,000 hectares of forests and 33,000 hectares of green land and a carbon sink of over 1 million metric tons.

In terms of regional development, preparation for the Games has accelerated the completion of a time and energy-effective transportation network. The development of a regional sport, tourism and cultural belt and leading-edge urban regeneration projects are underway.

In terms of social development, local communities are restructuring to fully and appropriately take part in the opportunities provided for housing, employment, education and attaining a work/life balance. Participation in national fitness and community winter sports activities continues an upward trend, in line with Beijing's vision of engaging 300 million people in winter sports in China. Of course, each and every Olympic and Paralympic gathering is not only a tremendous opportunity, but it is also filled with challenges and as Murphy's Law reminds us, if anything can go wrong it will. Nonetheless, the Games can deliver lasting benefits.

The 2022 Beijing Winter Games are a work-in-progress and will be a learning experience even after the Olympic flame leaves Beijing to begin the journey to

Paris and then two years later to Milan. However, the legacy of the 2022 Winter Olympics and Paralympics will continue to enrich Beijing, China and the world long into the future.

February 11, 2022 China Daily global edition

Ⅲ Duty and Commitment to Sustainable Development

Holistic healing

By ZHU LI, NIU HONGWEI and TERRY TOWNSHEND

Financing needed for biodiversity and ecological protection as well as climate-related projects

A Chinese saying best sums up half measures and haphazard actions: "Treat the head when the head aches, and treat the foot when the foot hurts." Treating human bodies holistically is more effective in restoring a patient's health. Similarly, our planet, now threatened by climate change and biodiversity loss, also needs healing in a holistic way.

We are beginning to realize the intertwined nature between climate and biodiversity. Climate change aggravates biodiversity loss and weakens nature's capacity to absorb carbon, further hastening climate change. To break this vicious cycle requires addressing these two challenges simultaneously and with equal vigor.

Although there is growing consensus on this among scientists, policymakers, and financiers, globally financing for climate and biodiversity remains lopsided.

Global climate financing reached $632 billion in 2019/2020, while biodiversity financing totaled just $124-$143 billion.

This contrast also exists in the deployment of green finance, where financing for climate efforts dwarfs that for biodiversity. According to the International Development Finance Club, of a total of $185 billion green finance commitments its members made in 2020, $179 billion or 96 percent went to climate finance, and only a meager $5.4 billion or 3 percent to biodiversity.

It is the same with green bonds issued in China. According to the China Green Bond Market Report 2020, of the $44 billion green bonds issued by Chinese entities in 2020, only about 5 percent were allotted for biodiversity or ecological protection, with the rest largely going to climate-related projects.

Many reasons drive this imbalance. In the climate space, greenhouse gas emissions can be credibly converted to CO2 equivalents, now a common currency to measure the contribution to climate change. This makes designing, financing, and monitoring climate-focused projects feasible. In contrast, quantifying ecosystem services and biodiversity (in either biophysical or monetary terms) is fiendishly difficult. Inevitably, this impedes investments that rely on quantifiable results.

Thanks to regulation to internalize the cost of carbon emissions, climate-focused projects (e.g., renewable energy development and energy efficiency) already have proven cash flows and attract sizable private investment. On the other hand, biodiversity still struggles to convert its benefits to human societies into financial revenue. Except for sustainable forestry, eco-tourism, mitigation banking, and a handful of other examples, "bankable" biodiversity projects are generally few and far between. This explains why most financing for biodiversity still comes from public sources.

Finally, biodiversity is often uniquely local, and projects designed for one place are therefore rarely directly replicable or scalable in other places. For their generally modest size and disparate nature, biodiversity projects don't conveniently fit the parameters of existing financial products and markets that favor standardization and economies of scale. So, biodiversity projects have a long way to go to take full advantage of modern financial markets' efficiency, reach and vast resources.

Nevertheless, ways to channel more financing into biodiversity conservation and bring about better alignment between climate and biodiversity do exist. To begin with, efforts to address climate and biodiversity must not undercut each other. For example, the land footprint of some clean energy infrastructure can be up to 12 times that of traditional energy sources, so where we place it is crucial. Without careful planning, well-intentioned clean energy infrastructure could endanger biodiversity and create additional financial burdens to restore impaired biodiversity.

We must step up efforts to explore the benefits of tackling both climate and biodiversity challenges with nature-based solutions. For example, restoring mangrove forests can deliver multiple benefits, from enhancing fish nurseries to storing carbon to mitigating the impacts of storm surges.

Encouragingly, China is jump-starting this effort by launching its National Mangrove Conservation and Restoration Action Plan, an initiative informed in part by a strategic study completed by the Paulson Institute and its partners. Under this plan, a total of 18,800 hectares of mangrove forests will be rehabilitated and planted by 2025.

In addition, China's national carbon emission trading system inaugurated in July 2021, and its planned expansion to cover eight high-emission sectors, has immense potential for scaling up nature-based solutions as it is expected to allow carbon credits generated from ecosystem-based projects to offset carbon emissions. Moreover, experts are also calling for the introduction of emissions allowance auctioning and allotment of a portion of the proceeds to ecosystem protection and restoration, which will help boost financing for biodiversity.

Seeking innovative ways to bridge the gap between biodiversity projects and existing financial markets is also imperative. For example, by combining replicable homogenous projects or bundling multiple heterogeneous projects into one diversified product, conservation projects may be structured into more marketable financial products, thus unlocking the vast financial resources that are increasingly looking for environmental, social and governance-themed investment opportunities. An example of this is the mangrove bonds that are gaining interest among financial institutions in and outside China.

Last but not least, exploring innovative mechanisms that help realize the economic value of ecosystem services by either leveraging existing markets or creating new ones must continue. For example, the New York Stock Exchange is exploring a new nature-based asset class in the form of Natural Asset Companies designed to capture and store nature's intrinsic and productive value.

Of course, for biodiversity finance to grow at scale, many other challenges must be addressed, such as strengthening the regulatory framework to value natural capital, building capacity, and implementing de-risking measures to incentivize private investment. In addition, reforming subsidies harmful to climate and biodiversity in the energy, agriculture, and fishery sectors and eliminating deforestation from soft commodity supply chains are essential to achieving climate and biodiversity goals more broadly.

Fundamentally, the climate and biodiversity crises are consequences of our current economic systems' failure to sufficiently value nature in all economic activities. To remedy this, we must transform our economies to recognize our natural capital's finite resources and services.

Healing our planet will take time and requires a holistic approach. Green finance and nature-based solutions already demonstrate their potential in achieving both climate and biodiversity goals, so we must speed up and scale up our actions. "Time and tide wait for no man" never rings truer than today.

July 11, 2022 China Daily global edition

Visible confidence booster

By REBECCA IVEY

China's fight against air pollution lends credence to trust that a greener future is attainable

From my window on the 18th floor of a Beijing office building, I can see distant mountains on three sides, standing out against a clear blue sky. The contrast is striking compared to the smog-wrapped city I first visited in the years running up to the 2008 Summer Olympics. As athletes, sports fans and political commentators prepare for the 2022 Winter Olympics in Beijing, amid geopolitical tensions and climate risks, what lessons have been learned from the two-decade effort to clean up Beijing's skies?

Efforts to improve the air quality have resulted in clear skies known as "Beijing Blue" which became the new normal after the Chinese government intervened. According to the International Olympic Committee, to fulfill its commitments made in the 2000 bid, China invested $21 billion in air quality improvements, including upgrading 60,000 coal-burning boilers and converting more than 4,000 public buses to run on natural gas.

Concrete achievements, not just rhetoric, are what enabled China to gain international acknowledgment and create "a lasting environmental legacy", according to a United Nations Environment Programme report. As anyone who has breathed Beijing air for the past decade can attest, the path to blue skies has not been linear, but China's commitments highlight measurable progress.

The fight against air pollution is an example that foreshadows China's ability to take action on climate change and redeem global trust for a more inclusive, resilient and sustainable future. President Xi Jinping's ambitious pledges that China will peak emissions before 2030 and achieve carbon neutrality before 2060 have motivated industries to take action and prompted other countries to up their game on emissions.

Figures show that China's carbon intensity in 2020 was 48.4 percent less than that in 2005, fulfilling China's commitment to the international community to achieve a 40-45 percent reduction in carbon intensity from the 2005 level by 2020. Now the"1+N" policy framework, meaning a general guideline plus various specific action plans, is dedicated to putting actionable policies in place in response to President Xi's initial commitment.

This Herculean task gained momentum with the China-US Joint Glasgow Declaration on Enhancing Climate Action in the 2020s during the United Nations Climate Change Conference (COP 26) in late 2021. The two nations have also reached a consensus on climate finance and nationally determined contributions under the Paris Agreement. As the World Economic Forum (WEF) President Borge Brende has said, future cooperation between China and the United States is crucial. "The only way (to move) forward is to realize that we are in the same boat and we have to collaborate."

However, the picture is not entirely rosy. PricewaterhouseCooper's 2021 Net Zero Economy Index shows that currently we are reducing the carbon intensity of our activities at less than one-fifth of the rate we need—12.9 percent a year. Along with other studies, the report concludes that such a huge transition cannot be achieved without a systematic and complex rewiring of the entire global economy. But declining trust among the public further dampens this prospect. A global climate study by the WEF, covering 28 countries, found that only around one-fourth of respondents trust business sustainability claims and most participants feel strongly that current environmental protection efforts are not sufficient.

To restore trust, the WEF is committed to supporting all stakeholders to find a common language on sustainability targets and actions. In 2020, in collaboration with other leading institutions in the field, the WEF co-developed a comprehensive set of metrics to fill the gap in consistent environmental, social and governance (ESG) reporting standards. A follow-up report on the ESG landscape among Chinese companies concluded that a measurable global language of sustainability that accords with global green investing priorities while helping Chinese companies along the journey to reach national environmental targets is increasingly relevant and would be appreciated by Chinese stakeholders. Meanwhile, the Green Investment Principles for the Belt and Road demonstrate the commitment of Chinese stakeholders to uphold climate action beyond its borders by supporting developing and emerging countries to harness green finance and technology to scale up low-carbon infrastructure.

Not only climate, but other global environmental concerns such as biodiversity, are high on China's priority action list. The WEF began publishing its New Nature Economy Report Series in 2020, using data to identify pathways for businesses and governments to join the transition to a nature-positive economy.

Looking back at events over the past two years, it is clear to the world that collaboration and trust are not just important—they are essential—if human beings are to survive and thrive.

Outside, the cloudless sky gives an impression of timelessness, but we should not forget that it was not achieved instantly, effortlessly or single-handedly. To ensure that future generations can still enjoy the gifts of nature, we must shoulder the responsibility: working together, restoring trust.

January 17, 2022 China Daily global edition

Sharing of low-carbon dividend

By YU ZIRONG

China's expertise and experience can help other developing countries with their energy transitions

Addressing the general debate of the 76th session of the United Nations General Assembly via video link on Sept 21, 2021, Chinese President Xi Jinping proposed a Global Development Initiative.

He pledged that China will step up its support for the development of green and low-carbon energy in other developing countries. It demonstrates China's commitment to supporting developing countries in responding to the novel coronavirus outbreak and promoting green and sustainable recovery.

Energy shortage is one of the major bottlenecks that has a detrimental effect on economic recovery in the post-pandemic era. As one of the first major economies to largely contain the pandemic, China is working to help other developing countries realize energy transformation and promote green development in the face of the COVID-19 by sharing its experience in low-carbon development and providing assistance in this regard.

The importance of stable and sufficient energy supply was realized in the early days after the founding of the People's Republic of China. As China started providing assistance to other developing countries shortly after its founding, energy access and related infrastructure were among the top priorities. Between 1956 and 1985, China helped 16 countries build 52 energy projects with a total installed capacity of 1.1 million kilowatts. Besides, 18 power transmission projects, which had transmission lines extending more than 2,400 kilometers, were initiated. China also offered convenience for production and living by carrying out off-grid renewable energy projects, such as methane power plants and small hydropower stations.

With the country's economy taking off, China's renewable energy industry has made remarkable achievements that offer strong support for its green and low-carbon energy transition domestically, as well as in other developing countries through foreign assistance. Through multilateral channels, under the framework of the China South-South Climate Cooperation Fund, the country continues to organize training for officials and technicians of developing countries, while providing photovoltaic equipment for generating power. Green energy assistance has also been enhanced bilaterally, such as the building of a photovoltaic system with a total installed capacity of 1 megawatt in Nepal, and a 50-MW solar power plant in Garissa, Kenya, the largest photovoltaic power station in East Africa. China's rapidly iterating energy technologies and economies of scale have greatly reduced the cost of renewable energy utilization; as the development and commercial cooperation scales up, more developing countries can share the benefits of China's renewable energy development.

Developing countries often suffer from the imbalance of high energy demand and insufficient supply, not to forget the challenges of controlling greenhouse emissions amid the growing threats from global climate change. The outbreak of the COVID-19 has only exacerbated the problems. Some renewable energy projects in developing countries have been suspended in the planning stage because of the rising debt burden, sovereign risks and financing costs. With long-term investments in energy and power infrastructure losing their appeal, private capital is even withdrawing from the market.

On the flip side, the pandemic has created opportunities for developing countries to switch to clean energy in the face of reduced willingness to invest in traditional energy systems. Major economies have reached agreements on a shift away from coal power to renewable energy in terms of overseas financing.

Responding to the demand for energy transformation in developing countries amid the pandemic, China can provide more targeted assistance that helps developing countries make full use of their renewable energy resources, choose an energy transition path that is consistent with their own resource endowments and development plans, and strive to realize late-developer advantages for its green and low-carbon transition, with the following approaches:

First, the designing of energy assistance must align with the energy sector development plan of the host country and respond to its call for cooperation. The assistance should be aiming for higher standards and higher quality and be a role model for commercial cooperation.

Second, the assistance should share methods for tackling the problems in exploiting low-carbon energy. China's progress in renewable energy is not limited to the growing installed capacities, it also includes its stimulating environment for innovative technology and green financing mechanisms.

For instance, China can help countries with favorable market mechanisms and business environments, and carry out exchanges and talent training on green finance. For fossil fuel projects that are already established, the assistance could target for energy efficiency and pollutant control system upgrading and coal-fired power plant flexibility retrofits. The assistance could also help developing countries approach expensive emerging technologies such as carbon capture, utilization and storage, laying the foundation for future commercial cooperation.

Third, China's experience in tackling poverty alleviation programs based on energy development and energy transformation is also worth sharing. For instance, the "No 1 central document" for 2021, released in February, stressed implementing an action plan for rural vitalization and setting up targets for better rural public infrastructure through initiating projects on rural clean energy. It proposed the establishment of a high quality energy mechanism in rural areas, including photovoltaic and wind power. Such action plans should be included in the cooperation to strengthen capacity and policy exchanges with other countries under the framework of South-South cooperation.

Last but not least, through providing assistance in renewable energy, China can also further contribute to the prevention and control of the pandemic in developing countries. Renewable energy and distributed power facilities in the remote areas of developing countries can better meet the needs of healthcare and daily production, compared to the large centralized ones driven by fossil energy. China's established assistance in the renewable energy sector should be followed by upgraded cooperation between the energy and public health authorities to ensure services such as lighting and refrigeration equipment for the vaccine transportation cold-chain.

The dividend of China's low-carbon development has become a global public good shared by the international community, especially other developing countries. Based on its proven approaches, they can seek a path to green recovery in the post-pandemic era and sustainable development that suits their conditions.

October 18, 2021 China Daily global edition

Green Exploration

Reform and Innovation Trials in Various Fields

I Beyond Promises: Low Carbon and Green Transformation

Gas cuts

By YAN TIAN and LONG DONGQUAN

Certification of offset tree planting is a pragmatic market-based approach Brazil and China are cooperating on to reduce methane emissions by cows

It was exciting to hear Brazil's Environment Minister Joaquim Alvaro Pereira Leite announce freshly formalized national commitments for tackling greenhouse gas emissions and deforestation at the 26th United Nations Climate Change Conference of the Parties, or COP 26, in Glasgow on Nov 13, 2021.

These commitments, including halving greenhouse gas emissions by 2030, realizing carbon neutrality by 2050, and ending illegal deforestation by 2080, can help save the seven biomes in the world and control the global rise in temperature.

China and Brazil have developed a comprehensive partnership at many different levels. Both public and private stakeholders from China have invested in Brazil's agribusiness and agriculture-linked infrastructure building since

2014. Maintaining economic growth while promoting food security plays an increasingly important role in this bilateral relationship. Brazil has established instruments, mechanisms and programs to meet its targets. These experiences are referential to sustaining China's imports, the sectoral development in China and of value for China to achieve its carbon emissions reduction goals.

One of the most eye-catching public-private initiatives is the production of the first carbon-neutral beef product in the world-Viva-by Brazilian agricultural research company Embrapa, and a leading beef company, Marfrig. After spending five years and 10 million reals ($1.8 million) on investigating the concept, protocol, techniques and the certification mechanism, Viva-certified meat has been available in over 10 supermarkets in the state of Sao Paulo since 2020.

There is little doubt that addressing greenhouse gas emissions from the livestock sector, which accounts for 14.5 percent of man-made emissions according to the Intergovernmental Panel on Climate Change's calculation, is a significant challenge. This number is larger for leading agricultural production countries such as the United States, New Zealand and Brazil.

In the livestock sector, cattle ranching is responsible for methane emissions, which is directly responsible for habitat conversion. The whole life of beef production, from the beginning of ranching-induced land-use change to food wastes, emits the highest amount of greenhouse gas compared to other ruminants, according to statistics from Our World in Data. Decarbonizing the farming stage, especially cattle's enteric methane emissions, is an essential step for combating climate change.

Brazil took the first-mover position in addressing beef-pertinent greenhouse gas emissions.

Its designed methodology is to neutralize the enteric methane of cows by planting trees in pastures, called Livestock-Forestry or Crop-Livestock-Forestry system. Embrapa found that methane emitted by 11 adult cattle per hectare per year could be offset by 200 fast-growing trees such as eucalyptus per hectare, bearing in mind Brazil's average stocking rate of 1.2 cattle per hectare.

The logic of planting trees in the agricultural system indicates reducing logging and sequestering emissions. Eucalyptus also increases or maintains organic carbon in the soil and is harvested for making value-added wood products such as furniture, which stores carbon even longer. This further provides additional income to farmers and producers.

This quite comprehensive system is a smart agricultural technique, the rationale of which technically facilitates Brazil to achieve its new ambitious goals as confirmed by Brazil's Ministry of Agriculture, Livestock and Food Supply.

Several stakeholders in both Brazil and China are cooperating to promote this innovative practice and to enable Brazil to enjoy first-mover advantages.

On the one hand, to green the trade relationship, both sides from the ministerial level at the COP 26 to institutional level are negotiating on the potential distribution of carbon-neutral soft commodities, including farm produce. This ensures the incorporation of criteria such as low carbon and carbon neutrality into the current business model. On the other hand, scaling up and localizing Brazil's carbon-neutral methodology in China's livestock sector are of great interest to many stakeholders in China as this aligns with China's carbon emissions peak and neutrality targets.

At the trading level, for China's business sector, sealed commodities with a carbon-neutral certificate are appealing. Certification is a pragmatic market-based approach with an instrumental function. Many members of the China Chamber of Commerce of Import and Export of Foodstuffs, Native Produce and Animal By-Products prefer holding sustainability-linked certification just like purchasing American soybeans with Sustainability Soybeans Assurance Protocol.

Domestically, to certify China's beef sector and to notarize Brazil's certificate, the China Environmental United Certification Centre thoroughly analyzed the methodology and believed that a complicated and comprehensive methodology could be developed, although it is hard for farmers achieving it on the ground to apply for the certificate. However, the essence of certification is to raise the bar and provide a level playing field in the industry.

January 17, 2022 China Daily global edition

Helping hands for Small Island Developing States

By SHI JIAOQUN

Nearly 30 years ago, given their unique environmental and developmental needs, Small Island Developing States (SIDS) were recognized as a special category at the 1992 United Nations Conference on Environment and Development. The SIDS are a group of developing countries characterized by small populations and numerous atolls spanning geographic regions—the Caribbean, the Pacific, the Atlantic, Indian Ocean, Mediterranean and South China Sea.

Although small individually, when looked at as a whole, the population of the SIDS represent 1 percent of the world's inhabitants, or around 65 million people.

But these islanders face unique social, economic and environmental challenges due to the inherent vulnerabilities of the SIDS, including their small geographic size, their remoteness, the disproportionate impact climate change is having on their ecosystems, biodiversity loss and narrowing of their resource base.

With limited arable land, many of the SIDS are dependent on small-scale agriculture and ocean resources. They also rely heavily on imported foods, often foods that are processed with high amounts of sugar and salt content, leading to health issues. Statistics from the Food and Agriculture Organization of the United Nations show that almost all Caribbean and Pacific SIDS import over 60 percent of food; 50 percent of islands import over 80 percent. Despite the food availability through imports, levels of hunger across the SIDS remains at alarming 17 percent.

The COVID-19 pandemic is further threatening the food security, nutrition and climate resilience of the SIDS.

Their collective GDP shrank by 6.9 percent in 2020 versus 4.8 percent for that of the other developing countries. This is mainly due to global contractions in two ocean economy sectors that are key to many of the SIDS: coastal tourism and fishery. For two out of three SIDS, tourism accounts for 20 percent or more of their GDP, according to an Organization for Economic Cooperation and Development report. Since the COVID-19 outbreak, the United Nations World Tourism Organization estimates that international tourist arrivals declined by 47 percent in the SIDS from January to April 2020, and warned that the road to recovery is set to be long and uncertain. The fishery sector has also been significantly impacted by the COVID-19 pandemic, adversely affecting domestic employment and nutrition.

In this challenging context, South-South and Triangular Cooperation has the opportunity to step in and demonstrate its unique advantages by addressing the agriculture, food, nutrition, environment and health issues of the SIDS. SSTC can enable the SIDS to acquire and adopt relevant solutions from other countries that have more recent experience in tackling development issues in similar socioeconomic contexts and agro-ecological zones.

The FAO has identified and mobilized knowledge, skills, and experience from developing countries to support the SIDS in scaling up both adaption and mitigation measures in the agricultural sector. In 2013, it supported the Samoa Farmers' Association to conduct a biogas feasibility study including a field trip to biogas cities in China. On that basis, China's Biogas Institute of the Ministry of Agriculture and Rural Affairs and the SFA, supported by other development partners, have brought China's sustainable animal waste management technologies to Samoa through the China-Samoa Agricultural Technical Aid Project (2018-2019). On completion, 21 animal waste digesters were shipped to Samoa and operated locally, and a total of 22 trainees have enhanced their skills under the tutelage of Chinese experts. Economically and socially, the project resulted in savings of around $25 on a household's average monthly cost of liquefied petroleum gas and relieved women from hard work of firewood collection.

Going forward, in promoting the Global Action Programme on Food Security and Nutrition in the SIDS, the FAO should also utilize the SSTC to promote sustainable and localized food and agricultural systems across the SIDS. Many completed and ongoing SSTC activities have promoted knowledge sharing, technical exchanges for enhancing traditional production systems, developing integrated approaches to pest, land and water management, and reviving interest in nutrient-rich traditional food crops such as root and tuber crops, plantains, and breadfruits across the SIDS.

Previous experience and achievements have further generated concrete recommendations on leveraging SSTC to promote sustainable agricultural development in the SIDS in the post COVID-19 era.

First, more proven solutions could be harnessed through the SIDS Solution Platform and be shared, exchanged, and practiced in other SIDS under the SSTC mechanism. On the occasion of the high-level SIDS Solutions Forum that was held on Aug 30 to 31, organized by FAO and co-hosted by the Government of Fiji, this is an opportunity for more proven solutions to be shared, exchanged, and practiced in other SIDS countries under the SSTC mechanism.

For instance, in Samoa, female farmers are leveraging social media to expand their access to the local vegetable, fruit and handicraft markets. Most of these initiatives are launched in countries such as Fiji, Samoa and Vanuatu because of their unique capacities. There is an opportunity to nurture and scale up such initiatives to other SIDS through the SSTC. There are also many science and technology initiatives in Asia, Africa and the SIDS across the globe that could contribute to sustainable and resilient agri-food systems.

Second, the SSTC should and will continue to align with the SIDS' development priorities and respond to the unique challenges they face. The SIDS are among the least responsible of all nations for climate change but are among the hardest hit. The SIDS are also among the most vulnerable countries to the impacts of the COVID-19 pandemic, which is disrupting key sectors that the SIDS' undiversified and already fragile economies strongly rely upon. Globally, all SIDS could benefit significantly from exchanges of knowledge and technologies.

Third, being positioned as a global advocate and partner for SSTC, the FAO plays a unique role in grouping multiple stakeholders together to promote sustainable food and agricultural development in the SIDS. According to the OECD, the total support for the COVID-19 crisis to the SIDS in 2020 is conservatively estimated at $2.8 billion. The FAO is mobilizing finance from resource partners to work on addressing capacity and investment through horizontal Southern Partnerships (it refers to partnerships driven by global south countries and among global south countries that are recognized horizontal). Additionally, it is also working with island governments to improve productivity and efficiency at each stage of the food value chain, especially by exploring the potential impact of public-private business models and engaging the broad range of stakeholders involved in getting products from farm to fork.

September 1, 2021 China Daily global edition

Ⅱ Exploring Chinese Solutions for Low Carbon Transformation in Different Industries

Resolve to green the Belt and Road

By DIMITRI DE BOER/CHRISTOPH NEDOPIL WANG

China becoming more and more proactive in aligning its overseas investments with the Paris Agreement

The Chinese government issued a policy on July 16 2021, encouraging Chinese businesses to integrate green development throughout the whole process of overseas investment and cooperation. The document, titled "Green Development Guidelines for Overseas Investment and Cooperation", was jointly issued by the Ministry of Commerce and the Ministry of Ecology and Environment. It is an excellent step to accelerate green development not only in China, but internationally.

The guidelines recommend that Chinese enterprises "follow international green rules and standards" in overseas activities, particularly in countries where local standards are insufficient. The guidelines encourage the practice of environmental impact assessments in accordance with internationally accepted standards—a clear move to promote green development. By including the three environmental aspects of pollution control, ecological protection and climate change, the guidelines break new ground by aligning Chinese overseas investment with the Paris Agreement.

The guidelines recommend that Chinese businesses support investments in solar, wind and other forms of clean energy. This is absolutely essential as the risks of climate change are becoming painfully obvious around the world, including in China. The likelihood of extreme weather including droughts, heat waves and floods, is greatly increased by climate change. All countries should stop building new high carbon infrastructure, and quickly start to reduce greenhouse gas emissions.

The guidelines also cover trade, by requiring companies to speed up integration with the global green supply chain, carry out green procurement and purchase environmentally friendly products and services. If implemented well, this could be a game-changer for the biodiversity on our planet, which continues to suffer heavily from deforestation.

The guidelines come at a time when the world hopes to recover after the novel coronavirus pandemic has left many economies struggling. By publishing the guidelines, China shows its willingness to play an important role in supporting sustainable development.

The guidelines are specifically addressed to some of the most important financial institutions: the China Development Bank, China Import-Export Bank and Sinosure, China's export credit agency. This policy gives a boost to their efforts to go green and helps to set their expectations that stricter measures are likely to follow. In fact, many of these financial institutions are already actively working on going green.

In June 2021, the Belt and Road Initiative International Green Development Coalition, ClientEarth and the Beijing Institute of Finance and Sustainability conducted a two-day workshop on environmental and climate risk mitigation with the largest financial institutions in the Belt and Road Initiative. Although the process is not without difficulties, these institutions are developing key policies, such as categorization of projects based on environmental risks, requirements for environmental standards, impact assessments, third-party evaluations, information disclosure and public participation, grievance mechanisms, and even potential fossil fuel exclusion policies. They are also making rapid progress in developing green loans and bonds, backed by a strong push toward climate finance from the People's Bank of China, China's central bank.

Looking at current investment trends, we're already starting to see this transformation on the ground. According to the China Belt and Road Initiative Investment Report H1 2021 released by the International Institute for Green Finance, 2020 was the first year when renewable investments in the Belt and Road countries exceeded investments in coal, while in the first half of 2021, no coal-related financing went into the Belt and Road countries. For example, the Industrial and Commercial Bank of China pulled out of financing for a huge coal plant in Zimbabwe in June 2021, and China already supports the energy transition of many Belt and Road countries. This shift away from climate-harming projects makes economic sense, as electricity from new solar power is already up to five times cheaper than from new coal power.

We expect that this positive trend will continue, with China becoming more and more proactive in greening its overseas investments. The new guidelines allude to "relevant environmental protection requirements on overseas projects". These currently don't exist, which leads us to believe that they may be issued in the near future. Furthermore, in the run-up to the upcoming climate conference in Glasgow in November, we anticipate that China may announce further steps to make the Belt and Road Initiative even more climate-friendly. China's leadership on climate action and biodiversity protection is the key to the global green transition.

August 9, 2021 China Daily global edition

Cleanly energized

By LIN BOQIANG

China's third-generation nuclear power technology can play a big role in the global endeavor to achieve carbon neutrality

By the end of 2020, 27 countries and regions had put forward their carbon neutrality goals. China is one of them. But compared with the advanced economies, China's road to carbon neutrality is more difficult and challenging. On the one hand, fossil fuels account for 85 percent of China's total energy consumption, with coal, the fuel having the highest carbon intensity, accounting for 58 percent of its energy consumption. On the other hand, China is still experiencing medium-to-high speed of economic growth, with its energy sector expanding. The relatively high energy intensive industrial structure and expanding energy consumption are obstacles that China must overcome to achieve its carbon neutrality goal.

China is shifting to an energy mix with lower carbon intensity by investing heavily in clean energies such as wind, solar and hydro power. In 2019, the country's installed solar and wind power capacity was 204 and 210 gigawatts respectively. The solar and wind power combined made up for about 21 percent of the nation's total installed power capacity. However, the electricity generated by solar and wind power only accounted for 8 percent of the total, due to their instability and low operation hours. The use of hydropower is also constrained by its limited potential for development and the environmental protection pressure it faces.

In comparison, nuclear energy still has huge room for development in China. In 2019, the country's installed nuclear power capacity was 48 GW, accounting for just 2 percent of the total installed capacity. But it produced 5 percent of the country's electricity. With its high efficiency and low carbon emissions, nuclear energy could play a bigger role for China to achieve carbon neutrality. When China started constructing its first nuclear power plant, the Qinshan Nuclear Power Plant, in 1983, the technologies and equipment used in the facility, including the reactor pressure vessel, were all imported, and the installed capacity was only 300,000 kilowatts. After more than three decades of development, China has rolled out Hualong One, its indigenous third-generation nuclear power technology. Hualong One meets the strictest safety standards in the world, with each unit having an installed capacity of 1.16 million kilowatts.

The 2011 Fukushima nuclear disaster in Japan greatly held back China's nuclear development. Coupled with a relatively abundant power supply, nuclear power in China has witnessed lukewarm growth over the past decade. However, China's nuclear power generation still expanded by around 10 percent annually. Currently, the country has a total installed nuclear power capacity of 52 GW in commercial operation, with another 19 GW under construction. The installed nuclear power capacity of the country is projected to hit 70 GW by 2025.

All the benefits of using nuclear power are based on safety. It is well known that a nuclear accident would not only bring huge economic losses, but also seriously hinder the progress of the whole industry. After the Three Mile Island nuclear accident and the Chernobyl disaster, major nuclear power countries have worked to develop safer standards, which resulted in the Utility Requirements Document (implemented in the United States) and the European Utility Requirements (implemented in Western Europe). The nuclear technologies that meet both the two safety standards are called third-generation nuclear technology. Hualong One, which is a third-generation reactor design, adopts a double-layer safety shell, and innovatively uses a combination of "active and passive" safety systems. Meeting the highest safety standards in the world, Hualong One marks a new milestone in terms of safety for China's nuclear power development.

Moreover, the first reactor unit using Hualong One design—Unit 5 of China

National Nuclear Corp's Fuqing nuclear power plant in Fujian province—was put into operation on Jan 30, 2021, four months ahead of schedule—it only took 68 months for the project to be completed, making it world's first unit of a nuclear project using the third-generation nuclear technology to be put into commercial operation within the set schedule. Previously, construction of the first reactor units adopting third-generation nuclear technology was delayed without exception due to the difficulties brought by the application of new equipment and technology. For example, two units in Sanmen, Zhejiang province, using US nuclear giant Westinghouse's AP1000 nuclear reactor design and the nuclear plant in Taishan, Guangdong province, using the third-generation European pressurized reactor were finished four to five years behind schedule, causing huge financial losses. The timely completion of the first unit using Hualong One technology indicates that China has joined the ranks of global leaders in nuclear technology.

China needs nuclear power to realize the goal of carbon neutrality. With renewable energy resources such as wind, solar and hydro power facing different development bottlenecks and difficulties, nuclear power, which is clean and stable, offers an important alternative for China.

Globally, Hualong One technology, which is safe, efficient and cost-effective, provides a low-carbon power supply solution for countries plagued by electricity shortages, whose demands for energy in the medium run could otherwise not be met by other renewable energy sources. China has already received orders for its Hualong One reactor, marking a remarkable transition from "importing nuclear technology" to "exporting nuclear technology". It is foreseeable that with Hualong One's gradual improvement, nuclear power will become the choice of more and more countries.

The world needs nuclear power to achieve carbon neutrality. Currently, it is reported that a total of 72 countries are considering developing nuclear power, including 41 countries participating in the Belt and Road Initiative. Hualong One will surely help the world realize the imperative green transition.

February 26, 2021 China Daily global edition

Urgent to tame embodied carbon

By WANG YUANFENG

The building and construction sector's performance is critical to China achieving carbon neutrality by 2060

By vowing to achieve carbon neutrality by 2060, China has strengthened the global fight against climate change. Yet the building and construction sector's role will be critical to China's successful pursuit of the carbon neutrality goal.

The building and construction sector accounts for nearly 40 percent of global energy and process-related carbon dioxide emissions. According to the 2019 Global Status Report for Buildings and Construction issued by the International Energy Agency (IEA) and the United Nations Environment Programme (UNEP), the global construction sector's emissions increased 2 percent from 2017 to 2018, reaching a record high. Worryingly, 230 billion square meters of new floor area and double the existing global building stock will be required by 2060 to accommodate two-thirds of the expected 10 billion global population in urban areas.

Such a huge construction demand, thanks to increasing urbanization, means continuous rise in the construction sector's emissions.

China's construction and building sector is the largest in the world. To build the existing about 65 billion sq m of floor area, the sector discharged about 2.1 billion metric tons of CO_2 emissions (operational emissions), roughly 20 percent of both China's total emissions and global construction emissions. And since about 2 billion sq m of new floor area are built in China every year-almost one-third of the global total of 6.13 billion sq m—the construction sector's annual carbon emissions accounts for about 11 percent of global total thanks mainly to manufacturing and transportation of building materials such as steel, cement and glass, as well as on-site construction. These emissions are called embodied carbon emissions.

As the construction sector is a major contributor to emissions, to achieve carbon neutral by 2060 and better cope with climate change, China has to dramatically reduce the sector's CO2 emissions in the coming decades. The IEA and UNEP reports suggest that the sector needs to take appropriate measures to reverse the trend of rising carbon emissions, and enhance energy efficiency at a rate of 3 percent a year.

But nearly two-thirds of the floor area that exist today will still be used in 2050, and new buildings are only likely to be zero-carbon by 2030.

Also, the building sector's current emission level poses a challenge to China. According to the 2019 research report on China building energy consumption released by the China Association of Building Energy Efficiency, the construction sector's carbon emissions will continue to increase and peak probably in 2039—nine years after the entire country's CO2 emissions peak. Therefore, whether China achieves carbon neutrality by 2060 will partly depend on the construction sector's performance.

As a report released by the Energy Transitions Commission in 2019, Fully Developed Rich Zero-Carbon Economy says, China's building and construction sector can achieve carbon neutrality. But decarbonizing buildings across generations would require a complete overhaul of the building and construction sector. For instance, driven by clear and ambitious policies, the sector should take a range of measures to promote "passive building" designs (extremely energy-efficient buildings that require little energy for space heating or cooling), material efficiency, use of low-carbon materials, insulated building envelopes, and highly efficient lighting and appliances.

To begin with, the plan to make the building and construction sector carbon neutral should have a specific timetable and road map, because the sector has to become carbon neutral by 2060 to ensure China fulfills its green commitment.

Second, there is a need to measure carbon emissions of all components of the building and construction sector, and quantify them by using the life-cycle assessment method.

Third, the building and construction sector's standards and codes should be thoroughly revised, because to achieve carbon neutrality, almost all the standards and specifications of the sector need to save energy and reduce emissions.

Fourth, policies and regulations for achieving carbon neutrality should be fully spelled out, along with economic, fiscal, financial, and voluntary labeling policies—especially green finance policies—to achieve carbon neutrality.

Fifth, carbon pricing, including carbon tax and carbon trading, is a very important and effective means to compel industries and enterprises to reduce emissions. So carbon emissions—both embedded and operational—from the entire sector should be incorporated into the national and pilot carbon trading markets as early as possible.

Sixth, since stakeholders, including governments, developers, design institutes, contractors, and users do not have enough knowledge about carbon neutrality, the government should disseminate more information and organize training programs to enhance their knowledge.

Seventh, publicity can help people realize the importance of carbon neutrality, and encourage them to adopt eco-friendly habits. While environmental courses and majors with a focus on carbon neutrality should be introduced in universities to prepare talent for the future, it is also important to include such courses in primary and middle schools.

In addition, China should pursue global cooperation to boost the global fight against climate change, not least because cooperation with economies such as the European Union and the United Kingdom will help put China's carbon neutrality work on the right track at an early date. And after China learns how to become carbon neutral, it can help other countries to meet their Paris Agreement requirements.

In other words, although achieving carbon neutrality is an arduous task, the building and construction sector can realize this great goal.

November 19, 2020 China Daily global edition

Healthy oceans matter

By XIE XI/CHEN JILIANG

Sustainably managing the world's sea areas will help preserve marine ecosystems and fight climate change and biodiversity loss

The whole world has been overwhelmed by the urgent challenges brought by the COVID-19 pandemic. But while this crisis is preoccupying the world, there are graver long-term risks from climate change and biodiversity loss that should not be ignored.

More and more countries have committed to carbon neutrality, and a carbon-neutral future points to a vision of the future in which humans live in harmony with nature.

Oceans are a dominant feature of our planet, covering 70 percent of its surface and driving its climate and biosphere. But the world's oceans are in peril from human activities and climate change. Urgent action is required to put the oceans on the path to recovery. Healthy oceans matter.

The newly released Guidance on Integrating and Strengthening Efforts Related to Climate Change and Ecological Protection by the Ministry of Ecology and Environment of China explicitly emphasizes the synergy of marine and coastal ecological conservation and restoration with climate change adaptation.

China has invested heavily in marine science over the past few decades and has also strengthened its regulations to manage its waters.

Since the 1980s, the number of marine protected areas (MPAs) in China has grown rapidly. By the end of 2019, China had established 271 MPAs, mostly located in coastal waters, with a total area of about 124,000 square kilometers, accounting for 4.1 percent of the marine area under its jurisdiction.

While China is moving toward a protected area system based on national parks, both the scale and quality of the MPAs need to be enhanced. The further investment in science should better support the designation and management of domestic MPAs and contribute to MPAs in international waters.

As the biggest consumer and processor of seafood and the country with the largest aquaculture industry, China needs to reform its fishing industry for the industry's quality-oriented growth.

Stricter rules have been issued to combat illegal, unreported and unregulated fishing. In 2020, there were several such allegations against China in waters beyond its jurisdiction, and there was a firm response from the Chinese authorities, indicating its resolve to curb such activities. China's fishery authorities have introduced hard-hitting punishments for illegal fishing by the country's distant water fishing vessels.

The white paper on the Compliance of China's Distant Water Fisheries 2020, released by the Ministry of Agriculture and Rural Affairs of China, is a strong statement of China's principles, positions, policies and measures on the management of pelagic fisheries and the effectiveness of its implementation, while China is also actively seeking the ratification of the Port State Measure Agreement. It will take some time to have a pronounced effect, but China seems to be on the right track.

Limiting fishing is critical for the quality of the ocean ecosystems. Input control, seasonal bans and fishery subsidy reforms are the main tools applied. The white paper on the Compliance of China's Distant Water Fisheries 2020 has called for the integration of climate risk management into fishery decisions, which indicates that more precaution is being taken into account.

We can develop solutions to preserve the environment and fight climate change by sustainably managing the oceans. While China is pioneering the discussion of nature-based solutions, more attention and confidence is needed on ocean-based mitigation options and their potential contribution to closing the emissions gap.

Five opportunities for action were raised in the report Ocean as a Solution to Climate Change released by the High-Level Panel for a Sustainable Ocean Economy, a unique initiative established in September 2018 by 14 world leaders. Among them, ocean-based renewable energy is no doubt central to China, as its research on coastal and marine ecosystems and carbon storage in the seabed is increasing.

The sustainable blue economy foresees economic opportunities and emerging trends in the decades ahead, including the greening of shipping, offshore renewable energy, carbon sequestration, eco-friendly tourism, use of genetic marine resources, sustainable aquaculture and the development of new types of marine food. As long as there is a clear policy framework, strong incentives and high environmental and social standards, investing in a sustainable ocean economy will lead to the integration of economic, social, environmental and climate impacts.

A healthy ocean economy is particularly important for China, a rapidly growing maritime power, with a coastline of 18,000 km, and a country that will play a critical role in the journey to carbon neutrality.

To further enable the role of oceans in a carbon-neutral future, China needs a more robust science and precaution-based, decision-making process for domestic and international policies. It is also important to have smoother cross-sector coordination at all levels through legislation and marine spatial planning.

The Guidance on Integrating and Strengthening Efforts Related to Climate Change and Ecological Protection is a great step forward, and more joint policies and actions are expected.

January 27, 2021 China Daily global edition

Key to unlock dual-goal scale-up

By MA JUN

China's green financial system needs refining so it can better support the efforts to realize the carbon peak and neutrality objectives

China's green finance market has grown rapidly over the past few years. At the end of September 2021, the outstanding amount of China's green loans reached 15 trillion yuan ($2.4 trillion), ranking first in the world. The cumulative issuance of green bonds in China reached about 2 trillion yuan from 2016 to 2021. And the growth of the green finance instruments accelerated in 2021. Green loans rose 28 percent year-on-year as of September, and green bond issuance rose nearly 170 percent in 2021 compared with the previous year. These rates far exceeded the overall growth of bank lending and bond issuance.

However, to meet the massive green financing demand arising from China's carbon peak and neutrality goals, the green finance market needs to be further scaled up-many fold-in the coming years and decades. A recent study, conducted by the Green Finance Committee of the China Society for Finance Banking, finds that China's green and low-carbon investment demand during 2021-2050 could reach 487 trillion yuan (in 2018 constant price terms). This means that the annual average demand for green and low-carbon investment could amount to 16 trillion yuan per year during the next 30 years. The majority of these investments will go into projects such as renewable energy, energy efficiency, new energy vehicles, green buildings and low-carbon technologies for manufacturing. About 90 percent of the funds for these projects will need to be mobilized by the financial system, with only about 10 percent of the funding coming from the government.

Therefore, mobilizing private capital is the key to successfully achieving the carbon peaking and carbon neutrality strategy (the "dual carbon targets"). The study by the Green Finance Committee argues that some key elements of the current green finance framework need to be modified to enhance its ability to mobilize larger amounts of private capital and to be further aligned with the requirement of carbon neutrality.

It calls for refining the green finance taxonomies, according to the no-significant-harm principle, to ensure that all projects included in the taxonomies deliver some environmental benefits while doing no harm to any environmental goals, including the emissions reduction goals.

Mandatory environmental and climate information disclosure requirements should be introduced, based on the Task Force on Climate-related Financial Disclosures recommendations, for entities that are seeking finance from banks and the financial market. Key to effective disclosure is the requirement for corporates and financial institutions to report the carbon intensity (footprint) of their operations and the financial assets on their balance sheets.

Stronger policy incentives should be introduced to enhance the expected returns of green and low-carbon projects. These incentives could include targeted central bank facilities, interest subsidies and guarantees from the government, as well as the emissions trading system.

Innovation of green finance products, such as sustainability-linked loans and bonds, green mortgage loans, secured loans using carbon credit as collaterals and green supply chain financing, also needs encouraging. And a transition finance framework should be established to scale up funding for transition activities toward net zero. This framework should include a taxonomy of transition activities, disclosure requirements, relevant financial instruments as well as incentives pertinent to the climate transition.

Various pilot programs have already been launched in some of the above-mentioned areas. For example, the China-UK green finance task force has initiated a Task Force on Climate-related Financial Disclosures pilot among 20 Chinese and UK financial companies, and its experience has provided an important basis for the People's Bank of China's policy preparation on mandatory disclosure requirements. A few months ago, the PBOC announced a new incentive, namely the carbon emissions reduction facility (CERF), that provides low-cost financing via commercial banks for decarbonization projects. Huzhou of Zhejiang province, a green finance pilot city, is now working on a policy framework to support transition finance.

In addition to mobilizing private capital to finance green and sustainable activities, another major task of green finance is to protect the financial system from risks arising from low-carbon transition. As carbon neutrality policies are implemented, firms in carbon intensive sectors such as coal mining, coal-fired power generation, steel, cement, and petrochemicals may face significant pressures in the form of increased costs and/or revenue reduction. The deterioration of carbon intensive companies' financial performance may eventually lead to financial risks for banks and investment firms, as some of these companies could default on bank loans and see their equity valuations decline.

Recently, the PBOC has requested 21 major banks conduct a climate stress test exercise on financial risks arising from their exposure to assets in coal-fired power generation, steel and cement sectors. This is only the beginning of a more systemic effort of measuring and managing climate risks. Going forward, the sector coverage of the climate risk analysis should be expanded, a wider range of scenarios or policy/technological shocks should be considered, and other types of financial firms (for example, asset managers) should also be required to conduct such analyses. Once the climate risk exposures are identified, financial firms will then need to develop a strategy to manage these risks, including via limiting exposures, assisting the decarbonization of carbon-intensive companies, and employing hedging instruments against climate risks.

"The dual carbon targets" present huge opportunities as well as significant challenges to the Chinese financial industry. Grasping the opportunities and meeting the challenges require greater and collective efforts from all levels of the financial community and the corporate sector. The good news is that we have the great passion from financial market players to participate in this endeavor. In September 2021, more than 400,000 people attended (most online) the Annual Forum of the Green Finance Committee of China Society for Finance and Banking, which focused on the topic of financing carbon neutrality.

January 18, 2022 China Daily global edition

Power adapter

By ZHOU QIN and LIU YUJING

Consensus needs to be reached on how to overcome a number of pressing challenges in order to successfully decarbonize China's power sector

China has pledged to peak its carbon emissions before 2030 and achieve carbon neutrality before 2060. Power system decarbonization will be one of the main focus areas for achieving the "dual carbon" target since it accounts for about 40 percent of China's overall carbon emissions.

To achieve the decarbonization goals, the characteristics of China's existing power system and the challenges of its decarbonization have to be analyzed and identified and a suitable new power system has to be explored and established.

Although the physical laws governing power systems are universally the same, the characteristics of each power system can be quite different. China's power sector is characterized by its heavy dependency on coal power generation, the remoteness of sources of renewable energy generation from major load centers, and the lack of exposure to price signals for the end-users.

Given the characteristics of its power system and its ongoing industrialization and urbanization, which mean its electricity demand continues to grow, China inevitably faces a number of critical challenges. Renewable energy must be developed on a large scale not only to replace the existing coal power plants but also to meet the additional demand growth in the future. Greater power system flexibility is critical because of the need for balancing the volatility on both the supply and demand sides. But the transition from coal power is lacking short-term alternatives to provide the system the kind of flexibility traditionally borne by coal-fired power plants. Long-distance renewable energy transmission is much needed since China's renewable energy and load centers are located far apart. Reform of the electricity market needs to be accelerated to achieve optimal resource allocation for power production, transmission and consumption.

To meet all these challenges and construct a new power system suitable for China's national situation, the focus needs to be on the following four key areas: Ensuring sustainable development of renewable energy, clarifying the pace of the coal power transition, keeping the grid planning and system dispatch operation up to date and enabling elasticity on the demand side.

Although the levelized cost of energy of wind and solar power has been reduced dramatically, renewable energy developers still have concerns about future investment because of the uncertainty of cost recovery caused by the removal of government subsidies. Thus, long-term contracts or auction mechanisms are needed to provide certainty for investment in renewables. Besides, government incentive measures are still needed for certain promising renewable technologies that are not yet cost-effective at their early stage, such as offshore wind power and solar thermal power.

Since offshore wind power is closer to the major load centers in the eastern region of China, it should be the next major renewable technology to be focused on with favorable policies and incentives.

The alarming power crunch in 2021 underlines the fact that when phrasing out coal to ensure climate security, it is equally important to secure a reliable supply of power. To support system flexibility, a certain portfolio of coal power plants will continue to play the role in providing such needs, and diversified energy storage technologies have to be developed at scale to provide daily and seasonal system flexibility before coal power is phased out at scale. Also, carbon capture, utilization and storage should play an important role in keeping a small fleet of coal power plants in service to guarantee system flexibility and reserve capacity.

China's grid companies have already adopted the most advanced technologies. Still, to significantly increase the proportion of renewable energy in the country's power generation mix, grid planning and operation have to be further improved in a way that can meet the changing dynamics. Economic power dispatching based on market signals should ultimately be the norm for system operation. Also, the sustainability of the existing pattern of large-scale west-to-east renewable energy transmission needs to be reconsidered. One alternative could be to develop large scale offshore wind power as well as distributed renewables that are much closer to the load centers to avoid the costly long-distance energy transmission.

Also, a low-carbon, high-efficiency power system can only be achieved if the demand side is participating in the power balancing.

A variety of technical solutions including micro-grids, virtual power plants, and other things need to be developed on an economic scale to make the demand side controllable, so it can be adjusted by the grid operator for real-time power balancing.

The steps for power market reform are expected to focus on establishing real-time price signals to prompt electricity users to adjust their power usage and to enable buyers to be able to purchase green power under longer term contracts which will help accommodate the price premium.

In conclusion, despite the strong willingness and diverse practices, there is still a lack of an industry-wide consensus on a comprehensive response strategy to the challenges before the decarbonization of China's power system can be realized. Therefore, there is an urgent need to bring together decision-makers, top industry experts, and policy designers to explore the concepts, promote the best practices, and jointly plan the road map for China's new power system with renewables as the mainstay.

February 9, 2022 China Daily global edition

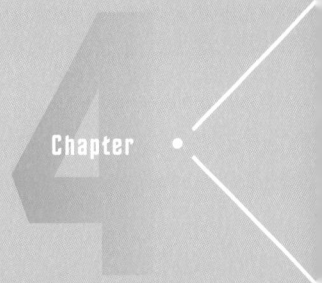

Multilateral Cooperation

No Border for the Exploration of Low Carbon
and Green Development

Ⅰ Advocating Dialogue: One World, One Family

China steps up to the plate

By NICHOLAS STERN and ZOU JI

The world has reached a critical moment in history. As we recover from the COVID-19 pandemic, we have an opportunity to create a safer and more prosperous world by pursuing a new model of sustainable, inclusive and resilient economic development and growth.

This new form of growth offers the chance to make the global economy cleaner and more efficient based on strong investments and innovation. It will allow us to effectively tackle the global threats of climate change, biodiversity loss and environmental degradation.

We will be able to create new jobs and new markets for products and services as we develop and deploy the technologies of the future. Critically we will be able to transform our energy systems away from wasteful and polluting forms of generation and consumption that are based on fossil fuels.

Instead we can power our economies with alternatives that do not damage lives and livelihoods through climate change and air pollution.

The World Health Organization estimates that more than 7 million people die each year worldwide from local air pollution, mostly due to the burning of biomass and fossil fuels. Many rapidly growing cities of developing and emerging market countries are suffering severe social and economic harm because workers and their families become sick or die from breathing dirty air.

In August 2021, the Intergovernmental Panel on Climate Change published its latest assessment of the science of climate change, and concluded that rising levels of carbon dioxide and other greenhouse gases in the atmosphere are now affecting every part of the world, particularly by making many extreme weather events more frequent and intense.

In 2021 summer we have witnessed heatwaves, flooding and wildfires across the world that have been made more severe by a rise in global temperature of just 1 C. The lives and livelihoods of millions of people are being damaged and destroyed. No country is too rich to be affected, but we also know that the poorest people are least able to protect themselves from these impacts.

The United Kingdom has set the goal of keeping within reach the goal of limiting the rise in temperature by the end of this century to no more than 1.5 C. As the IPCC has pointed out, beyond this level of warming there are dangerously rising risks of potentially catastrophic impacts, such as destabilization of the polar ice sheets and profound disruption of both river flows from the Himalayas and of the monsoon season.

To have a reasonable chance of limiting warming to a rise of 1.5 C, global emissions of carbon dioxide, the main greenhouse gas, will need to be eliminated by the middle of this century. Many countries have now committed to a target of net zero emissions where the amount of greenhouse gases added to the atmosphere each year is reduced to the same level as the amount removed annually through planting more trees and vegetation or technologies such as direct air capture.

The success of COP 26 is not guaranteed. The developed countries have not yet honored their commitment to mobilize $100 billion annually from public and private sources to support climate action by the developing countries. The developed countries must demonstrate that they have kept their promise ahead of COP 26 and should lay out plans to increase financial support in subsequent years. They could, for instance, commit to providing $60 billion from bilateral sources and $90 billion from multilateral sources each year by 2025.

But the new pledges for emissions cuts by 2030 that have been submitted ahead of COP 26 are collectively too weak and only consistent with a pathway to a potentially catastrophic warming of 2.7 C by the end of the century, according to the United Nations.

China is already showing global leadership on climate change. President Xi Jinping made a truly historic announcement in September 2020 at the UN that China will achieve carbon neutrality before 2060. Similarly, it was extremely significant that President Xi declared at the UN General Assembly recently that China will end all financial support for new coal power plants overseas.

China can also show other countries how a large economy can be transformed by moving away from fossil fuels. Although it remains heavily dependent on coal for its energy, it is rapidly developing alternative sources of energy, such as renewables, and investing strongly in forms of transport such as electric vehicles that rely on clean power. As it makes that transformation, China will also benefit in the medium term from a diversification of energy sources, which will make market crises less likely.

President Xi has also indicated that China will control the development of its domestic coal power, and will strictly regulate projects that result in both high energy consumption and high carbon emissions. As the costs of new technologies fall and the leading group on carbon peaking and carbon neutrality increases coordinated action across government, the transition to sustainable growth should accelerate.

If China is able to bring forward the peaking of its carbon dioxide emissions from 2030 by accelerating the transition to a strong, sustainable and resilient economy during the 14th Five-Year Plan period (2021-2025), it will help to make the whole world a more prosperous and peaceful place.

October 13, 2021 China Daily global edition

Paradigm shift

By DONALD RAMOTAR

Addressing the climate crisis requires a fundamental change to the way we do business not just technological Band Aids

Climate Change is so important that it can spell the end of life as we know it on Earth and therefore demands immediate action, not just talk.

This is already a real tragedy. I say this because we have been warned about this situation for decades. Since the late 1960s and early 1970s scientists have been warning us about the terrible dangers that would befall us if we did not change our relations with nature.

The world leaders have met on many occasions. Since 1995, the United Nations has convened 25 such conferences, the year of 2021 is the 26th. At all of these conferences commitments were made but not kept or only partially kept. Despite the many convincing speeches that were made in the past, despite a full understanding of the cause of the problem and the cure, the situation continues to get worse.

This is manifested in the increasing frequency and intensity of natural disasters. It breaks the heart to see how much suffering is caused by these phenomena.

The cause is fundamentally due to human economic activities and the pursuit of wealth that is unsustainable. This has resulted in serious damage to the world's ecology. Carbon stored in forests, the oceans and in the earth is being released as we overexploit the resources of the world.

Added to this is industrialization that has pumped millions of tons of toxic gases into the atmosphere.

The cure is also clear. We have to preserve and protect nature so that the Earth can sustain our activities. We must live more harmoniously with nature. We have to understand nature's laws and co-exist with them.

We may well ask why has mankind failed to arrest the situation seeing that we know the causes and the cure.

In my view, it is because we have been putting forward only technological solutions to deal with the problem. We have heard talk and we have seen the implementation of new technologies, solar power, wind power, thermal power, nuclear power and much more to generate energy. That is indispensable to our existence for we do need clean nonpolluting energy generation.

Scientists have also built cars and other motor vehicles that are not polluting the atmosphere.

But despite all of these marvelous technological advances the situation is deteriorating at a rapid pace. Indeed this conference that is being held in Scotland will call for bringing forward the time frame for countries to arrive at net-zero emissions.

What is abundantly clear is that the technological approach, important as it is, is not the solution on its own. Never before in our history have we had at our disposal so much fantastic technology. Yet our world is in a worse condition environmentally than it has ever been.

That is not to downplay the importance of technological solutions. They are vital. But they do not address the main problem.

The main issue is the socioeconomic relations that dominate our world. It is fundamentally a system controlled by very powerful corporations whose main objective is the maximization of profits. They always pay lip service to environmental issues, but as soon as they think that it will affect their bottom line, environmental issues are promptly ignored. This is the nature of the system that dominates and controls the world.

More than 100 years ago, J.P. Dunning wrote: "Capital is said to fly turbulence and strife and to be timid, which is very true; but this is very incompletely stating the question. Capital eschews no profit or very small profit, just as nature was formerly said to abhor a vacuum. With adequate profit, capital is very bold. A certain 10 percent will ensure its employment anywhere; 20 percent certain will produce eagerness; 50 percent, positive audacity; 100 percent will make it ready to trample on all human laws; 300 percent, and there is not a crime at which it will scruple, nor a risk it will not run even to the chance of its owner being hanged. If turbulence and strife will bring a profit, it will freely encourage both."

We also know from our own experience that this is true. For instance we can recall the case of the US vs. Reynolds Tobacco, Lorillard and Phillis Morris. The tobacco companies knew that cigarettes were the main cause of some types of cancers, lung and stomach. Yet they lied about it and aggressively marketed them. The profit they were making was so huge that they hired the best lawyers to be their lobbyists. No lives mattered to them.

We also know that the oil companies were aware of the danger to the Earth that their extracting oil was creating. It is among the main reasons for climate change. They knew this more than 40 years ago. Instead of trying to correct it and to look for solutions, they have spent billions to discredit the findings of the scientists who first raised the alarm. They spend billions on lobbyists and have invested heavily in political parties by financing election campaigns. Even now they are investing heavily in more extensive exploration and exploitation of hydrocarbon resources. This means that they have no intention to observe any restraint.

Clearly therefore for these huge profit-making organizations nothing is more important than making money. Human lives mean nothing to them. The Mighty Sparrow's 1970s Calypso hit Capitalism Gone Mad is playing out before our very eyes.

Therefore we have a fundamental contradiction. The drive for profits is pushing the corporations to disregard the environment; to overexploit the world's resources. On the other hand to slow down and reverse climate change we have to think and act more to conserve and preserve nature. This environmental crisis is telling us that the international economic system that we have been operating under has outlived its usefulness and, for the sake of life on the Earth, must be changed.

Without doubt the conference in Scotland is useful but it will not deliver the solution. This calls for mass action and a demand for an economic paradigm shift. The author is former president of the Cooperative Republic of Guyana and former general secretary of the People's Progressive Party.

November 8, 2021 China Daily global edition

Green Empowerment

By ERIK SOLHEIM

Proficiency China has demonstrated in its fight against the novel coronavirus can be leveraged to lead the way in addressing the climate challenge

It is said that there are decades where nothing happens, and there are weeks where decades happen.

One important lesson from history is that sometimes development is very slow until it becomes extremely fast. I believe that is where we now stand on the environment. After a long period of sluggish progress, in the years of COVID-19 decades happened. When President Xi Jinping announced at the United Nations General Assembly in September 2020 that China will strive to peak carbon emissions before 2030 and achieve carbon neutrality before 2060, a green shock wave passed through the international system.

We are a much bolder world fighting for the environment on our way out of the pandemic. Within a month after China's decision, then President Moon Jae-in of the Republic of Korea and Prime Minister Yoshihide Suga of Japan announced carbon neutral goals for their countries. Joe Biden drives an ambitious climate program even if he struggles to get laws passed in Congress. In the European Union, member countries are working on the Green New Deal and a green taxonomy, an amazing ambition to put green development center stage in European integration. In India, Prime Minister Narendra Modi is scrapping one planned coal plant after another, and taking his nation into the global lead on solar energy and green hydrogen.

Green is gold. In order to help establish a global low carbon economy and a beautiful China, China should embrace this concept, first launched by President Xi when he was Party chief in Zhejiang province. Fighting against climate change and protecting nature is not a cost to humanity, but a great opportunity for creating jobs, bringing prosperity and improving living conditions. It is a win-win-win policy, good for the environment, the economy and jobs, and social lives. Interestingly, Biden has presented his climate program with a focus on all the benefits for US citizens. The US and China are on the same wavelength: Climate change is an opportunity to embrace as well as a problem to solve.

Indeed China's special envoy for climate change Xie Zhenhua and the American envoy John Kerry met many times last year and were instrumental in finalizing the US-China Joint Glasgow Declaration on Enhancing Climate Action in the 2020s, which was announced at COP26. They have shown ways to reduce geopolitical tensions which should be embraced in other areas as well.

What drives the global environment agenda today is the political economy, not UN climate talks. The price of solar energy has decreased 90 percent in a decade, the price of wind 60 percent and electric batteries 85 percent. China is an immensely innovative nation. The sheer size of the Chinese economy makes every innovation cheaper, because it can produce for so many customers. Also globally, we see private business running ahead of politicians in many other countries. It's all about innovation and scale.

Western companies have made strong commitments to the Green Agenda. American Microsoft promises to go carbon neutral by 2030, to even compensate for all emissions in the company's history. Swedish Ikea has an amazing strategy for the circular economy.

In China, there is the same trend. Companies such as Tencent, Alibaba and Huawei are rapidly moving into the Green Agenda. Huawei helps solar plants become more effective and uses its amazing AI to protect nature. CATL has over a few years grown to become the world's biggest electric battery company, far ahead of any rival. This needs to be accelerated and expanded.

Time is up for the "pollute first, clean up later" development model.

China's response to the novel coronavirus outbreak has been the most effective in the world. Other East Asian nations including the ROK, Vietnam and Singapore have delivered similar impressive performances.

The same competence China has shown in its fight against COVID-19 can be leveraged to address the greatest challenge of the 21st century: protecting Mother Earth. The Ministry of Ecology and Environment has started to promote legislation to ensure China will peak its carbon emissions fast, setting targets for provinces, cities and businesses. Four Chinese ministries have issued brilliant guidelines for making sure Belt and Road becomes a vehicle for green development. These are goal-oriented strategies focusing on accountability and measurement. The People's Bank of China is working on green standards for finance as well as guidelines for banks and financial institutions to disclose environment-related information. The low-carbon green strategy was integrated in every aspect of the 14th Five-Year Plan (2021-2025) whereby provinces, cities and businesses will be required to set their own targets. If China's emissions are to peak before 2030, front runner provinces and cities will need to peak fast.

For the vast majority of people in every country, going green is positive. It brings jobs, better social practices and reduces pollution. Still, some people will be left vulnerable during the transition. In China, the transition may be easier for Guangdong and Jiangsu provinces than for Liaoning or Shanxi provinces, if only because of their different economic structures. The transformation may be easier for people in hightech cities such as Shenzhen or Suzhou than in the heavy industrial parts of northern China. The transition needs to be fair. Europe and North America are facing a mirror challenge. It may be helpful to exchange best practice.

Social fairness is vitally important because it will make the transition easier. The more people on board, the fewer obstacles and less pushback there will be. I was impressed when visiting Didi, the Chinese car-hailing company, when they told me they have programs for employing former coal workers. Such initiatives will ensure a fair and social transition.

Finally and most importantly, China should take upon itself to help lead the world. Through cooperation with the US, Europe and other countries, China can share its unique ideas and experience, such as the huge progress fighting against air pollution in cities, the desert greening endeavor in Northwestern China, the fishing bans of the Yangtze, the new national park program or green developments in cities like Hangzhou or Guangzhou. China can be a global green leader by showing the world that a green recovery from the pandemic is possible.

No one has the full answer as to what we should do. We would be wise to follow the advice given by former Chinese leader Deng Xiaoping: Cross the river by feeling the stones.

Led by that pragmatism we will in 2060 look back on a similar success of China protecting Mother Earth as we have seen in China lifting hundreds of millions out of poverty over the last decades.

December 29, 2020 China Daily global edition

Ⅱ Paths to Achieving Carbon Neutrality

Cleaner city leader

By NICHOLAS STERN and QI YE

China could demonstrate international leadership in the collective fight against global threats by focusing on sustainable urban development

Having done a good job in controlling the novel coronavirus and restarting its economy last year, China is leading the world's economic recovery, and it now has a critical opportunity to demonstrate to the rest of the world how to make the transition to sustainable and resilient growth, particularly in its cities.

New figures show that China's economy grew by 2.3 percent in 2020. Although this was sharply down on the growth rates over the past few years, it is a better performance than the contractions recorded by many other countries, including the advanced economies. In particular, China's GDP increased by 6.5 percent in the last quarter of 2020, higher than the annual growth rate in 2019.

The flip side of China's rapid economic recovery in 2020 was the continued rise in its carbon dioxide emissions, as its consumption of coal increased by 0.6 percent last year, oil by 3.3 percent and natural gas by 7.2 percent.

It is a reminder of the challenge that China still faces to realize President Xi Jinping's vision of an ecological civilization.

China's growth in recent decades has helped to lift hundreds of millions of people out of poverty and improved living standards across the country. This economic miracle has mainly been powered by the growth of its cities, with many workers migrating from rural to urban areas.

But much of this urban development has created pollution, waste and inefficiency. The 14th Five-Year Plan (2021-2025), which has been adopted at the just—concluded session of the National People's Congress, offers a chance for China and its cities to move toward higher—quality growth, with sustainable urban development at its center.

Many of China's cities, particularly those along its coastline, have become sprawling metropolises, as local authorities have attempted to generate revenues, including from land sales, by encouraging rapid outward development.

But this has been at the expense of the destruction of arable land, natural ecosystems and biodiversity in the surrounding rural areas. It has also locked in inefficiencies and pollution with longer commuting times for many workers, and higher consumption of energy and fossil fuels.

As recent studies by the Coalition for Urban Transitions have outlined, China has much to gain if its future growth is focused on clean, compact and connected cities where it is easier to move, breathe and work productively.

Such a new paradigm of urban development is urgently needed in China as it moves away from massive investment in high-carbon sectors. Stronger spatial planning policies and improvements in the energy, buildings, materials and transport sectors would support this.

Some of China's cities are already embracing a more sustainable model for development, driven by cleaner energy, more efficient use of resources, and innovation in technology, finance and policy.

Shenzhen, for instance, has embraced low-carbon development, focusing on the greening of its industries. It has been continuously improving its economic quality, with innovation and industrial modernization at the core, rather than narrowly focusing on the pace of growth. For almost 10 years, it has been operating a trading system for greenhouse gas emissions, and it plans to peak emissions by 2022.

Sustainable urban development has boosted Shenzhen's competitiveness domestically and internationally. It provides important lessons for other cities in China.

China's huge and growing urban population, as well as its leading role in promoting green finance, means that it will likely play a particularly important role in pushing forward sustainable urban development across the world, including in the countries participating in the Belt and Road Initiative.

Sustainable urban development will be crucial to the achievement of President Xi's historic pledge, announced at the United Nations in September 2020, that China will strive to achieve carbon neutrality before 2060.

Given the aim of peaking national emissions of carbon dioxide before 2030, China will be attempting a transition over 30 years that other countries are planning to achieve over a significantly longer period.

For instance, the United Kingdom's territorial emissions of carbon dioxide peaked in 1972, and it plans to reduce its output of all greenhouse gases to net zero by 2050.

If China were to accelerate sustainable urban development across the country during the 14th Five-Year Plan, it would reinvigorate growth and put itself more firmly on the path to an ecological civilization.

It would mean, for instance, that many of its cities could peak their emissions before 2025, allowing the country as a whole to reach the milestone of peaking by 2025, and putting the 2060 target for carbon neutrality more firmly in reach.

If China's updated nationally determined contributions to the Paris Agreement includes a commitment to peak emissions by 2025, it would place pressure on the Biden administration to respond with a significantly more ambitious pledge by the United States.

Joint leadership by the world's two largest emitters of greenhouse gases is needed now more than ever.

And we have seen the growing cost of climate change impacts, which includes wildfires, flooding and storms, over the past 12 months, with 2020 ranking as the warmest year on record in both Europe and Asia.

Most of all, sustainable urban development would demonstrate how the world could benefit from China's international leadership in the collective fight against global threats including infectious diseases, biodiversity loss and climate change.

March 15, 2021 China Daily global edition

Key to reduce emissions

By JEFF HUANG

In March 2022, Hong Kong's first carbon futures exchange-traded fund was introduced. The ETF tracks the ICE EUA Carbon Futures Index, which measures the performance of a long-only basket of European Union Carbon Emission Allowances futures contracts.

In China, the accumulated trading volume of China Emission Allowances issued by the Ministry of Ecology and Environment to over 2,200 power generation companies nationwide under the National Emissions Trading Scheme, has reached 189 million metric tons from August 2021 to April 2022, valued at 8.2 billion yuan ($1.3 billion).

The emissions trading systems of the European Union and California indicate that regulated carbon trading in the over the counter (OTC) derivatives market and on-exchange futures market plays a crucial role in maintaining a functioning cap-and-trade system. Companies use these regulated markets to hedge their forward price exposure. In 2021, for instance, 18 billion tons of carbon allowances were traded on the Intercontinental Exchange, equivalent to an estimated $1 trillion in notional value. These allowances included 15.2 billion units from the EU, 2.4 billion from California, 255 million from the United Kingdom and 346 million of Regional Greenhouse Gas Initiative allowances.

In Europe and California, power companies acquired a toolset for trading and risk management in deregulated power markets. Years later, they applied the same toolset to carbon trading. In contrast, Chinese power companies have to explore both simultaneously. The Chinese energy spot markets have already developed price volatility. So will allowance prices, as expected, due to the incrementally tightening allowance allocation and gradual phase-out of free allocation for companies in the power sector. Although the wind and solar generation enterprises are trying to capture trading opportunities in the spot markets and offload their risks to financial institutions, building a robust risk culture with adequate human capital and protocols remains a big challenge. However, it also represents an opportunity to gain a competitive edge.

Take Shanxi province for example. The deregulated provincial wholesale power market just crossed into the second year of continuous spot trading. About 40 percent of the power consumed in Shanxi now is from renewable wind and solar sources. However, over the whole year of 2021, the spot settlement prices for renewable energy units have consistently been lower than the average provincial market prices.

To help power companies in Shanxi to close the skill gap in trading and risk management, the Carbon and Power Trading Lab was established by AEX Holdings and four Chinese partners with the aim of running a comprehensive OTC trading simulation that helps coal and renewable generators as well as electricity retailers to experience full-cycle OTC trading and risk management.

Institution participation is the key to the efficient pricing of commodity futures. Carbon futures and power futures are no exception. Here, open interest from multiyears forward contracts listed on futures exchanges are a good indicator. In China, total open interest from the five futures exchanges stands at 29.9 million contracts at the end of July 2021. This is only 2.7 percent of the global total of 1.1 billion contracts. In contrast, China's GDP is about 17 percent of the global total. Meanwhile, of the 90 futures listed on exchanges, few have forward price curves that go beyond 12 months.

The bottom line is: the exchanges need a new playbook and focuses on growing liquidity in longer-dated contracts beyond 12 months to attract more participants right from the start. The same is true for carbon and power futures contracts. Adequate participation in the price discovery process from institutions should be a defining feature of commodity "Trading 2.0" in China.

Over the past three decades, commodities futures trading has made significant progress. The National People's Congress, China's top legislature, just passed the Futures and Derivatives Law, commodities futures trading has entered a new phase. Over the past several years, OTC carbon allowance forwards trading was attempted in a handful of provincial ETS pilot markets. Trading liquidity did not emerge. The Futures and Derivatives Law, for the first time, promulgates a basic OTC derivatives trading regulatory framework that opens the door to new bottom-up initiatives, such as the Shanxi lab.

Efficient ETS carbon pricing in Europe and the US has presented a strong case for neutral, transparent and competitive futures exchange operators. Codification in the new Futures and Derivatives Law of the legacy practice of regulators appointing exchange leadership is anachronistic at best. Commodity "Trading 2.0" needs to rise up to meet the challenge of pricing carbon and power efficiently in the fight against climate change.

In 2008, the Chicago Climate Exchange came to Tianjin to explore implementing a carbon cap and trade system in China. Today, Chinese power companies and financial players are better served by adopting best practices to achieve efficient carbon pricing that guides the nation's energy transition toward the 2030 carbon peak and beyond.

April 22, 2022 China Daily global edition

Good business

By DEBORAH LEHR

Development and commercialization of green technologies has become a priority for both financial institutions and companies

We are facing a moment that only comes once in a generation. Another technology boom, but this time one driven by climate change.

Entrepreneurs, companies and governments are coming together to seek innovative ways to help the world transition to carbon neutrality.

The political will to address the challenge is growing. China has joined the European Union as a leader in green finance, and we are now seeing others follow: the Middle East, Latin America and Africa. Here in the United States, President Joe Biden has made climate an all-of-government affair.

Government policies, good governance and regulatory enforcement structures are all important components of the political will necessary for developing a successful green finance framework to support the transition to carbon neutrality. But as we all know too well, that is not enough-we also need to mobilize private capital.

And the good news is, this is happening. Green finance has moved from being a philanthropic activity into the mainstream for business.

The novel coronavirus outbreak and increasingly visual climate-related disasters have demonstrated the importance of long-term resilience. Financial institutions have realized the great threat that climate risks pose to financial stability.

Leading investment banks, hedge funds and other financial institutions around the world have made the green transition a growing priority and are using the power of their platforms to be advocates.

In short, climate change is now good business. According to Bloomberg NEF, a record $501 billion was pumped into the energy transition in 2020.

In addition to the priority that companies are placing on their own transition to net-zero emissions, we're seeing investment opportunities on a scale not seen since the technology boom in the 1990s.

Climate investing is no longer just about renewables and infrastructure. It is also going mainstream. The prime example is Tesla. Its stock surged 740 percent in 2020 and its market cap is now larger than that of General Motors.

China is going to be at the heart of this climate business boom. Not only because the scale of its emissions creates opportunity but also because it is becoming a leader in innovative green finance as well as clean tech.

Take, for example, the business of environmental goods and services, which China has started to open further to foreign companies. In a recent study, Goldman Sachs estimated that there is a $16-trillion opportunity in this sector and China could create up to 40 million jobs by 2060. That's good business.

The development and commercialization of new climate technologies is essential for us to reach carbon neutrality. It's in all of our interests to support deployment of these technologies. Yet, at the same time, we have to ensure that the climate business does not turn into a climate clash. Already we see competition in new energy vehicles, solar panels and lithium-ion batteries. Healthy competition is good because it drives down costs. But competition that leads to restricting technologies for reasons other than national security is not in anyone's interest.

There is increased demand on the client side as well. Assets in sustainable funds hit a record $1.65 trillion at the end of last year, up 29 percent from the previous quarter.

TPG, for example, a major US private equity company, is launching a global climate fund to invest in technologies and solutions that could help build green equity to balance the huge growth that we're seeing in green bonds.

The world's largest asset managers such as BlackRock have identified sustainability as a key priority and are pushing the companies they own to increase climate disclosures and using the platform of their own money to encourage change.

This is a wave that can't be turned back.

The launch of China's carbon exchange, planned for the end of June 2021, will also create new opportunities. When it launches, with just one industry, the power sector, it will cover not only about 45 percent of China's own carbon emissions, but 14 percent of global emissions. When the eight other industries, such as cement and electrolytic aluminum, are added to the exchange, it could potentially cover up to 30 percent of global emissions.

Carbon could become the new currency with China creating the terms, the standards and the pricing.

It is important, therefore, to continue discussions so that we can understand where some of the flashpoints might show up and hopefully find the right framework for dealing with the inevitable differences that will arise.

June 7, 2021 China Daily global edition

Ⅲ Collaborating for a Green Future

Out of dire straits

By JEFFREY SACHS

China and the US signal crucial cooperation to address the climate crisis

The agreement between China and the United States to cooperate on climate change is a very welcome development. We should recall how China-US cooperation was pivotal to the successful global negotiation of the Paris Agreement in 2015. Now, such cooperation is vital to the successful implementation of the Paris Agreement.

The climate situation is more dire than in 2015. The climate dangers continue to mount and accelerate. The Earth's average temperature has been rising by around 0.2 C per decade, but in the recent 10 to 20 years, by an even higher rate, perhaps up to 0.3 C per decade. The Earth is currently 1.2 C warmer than the pre-industrial average temperature, and could exceed the 1.5 C threshold within a few years.

The need for global action is urgent. Fortunately, most of the major economies of the world now recognize that essential fact. China, the European Union, Japan, the Republic of Korea, the US, and others, have all recently committed to reach net-zero emissions of greenhouse gases by around mid-century. China's commitment is to do so before 2060 at the latest.

I believe that the major countries will soon agree that the entire world can and should reach net-zero emissions even faster, by 2050 at the latest. There are two reasons why the agreed timeline to net-zero emissions is likely to be moved forward. The first is that the climate threats are even more dangerous than widely believed. The second is that the technological options to reach net-zero emissions are even better than widely realized.

Climate-related disasters are occurring in many forms. Hurricanes, droughts, floods, heat waves and forest fires are all becoming more intense and dangerous. Ominously, the sea level could rise by several meters as a result of the partial disintegration of the ice sheets of Antarctica and Greenland. Such a massive sea level rise would be utterly devastating to coastal societies around the world.

At the same time, the ability to reach net-zero greenhouse gases emissions is also easier than has been supposed until recently. Technological advances will enable the world to shift decisively from fossil fuels to zero-carbon energy by mid-century, and at very modest cost as a share of national income. The key is for all of the major economies to work out a clear transition pathway to zero-carbon energy.

The key to worldwide decarbonization lies in six main steps. First, all new power generation should be based on zero-carbon sources: solar, wind, hydro, nuclear, geothermal and others, and fossil-fuel-based power generation should be phased out. Second, transport should be electrified, with battery electric vehicles replacing those with internal combustion engines. Third, buildings should utilize electricity rather than fossil fuels for purposes of heating and cooking. Fourth, zero-carbon electricity should be used to produce other green fuels, such as hydrogen, for use in industry. Fifth, digital technologies such as smart grids should be deployed to conserve energy. Sixth, diets should shift toward more plant proteins and less animal proteins, for better health and to reduce the pressure on the environment.

One of the most important parts of the new agreement is the joint commitment of China and the US to "develop by COP 26 in Glasgow their respective long-term strategies aimed at net zero greenhouse gases emissions". Under the Paris Climate Agreement, countries are to submit "long-term" strategies, which are distinct from the shorter-term Nationally Determined Contributions, and should show their pathway all the way to net zero emissions.

When the Chinese and US governments work out their respective long-term strategies in the coming months, they will very likely reach two main conclusions. First, reaching net-zero emissions from the power sector will be easier than they currently expect. Second, the transition can also happen faster than they currently expect. China has committed to reach net zero by 2060. I believe that on close analysis, China's specialists will find that net zero by 2050 is both achievable and advantageous for China and for the world.

China is very well placed to make a rapid transformation to net zero, because it has strong technological and manufacturing capacities in all of the most vital areas: advanced photovoltaics, wind turbines, hydroelectric power, long-distance high-voltage transmission grids, 5G broadband, artificial intelligence systems, electric vehicles, advanced batteries, among other technologies. Moreover, under its 14th Five-Year Plan (2021-2025), China has committed added resources to technological advances in key areas, which will enable it to excel in low-cost rapid decarbonization.

Of course both China and the US face domestic challenges in shifting their respective coal-dependent regions and workforces to the advanced zero-carbon economy. Yet there is no country in the world with more experience and success than China in rapid structural changes that also support inclusive development. After all, China successfully reduced the rate of extreme poverty from 80 percent to zero between 1980 and 2020 in the midst of dramatic structural changes in urbanization and the labor market.

I am also gratified that the agreement signals the intention of the two countries to work together to support a successful COP 15 of the Convention on Biological Diversity (CBD) that China will host in Kunming in October 2021. The US is not yet a signatory to the CBD. I hope that President Joe Biden will submit the CBD to the US Senate for ratification so that the US can become a full member of the treaty. Sustainable land use under the Convention on Biological Diversity is not only vital to the protection of biodiversity, but also essential to reaching net-zero emissions. Unsustainable land practices are a major contributor to greenhouse gas emissions.

The shared commitment of China and the US to addressing the climate crisis should be a harbinger of active cooperation in many other areas. Both countries, and the entire world, have much to gain from cooperation, and much to lose from hostility. When China and the US work together, and bring in the rest of the world as partners, the benefits can be truly historic.

April 21, 2021 China Daily global edition

Three for all

By WOLFGANG RÖHR

China, the European Union (EU) and the United States was the most important participants at the United Nations Climate Change Conference (COP 26), for a simple reason: Together, they are responsible for over 50 percent of global greenhouse gas emissions. Currently, China contributes 28 percent of global greenhouse gas emissions, the US 15 percent and the EU 8 percent. Historically, however, a different picture emerges. Over time, the US has contributed 29 percent to all man-made greenhouse gases in the atmosphere, the EU 22 percent and China just 13 percent.

All three have set themselves ambitious emissions reduction goals for the next decade and beyond. In his address to the 2020 UN General Assembly, President Xi Jinping announced that China will peak of greenhouse gas emissions before 2030 and that it will become carbon neutral before 2060. The Joe Biden administration has pledged that the US will reduce its emissions by 50 percent by 2030 and become carbon neutral by 2050. The EU has pledged a reduction of 55 percent by 2030 and to also become carbon neutral by 2050.

Over the past years, China has seen a spectacular development of its low carbon technology. Today, 45 percent of all wind turbines and 72 percent of all solar panels worldwide are produced in China. But while China is clearly a world leader in renewable energy, it is still dependent on coal. In his address to the 2021 UN General Assembly, President Xi stated that China will not build new coal-fired power projects abroad. That is a significant development. Yet the importance of coal within China is considerable. In 2020, China commissioned more than three times as much power from coal than the rest of the world combined. As the concept of "ecological civilization" is enshrined in China's Constitution and has just again been stressed by President Xi in his address at the UN Biodiversity Conference in Kunming, it is to be hoped that the country can be weaned off coal.

The Donald Trump administration left the Paris Agreement, thus putting the sincerity of the US commitment to the fight against climate change in doubt. The Biden administration was quick to reverse that decision and announce ambitious undertakings. The problem with the US is that climate policy is a deeply partisan issue, with Democrats favoring ambitious goals and Republicans much more reluctant to subscribe to deep cuts in greenhouse gas emissions. With the midterm elections just a year away and the next presidential election in 2024, it is difficult to foresee the trajectory of US climate policy over the next decades. That, however, is a requirement if other countries are to be induced to make and implement major commitments.

The EU has been fairly consistent in its climate policy. Its 2021 Climate Law even makes adhering to its targets a legal obligation. The EU's problem, however, is—as so often—the divergence in the views of its 27 member states. While some countries, such as Germany, favor even more ambitious cuts, other countries, in particular those in Central Europe, are more cautious. And whereas Germany regards nuclear power as outdated and plans to switch off all its remaining nuclear reactors by 2022, French President Emmanuel Macron has announced a new policy under which France, now generating 70 percent of its electricity from its more than 50 nuclear reactors, may add a large number of small modular reactors over the coming years.

The EU and China have long established some degree of cooperation on climate issues. From the 2005 Joint Declaration on Climate Change to the 2018 Leaders' Statement on Climate Change and Clean Energy, there is a good basis on which further cooperation can be built. Collaboration between the US and China can be advanced with the Joint Statement Addressing the Climate Crisis released in spring 2021 as a starting point. The EU and the US also issued a joint statement in

2021 in which both sides committed to greater cooperation to counter the climate crisis.

Such cooperation will be necessary to tackle a number of contentious issues. One of them is the carbon border adjustment mechanism that the EU wants to introduce to stop "carbon leakage". It would essentially be a new tax on goods imported into the EU from countries with less stringent regulations on limiting greenhouse gases. China has already made clear that it does not favor the introduction of new instruments that could hinder trade, and the US, too, is less than enthusiastic.

Yet still larger challenges loom. The World Energy Outlook, released by the International Energy Agency, shows that global energy-related emissions, after a short fall due to the COVID-19 pandemic, will rise in 2021, and it will in absolute terms be the largest increase since 2010. Even if all announced pledges by governments were to be implemented, the demand for natural gas and oil until 2030 would be much higher than required to move toward a net zero scenario. Governments therefore need to do a lot more to fully deliver on their announced pledges.

The lofty goal that the international community has set itself can only be achieved by even more stringent national contributions, strict adherence to these pledges, and close cooperation, in particular among the three major players on climate policy. That, in turn, requires teamwork across the board: One cannot expect fruitful cooperation on climate while rivalry or even hostility on other issues persists.

October 28, 2021 China Daily global edition

COP 26 finally shakes the trees

By HANS FRIEDERICH

Multispecies afforestation is an imperative need to reduce carbon dioxide and protect biodiversity

One of the main outcomes of the UN Climate Change Conference (COP 26) was the agreement to stop logging forests. The countries that have signed the pledge, including Brazil, Canada, China, the Democratic Republic of Congo, Indonesia, Russia and the United States, are home to around 85 percent of the world's forests.

This agreement is an important achievement as retaining these natural forests are critical for a number of reasons. Old-growth or primary forests provide many services to mankind, such as the provision of water and soil protection, acting as refuges for endangered plants and animals, as well as their critical carbon sequestration role.

Clearing natural forests to create plantations, as has happened in many countries, is a harmful practice, and hopefully the new COP 26 agreement will curb it. But where natural forests have been logged in the past, where the remaining forests are degraded or where land is being eroded, planting trees is an important way of restoring the essential natural processes.

The scientific advisory body to the Paris Accord, the Intergovernmental Panel on Climate Change, has recognized tree planting as a particularly effective way of reducing carbon dioxide. In light of this, many countries have embarked on afforestation drives.

Planting trees to create carbon sinks to offset current emissions is, however, not enough. Offsets should be the last resort to deal with residual emissions, after serious efforts have been taken to mitigate and reduce ongoing emissions. The intention to reach carbon-neutrality within the coming years is actually far from sufficient to support the aim of keeping global warming within 1.5 C, as this means little or no reduction has taken place and the ongoing emissions are simply balanced by offsets.

Critics of tree planting for carbon sequestration also point out that there are serious questions about the environmental value of such planted woodlots as they are often monoculture plantations. Scientific studies have shown that woodlots of one or two species are more vulnerable to pests and diseases than mixed forests, and monoculture forests also have lower biodiversity benefits than mixed forests.

The choice of species is another aspect that can raise concerns. The introduction of eucalyptus gum trees throughout the world has not been beneficial in all cases. Leaf-fall from the gum trees does not help soil fertility as the leaves are poisonous, and not many plants can be intercropped with eucalyptus for the same reason. Eucalyptus plantations therefore have limited benefits, apart from fuel wood and poles for construction and infrastructure.

There is often a question of local ownership of new plantations, and without local involvement, planted forests may not flourish. One of the key challenges to planting trees on common land is the maintenance of the plantation, as young trees can be eaten by browsing animals, or uprooted by trespassers, and they typically need irrigation during the first years of growth. There are many examples of well-intended afforestation projects that failed because the trees did not survive. Involvement of local people is critical for the establishment and survival of planted woodlots.

But, there is more to planting trees than CO2, as China has shown during its "Grain for Green" afforestation program that was launched in 1990. Grain for Green involved 124 million people in 1,897 counties in 25 provincial-level regions and by 2010, around 15 million hectares of farmland and 17 million hectares of barren mountainous wasteland were restored for natural vegetation.

Some of these forests have bamboo as the main species, and bamboo development is another area where China is leading the world. According to the National Forestry and Grassland Administration, China now has nearly 7 million hectares of bamboo, half of which was planted specifically for human and industrial use. Their fast growth, resilience to changing weather patterns, extensive root structure and the ability to flourish in soils that are not of much use for other crops, have created the foundation for a national economic sector in China that is worth the equivalent of $50 billion. The trade comprises food, furniture, construction and interior design materials, textiles, pulp and paper and other products made from bamboo and bamboo fiber.

It is important to consider reforestation and afforestation in a wider landscape context. Many modern land use systems are a patchwork of natural protection areas, agriculture developments and other rural development, including infrastructure and villages. Plantations can form an important component of such a diverse landscape, and a combination of different species in different sections of the area will contribute to the overall health of the environment.

Tree planting should not be restricted to the rural landscape alone. A lot of recent research has indicated that trees are good for well-being and health, and trees in cities provide shade and keep the streets cool.

During its recent urbanization programs, China introduced the concept of sponge cities, an approach that is now being followed in other countries too. This type of urban development involves the restoration or creation of wetlands and green spaces to help with drainage and water absorption during periods of heavy rain. This is critical, especially in low-lying cities, with the increase in extreme weather events as a result of climate change.

Trees can also be used to help restore brownfields and regenerate polluted land. Existing forests must be protected where possible, but degraded land must be restored and cleared areas reforested.

Not all trees are good for every situation though. We need to find the right trees for the right place and the right time. And whatever initiatives are promoted, the involvement of local people is critical to ensure a successful establishment of a healthy woodlot.

December 22, 2021 China Daily global edition

Casualties of change

By YANG LICHAO and ROBERT WALKER

Drought this year in China, floods in Pakistan and forest fires across Europe demonstrate the need for an immediate global response to climate change. Yet, as the next United Nations Climate Change Conference (COP 27) to be held in Sharm El-Sheikh, Egypt, in November draws ever closer, signs of progress are slight.

Indeed, with the disruption caused by the COVID-19 pandemic and the vast increase in the wholesale price of natural gas, the risks of regression-increasing carbon emissions by reinstating coal burning plants or opening new gas fields-are very real.

Such slippage is dangerous in that it creates a precedent for again prioritizing the short over the longer term, favoring this generation at the expense of future ones. Even if the slippage is only temporary, the transition will need to be more rapid-potentially more brutal-if targets for carbon reduction are to be met.

There is much talk of a just transition in the context of the need to rapidly respond to climate change. As the term is used by the International Labour Organization, a just transition focuses attention on the loss of carbon-dirty jobs necessary to reach zero-carbon emissions, and on the importance of meaningfully compensating those people and communities affected. This is important in reminding policymakers that change can create casualties and do long-term damage unless managed justly.

Many of the regions in Europe and North America where carbon-heavy industries closed over 40 years ago are still characterized today by multiple deprivation. In China, income losses affecting workers in State-owned enterprises are minimized by redeployment and relatively generous social security payments but the consequences for private sector employment are less clear.

However, issues of justice in the global transition to a low carbon economy do not arise only with respect to the individuals immediately affected. Distributional justice-who benefits and loses, and which people and organizations are encouraged or required to change their behavior-is clearly important. So is procedural justice-who participates in the decision-making and how-and recognition of power asymmetries and institutional discrimination and oppression.

COP 26, held in Glasgow, Scotland, in 2021, demonstrated procedural injustice at a global scale with industrial might silencing valid complaints of longstanding exploitation. The fossil-fuel lobby had 503 delegates-more than any country-while the largest non-plenary room had just 144 seats, less than the number of parties to the Paris Agreement on Climate Change. With aspirations to limit temperature rises to 1.5 C in the year 2100, the most optimistic estimates after Glasgow suggested a 1.8 C increase.

Wang Yi, senior advisor to the Chinese delegation of COP 26, observed that "if we are going to aim for 1.5 C instead of 2 C, there has to be an increase in funds available to make that happen".

Developed countries at COP 26 deferred on their promise of jointly investing $100 billion in supporting developing countries to mitigate and adapt to climate change. No less than 11 African countries currently spend more on climate adaptation than on health. Additionally, there was no agreement on establishing finance for loss and damage. The United States alone is estimated to have inflicted $1.9 trillion in damage on other countries from the effects of greenhouse gas emissions.

Away from the disappointments of Glasgow COP 26, President Xi Jinping proposed a Global Development Initiative before the General Debate of the 76th Session of the UN General Assembly. In doing so, he reminded world leaders that combating climate change is one element in a much broader global agenda focused on 17 sustainable development goals to be achieved as early as 2030.

He advocated a "new type of international relations based on mutual respect, equity, justice" to "accommodate common development and progress of all countries".And to help address the "huge funding gap", he said that China "will allocate more of its own development cooperation resources" to the GDI.

At the launch meeting of the Group of Friends of GDI in January 2022, Zhang Jun, the permanent representative of China to the United Nations, reemphasized the importance of development, suggesting that the eight priorities of the GDI were chosen to ensure the achievement of all 17 SDGs. Of the eight priorities, climate change, poverty alleviation and food security reflect the challenge of the green transition, while industrialization, the digital economy, and connectivity are the means of facilitating it.

Zhang further opined that the GDI, "with development as its priority and commitment to people-centered development, aims to protect and promote human rights through development".

Some Western skeptics question the coupling of human rights with development and find difficulty in appreciating the importance of common development and common prosperity. In the former case, they overlook the core principle of progressive realization: a state's compliance with its obligation to take appropriate measures is assessed in the light of the resources-financial and others-available to it. Development is a fundamental prerequisite for the full realization of human rights.

In the latter case, they ignore the principle of a just transition: the fair treatment and meaningful involvement of all people with respect to the development, implementation and enforcement of policies pertaining to transition. Policies that benefit shareholders but not workers or those laid off are patently unjust; so are those that further enrich developed countries at the expense of developing ones. If all in a community cannot benefit from a transition, the disbenefits should at least be minimized and fairly allocated.

Principles of justice differ from other kinds of moral concern in that they establish-or should establish-rightfully enforceable expectations or entitlements. In more affluent jurisdictions, therefore, polluters are liable to punishment while consumers of carbon fuels miss out on the subsidies available to users of green energy. It is less evident, though, that procedural justice is invariably enforced or that the least powerful do not bear a disproportionate share of the disbenefits of transition.

Lacking resources and access to technical expertise and investment, developing countries find transition difficult. Additionally burdened by debt to the developed world, just transition becomes almost impossible.

National obligations with respect to tackling climate change and facilitating transition are, as yet, unenforceable under the COP process and, thereby, arguably inherently unjust. This will not change at Sharm El-Sheikh leaving developing countries again with insufficient international support. The possibility of funding and technical assistance through the GDI provides developing countries with a vital new means to achieve their just transitions to a green economy.

September 22, 2022 China Daily global edition